TASTE *and* SEE

140 MEDITATIONS

JOHN PIPER

Multnomah® Publishers *Sisters, Oregon*

TASTE AND SEE
published by Multnomah Publishers, Inc.

© 1999, 2005 by Desiring God Foundation
International Standard Book Number: 1-59052-449-7

Cover photograph by Stephen Gardner, PixelWorksStudio.net
Cover design by The DesignWorks Group, Inc.

Scripture quotations are from:
New American Standard Bible (NASB) © 1960, 1977, 1995
by the Lockman Foundation. Used by permission.
Revised Standard Version Bible (RSV) © 1946, 1952 by the Division of Christian Education
of the National Council of the Churches of Christ in the United States of America.
The Holy Bible, New International Version (NIV) © 1973, 1984 by International Bible Society,
used by permission of Zondervan Publishing House.
The Holy Bible, New King James Version (NKJV) © 1984 by Thomas Nelson, Inc.
The Holy Bible, King James Version (KJV)
The Holy Bible, English Standard Version (ESV) © 2001 by Crossway Bibles,
a division of Good News Publishers. Used by permission. All rights reserved.

Multnomah is a trademark of Multnomah Publishers, Inc.,
and is registered in the U.S. Patent and Trademark Office.
The colophon is a trademark of Multnomah Publishers, Inc.

Printed in the United States of America

For information:
MULTNOMAH PUBLISHERS, INC. • 601 N. LARCH ST. • SISTERS, OREGON 97759

Library of Congress Cataloging-in-Publication Data

Piper, John, 1946-
    Taste and see / John Piper.
        p. cm.
    ISBN 1-59052-449-7
    1. Spirituality. 2. Christian life.   I. Title.
BV4501.3.P557 2005
242—dc21

                                                                    2005008707

06 07 08 09 10— 12 11 10 9 8 7

Come, lay your head down, little lamb,
 And rest upon my shoulder;
It won't be long till you're too big,
 And both of us are older.

Come, lay your head here, little lamb,
 Your wool against my face;
And feel your father's silent love,
 Secure in my embrace.

Come, lay your head close, little lamb,
 And listen to my heart;
And memorize the message there,
 For when we are apart.

Come, lay your head now, little lamb,
 While there is still a place;
I cannot promise life or strength,
 Nor shape tomorrow's grace.

Come, lay your head, my little lamb,
 And listen on my shoulder;
The voice of Jesus deep within:
 "That's just the way I hold her."

BOOKS BY JOHN PIPER

The Pleasures of God

Desiring God

The Dangerous Duty of Delight

Future Grace

A Hunger for God

Let the Nations Be Glad!

Seeing and Savoring Jesus Christ

The Legacy of Sovereign Joy

The Hidden Smile of God

The Roots of Endurance

The Misery of Job and the Mercy of God

(with photography by Ric Ergenbright)

The Innkeeper

Recovering Biblical Manhood and Womanhood

(edited with Wayne Grudem)

What's the Difference?

The Justification of God

Counted Righteous in Christ

Brothers, We Are Not Professionals

The Supremacy of God in Preaching

Beyond the Bounds

(edited with Justin Taylor and Paul Kjoss Helseth)

God's Passion for His Glory

A God-Entranced Vision of All Things

(edited with Justin Taylor)

Don't Waste Your Life

The Prodigal's Sister

A Godward Life

Pierced by the Word

When I Don't Desire God

The Passion of Jesus Christ

Sex and the Supremacy of Christ

(edited with Justin Taylor)

Contents

PREFACE

Boston pastor John Cotton, who died in 1652, had spiritual tastes that are unintelligible to the average modern person. In his declining years he was asked why he read late into the evening. "Because I love to sweeten my mouth with a piece of Calvin before I go to sleep," he replied. I have felt that way about the prophet Isaiah and the psalmist David and the apostle Paul and Jonathan Edwards, who was born fifty-one years after John Cotton died.

There are bad reasons to turn to other writers besides the Bible. And there are good ones. One of the bad reasons we turn to other writers is that we find the Bible tame and tasteless. It is anything but tame and tasteless. One of the good reasons we turn to other writers besides the Bible is that we savor the taste of God not only in the Bible, but also in the way others savor him. The best writers intensify our taste for the Bible, and especially for God himself. Edwards has had that effect on me for more than thirty years.

"Taste and see that the LORD is good," says the psalmist (Psalm 34:8). This is what I mean by "*savoring* the supremacy of God"—the subtitle of this book. We taste the sweetness of God as he meets us in his Word. "How sweet are your words to my taste, sweeter than honey to my mouth!" (Psalm 119:103, ESV). It is not surprising, then, that those who are permeated with God's Word will have a certain taste, as Jesus said, "You are the salt of the earth, but if salt has lost its taste, how shall its saltiness be restored?" (Matthew 5:13, ESV). And if these savory, Bible-saturated Christians write as Jonathan Edwards wrote, there will be a kind of Godward flavor to what they say. This is what we love to sweeten our mouths with before we go to sleep.

I know that I am not Calvin or Edwards—I said this in Book One—but I do love the Bible and try to steep my mind and heart in it year after year. So what I have written here is partly meditations on biblical reality and partly applications to contemporary life. I hope that what pervades all the readings is a savoring of the supremacy of God. Jonathan Edwards said, "The creation of the universe is nothing but God's manifestation of his own perfection and excellency." This is true. And so the aim of all life is to see and savor and show this perfection and this excellency.

This is my aim. And if this book is seen on the bedside table of some battle-weary saints, I hope the reason they give is, "Because I love to sweeten my mouth with the supremacy of God before I go to sleep."

> May my teaching drop as the rain,
>   my speech distill as the dew,
> like gentle rain upon the tender grass,
>   and like showers upon the herb.

DEUTERONOMY 32:2, ESV

ACKNOWLEDGMENTS

As I write these thanks, I am nearing the end of twenty-five years of ministry as a pastor of Bethlehem Baptist Church. These are the people whom I love to serve week by week in the ministry of the Word and prayer. Thank you, my much-loved partners, for spreading a passion for the supremacy of God in all things for the joy of all peoples through Jesus Christ. You have favored me with your faithfulness and supported me in my writing through all these years without complaint.

To the Council of Elders, among the saints at Bethlehem, you have been a sweetness in my life and labor for twenty-five years. This is astonishing, and a great gift of grace to me, in a world of contention. The vision of God that unites us is precious and pervades this book. Thank you for the bounty of your blessing on my life.

To Aaron Young and Rick Gamache and Justin Taylor, thank you for your partnership in the making of this book. Your spirit and insight and vision and joy and encouragement and correction keep me on track and happy in the narrow way that leads to life.

To Carol Steinbach, if you ever weary of writing indexes and giving editorial counsel—after thirty years of friendship and partnership in the ministry—I don't know where I will turn. May the Lord continue to give you joy in the use of your remarkable gifts. And thanks also to Robert Williams and Nancy Markie for volunteering your time to assist Carol in assembling the indexes.

To the team at the Billy Graham Training Center, The Cove, thanks for a quiet place where the finishing touches could be put in place without distraction. Your kindness was beyond all our expectations.

Noël, God looked with great favor on me when I fell in love with you in 1966. I had no idea I was marrying a skilled editor and proofreader and theological consultant and author in your own right. I did hope that I was marrying a woman of God who would stand by me in all the unknown paths of our pilgrimage. This has come true. Thank you. I love you. The book is dedicated to the daughter you never bore and never ceased to ask God for. With God all things are possible. As the thunder rolled across those Blue Ridge Mountains of North Carolina the afternoon I finished this book, there you sat with Talitha teaching her the Lord's Prayer.

> Come, listen now, my little lamb,
>   This prayer is like no other;
> Come, learn to live a Godward life
>   From such a praying mother.

The Exuberant Omnipotence of God

Reasserting God's Rightful Place in All of Life

Where is God in your daily newspaper or in your talk radio show or the network TV programming or *Time* and *Newsweek* or the theater or the public school classroom? God is the most important reality in the universe. But he is almost totally ignored. And if not, he is as likely belittled as reverenced. Yet he is the most crucial factor in every issue facing the nation. There would simply be no nation without God. But he is disregarded by our cultural leaders in almost all they do. Disregard for God is the greatest evil in the West today. It is as though an ant on his anthill should disbelieve in the earth.

If the church is going to reassert God's rightful place in the soul of man and the center of all life, we will need a sharpened focus of who he is and what he is like. One of the reasons our witness to God's reality is minimal is that our *understanding* of God's reality is minimal. In the name of quick and relevant impact we minimize the very greatness that would be his renown. Without this, we will not boldly and graciously reassert his rightful place in all of life.

What we need is a big picture of a great God who is utterly committed to joyfully demonstrating his greatness in doing us good. That is, we need to see the majesty of God and know the splendor of God overflowing toward us with exuberant omnipotence. It is not enough to believe that God is big and strong and fearsome—which he is. We must experience this magnificence as the explosion of God's uncontainable zeal to satisfy his creatures by showing them himself.

We need the vision of God that Jonathan Edwards had already at age twenty when he preached a sermon titled "Nothing upon Earth Can Represent the Glories of Heaven." He reveled in the God of this sermon so much that he preached the same message in at least six towns outside his own parish of Bolton. The "doctrine" of the sermon he stated like this: "The godly are designed for unknown and inconceivable happiness." This he discerns from the purpose of God to glorify himself in creating the world and from his conviction that "this glory of God, [consists] in the creature's admiring and rejoicing [and] exulting in the manifestation of his beauty and excellency. For God has no glory actively from those that behold his glory and take no pleasure in it; but the essence of [the] glorifying of God consists, therefore, in the creature's rejoicing in God's manifestation of his beauty, which is the joy and happiness we speak of" (*The Works of Jonathan Edwards*, vol. 14, ed. Kenneth Minkema [New Haven: Yale University Press, 1997], 144). In other words, the certainty and greatness of the happiness of God's people is as sure as God's zeal for his own glory.

This is the vision we need. And we would do well to meditate on some of the texts that capture the wonder of God's exuberant omnipotence in doing good to those who hope in him.

- The LORD, your God, is in your midst, a warrior who gives victory; he will rejoice over you with gladness, he will renew you in his love; he will exult over you with loud singing as on a day of festival. (Zephaniah 3:17–18, RSV)
- I will make with them an everlasting covenant, that I will not turn away from doing good to them; and I will put the fear of me in their hearts, that they may not turn from me. I will rejoice in doing them good…with all my heart and all my soul. (Jeremiah 32:40–41, RSV)
- The eyes of the LORD run to and fro throughout the whole earth, to show his might in behalf of those whose heart is blameless toward him. (2 Chronicles 16:9, RSV)
- The LORD will again take delight in prospering you. (Deuteronomy 30:9, author's translation)
- For the LORD takes pleasure in his people; he adorns the humble with victory. (Psalm 149:4, RSV)

- His delight is not in the strength of the horse, nor his pleasure in the legs of a man; but the LORD takes pleasure in those who fear him, in those who hope in his steadfast love. (Psalm 147:10–11, RSV)
- Great is the LORD, who delights in the welfare of his servant! (Psalm 35:27, RSV)
- My God will supply all your needs according to his riches in glory in Christ Jesus. (Philippians 4:19)
- In the coming ages he [will] show the immeasurable riches of his grace in kindness toward us in Christ Jesus. (Ephesians 2:7, RSV)
- You shall no more be termed Forsaken, and your land shall no more be termed Desolate; but you shall be called My delight Is in Her, and your land Married; for the Lord delights in you.... As the bridegroom rejoices over the bride, so shall your God rejoice over you. (Isaiah 62:4–5, RSV)

God's omnipotent exuberance to do us good is one of the most freeing discoveries a human can make. Oh, that we might believe it and savor it and bring it to mind again and again until it is our very nature to feel the truth that "the godly are designed for unknown and inconceivable happiness." Unremitting confidence in this truth would surely transform our attitudes and keep us steady in the face of great adversity.

2

LESSON FROM A LOST MASTERCARD

"Cast All Your Anxieties on Him

Because He Cares for You"

I used to carry a MasterCard for identification and rare, unforeseen expenses. Noël and I quit using it for regular purchases after the personal finance seminar at our church that exposed our own foolish habits with credit. That solved the problem of overspending our monthly budget. We use checks and cash for everything now.

So we know how much we have spent before the horrible reckoning at the end of the month. But I still carried it. Then I took it to California on vacation and lost it—and I had no idea where. It could have been in the seal show at Sea World. It could have been in the fruit shop in Tijuana where the bees covered the watermelon. It could have been in who knows how many McDonald's or on the beach in Coronado, where the sand really is gold and the condos sell for half a million dollars. (We were swimming, not shopping.) I had no idea where it was.

But the wonderful thing is that I felt no worries. Now, mind you, that's not natural for me. I am by nature a pessimist, and under ordinary circumstances I would have concluded that someone had already charged the limit on my card. I would usually have gotten mad at myself or my family and taken out my frustration on everybody. I would have looked hard for some divine purpose in all the trouble and had an awful time being happy.

But this time it was different. I felt no worries at all. I didn't get angry with anyone. I never felt any frustration. I was happy the whole way through. What a victory! The whole time it was lost I went about my business as usual, trusted God, and loved my family.

And when I got back from vacation, there it was in an envelope. Daniel Fuller, my friend and former professor, had mailed it to me from California. I had dropped it in his car.

Do you know what the secret to my happiness was? I never knew I had lost the card until I saw it in the envelope in Minneapolis.

I stood there holding it in my hand and smiling. Just think of how feisty I might have been if I had known I lost it. Think how depressed and worried and angry and frustrated and irritable I might have been. And the whole time the card was safely on the way to Minneapolis. All my anger and frustration and discouragement would have been absolutely pointless.

Now, is there not a lesson in this? There is for me. It's this: As soon as we discover we have a problem, God has already been working on it and the solution is on the way.

I have seen it happen again and again in my life. A letter arrives with the solution to some problem. But just the day before I had been discouraged and downcast, not knowing that the letter was already in the mail.

If we believe in the God of Romans 8:28, we will always remember that by the time we know a problem exists, God has already been working on it and his solution is on the way. Ponder the eagerness of God to work for us. "From of old no one has heard or perceived by the ear, no eye has seen a God besides thee, *who works for those who wait for him*" (Isaiah 64:4, RSV, emphasis added). "The eyes of the LORD run to and fro throughout the whole earth, *to show his might in behalf of those* whose heart is blameless toward him" (2 Chronicles 16:9, RSV, emphasis added). "Surely goodness and mercy shall follow me [literally: pursue me] all the days of my life" (Psalm 23:6, RSV).

That is what was happening before I knew I had a problem. And that is what God is doing all the time for those who trust him. Of course, the point here is not that God spares his people trouble. And all of us know that a lost credit card is the least of our worries in a world of suffering like ours. The lost credit card is merely a parable of much greater things. They will not always turn out the way we think is best. But that does not mean God is not at work. He is always at work. And he is turning all our losses and all our pains into something good for us as we trust him. This is his promise.

Therefore, fret not. Cast all your anxieties on him. They are as unnecessary as mine would have been for the lost MasterCard. The time will come when you will see the wise and loving point of it all. By faith live in that moment now, even before you know.

⟨∞⟩

3

GOD IS LOVE, GOD IS GOD

Balancing Complexity and Simplicity in the Bible

One could easily dwell too long on the hard things in the Bible. They are there. Peter tells us so. He says that in Paul's letters "are some things hard to understand" (2 Peter 3:16). Some people are wired to see them. Others are wired to avoid them. The Bible is made for both types. How shall we say this in a balanced way that honors both?

Perhaps it would help to do it like this: Consider that "God is love," as it says in 1 John 4:8, and that God is God, as it says in Isaiah 46:9, "I am God, and there is no other; I am God, and there is no one like Me." The truth that God is God implies that God is who he is in all his glorious attributes and self-sufficiency. But the truth that God is love implies that all of this glory is moving our way for our everlasting enjoyment.

Now, those two truths unleash very different impulses through the Bible. And we will see that a balance is introduced here lest we make of Christianity an elitist affair, which it definitely is not.

That God is love unleashes the impulse of simplicity, and that God is God unleashes the impulse of complexity.

That God is love unleashes the impulse of accessibility, and that God is God unleashes the impulse of profundity.

That God is love encourages a focus on the basics, and that God is God encourages a focus on comprehensiveness. One says, "Believe in the Lord Jesus, and you will be saved" (Acts 16:31). The other says, "I did not shrink from declaring to you the whole counsel of God" (Acts 20:27, RSV).

That God is love impels us to be sure that the truth gets to all people, and that God is God impels us to be sure that what gets to all people is the truth.

That God is love unleashes the impulse toward fellowship, and that God is God unleashes the impulse toward scholarship.

That God is love tends to create extroverts and evangelists, and that God is God tends to create introverts and mystics.

That God is love helps foster a folk ethos, and that God is God helps foster a fine ethos.

One ethos revels in the intimacy of God and sings softly,

I love you, Lord
    And for you I wait:
Your promises
    And your power are great.
Make haste, my God,
    May I taste your ways
I will magnify your sweet peace
    All of my days.

JOHN PIPER

And the other ethos reveals in the transcendent majesty of God and sings with profound exultation,

Far, far above thy thought
    His counsel shall appear,
When fully He the work hath wrought
    That caused thy needless fear.
Leave to his sovereign will
    To choose and to command:
With wonder filled, thou then shalt own
    How wise, how strong His hand.

GIVE TO THE WINDS THY FEARS, PAUL GERHARDT, 1653

If any of you is saying to yourself, "I don't like this separation between God is love and God is God, between folk and fine, evangelists and mystics, fellowship and scholarship, accessibility and profundity, simplicity and complexity"— GOOD! Because, in my mind, every one of these things is precious, and both sides of all these pairs are indispensable in the ministry and mission of Christ in the world. So my prayer is this. For believers, I pray that, seeing these different impulses in Christianity, you will embrace both of them. If you lean toward one side (as we all do), that you will be respectful and affirming to those toward the other side. And that you will cherish the fuller manifestation of God in his church and in the world. And for those who may be reading this without love to Christ in your heart, my prayer is that what you have seen will help remove some caricatures or stereotypes of Christianity and the Bible—and open the way for you to see all that God is for you in Christ, so that you freely believe on him.

4

THE GREAT WORK OF GOD: RAIN

A Thanksgiving Meditation on Job 5:8–10

> *But as for me, I would seek God,*
> *And I would place my cause before God;*
> *Who does great and unsearchable things,*
> *Wonders without number.*
> *He gives rain on the earth,*
> *And sends water on the fields.*

If you said to someone: "My God does great and unsearchable things; he does wonders without number," and they responded, "Really? Like what?" would you say, "Like rain"? When I read these verses from Job recently, I felt, at first, the way I did on hearing some bad poetry that went something like this: "Let me suffer, let me die, just to win your hand; let me even climb a hill, or walk across the land." Even? I would suffer and die to have your hand, and *even* walk across the land? As if walking across the land were more sacrificial than dying? This sounded to me like a joke.

But Job is not joking. "God does great and unsearchable things, wonders without number. He gives *rain* on the earth." In Job's mind *rain* really is one of the great, unsearchable wonders that God does. So when I read this a few weeks ago, I resolved not to treat it as meaningless pop musical lyrics. I decided to have a conversation with myself (which is what I mean by meditation).

Is rain a great and unsearchable wonder wrought by God? Picture yourself as a farmer in the Near East, far from any lake or stream. A few wells keep the family and animals supplied with water. But if the crops are to grow and the family is to be fed from month to month, water has to come from another source on the fields. From where?

Well, the sky. The sky? Water will come out of the clear blue sky? Well, not exactly. Water will have to be carried in the sky from the Mediterranean Sea over several hundred miles, and then be poured out on the fields from the sky. Carried? How much does it weigh? Well, if one inch of rain falls on one square mile of farmland during the night, that would be 2,323,200 cubic feet of water, which is 17,377,536 gallons, which is 144,735,360 pounds of water.

That's heavy. So how does it get up in the sky and stay up there if it's so heavy? Well, it gets up there by evaporation. Really? That's a nice word. What's it mean? It means that the water stops being water for a while so it can go up and not down. I see. Then how does it get down? Well, condensation happens. What's that? The water starts becoming water again by gathering around little dust particles between .00001 and .0001 centimeters wide. That's small.

What about the salt? Salt? Yes, the Mediterranean Sea is saltwater. That would kill the crops. What about the salt? Well, the salt has to be taken out. Oh. So the sky picks up millions of pounds of water from the sea, takes out the salt, carries the water (or whatever it is, when it is not water) for three hundred miles, and then dumps it (now turned into water again) on the farm?

Well, it doesn't *dump* it. If it dumped millions of pounds of water on the farm, the wheat would be crushed. So the sky dribbles the millions of pounds of water down in little drops. And they have to be *big* enough to fall for one mile or so without evaporating, and *small* enough to keep from crushing the wheat stalks.

How do all these microscopic specks of water that weigh millions of pounds get heavy enough to fall (if that's the way to ask the question)? Well, it's called coalescence. What's that? It means the specks of water start bumping into each other and join up and get bigger, and when they are big enough, they fall. Just like that? Well, not exactly, because they would just bounce off each other instead of joining up if there were no electric field present. What? Never mind. Take my word for it.

I think, instead, I will just take Job's word for it. I still don't see why drops ever get to the ground, because if they start falling as soon as they are heavier than air, they would be too small not to evaporate on the way down. But if they wait to come down, what holds them up till they are big enough not to evaporate? Yes, I am sure there's a name for that too. But I am satisfied for now that, by any name, this is a great and unsearchable thing that God has done. I think I should be thankful—lots more thankful than I am.

CHHO

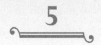

5

"THERE IS A LION OUTSIDE! I SHALL BE SLAIN IN THE STREETS!"

Pondering the Illusions Created by a Lazy Heart

Meditation on Proverbs 22:13, RSV

The sluggard says, "There is a lion outside!
I shall be slain in the streets!"

The sluggard says, 'There is a lion outside! I shall be slain in the streets!'" This is not what I expected the proverb to say. I would have expected it to say "The *coward* says, 'There is a lion outside! I shall be slain in the streets!'" But it says "sluggard," not "coward." So the controlling emotion here is laziness, not fear. But what does laziness have to do with the danger of a lion in the street? We don't say, "This man is too lazy to go do his work because there is a lion outside." The presence of a lion does not produce laziness, it produces fear. So what's the point of the proverb?

The point is that the sluggard creates imaginary circumstances to justify not doing his work and thus shifts the focus from the vice of his laziness to the danger of lions. No one will approve his staying in the house all day just because he is lazy.

But they might sympathize with him and approve his staying home if there were real danger outside. So, to hide his laziness and justify himself, he deflects attention away from the truth (laziness) to an illusion (lions).

If we would be wise people—people on the way to being "sages"—we must understand how our sinful human hearts and minds work. One profound biblical insight we need to embrace is that our heart exploits our mind to justify what the heart wants. That is, our deepest desires precede the rational functioning of our minds and incline the mind to perceive and think in a way that will make the desires look right. It is an illusion to think that our hearts are neutral and incline in accordance with cool, rational observation of truth. On the contrary, we feel powerful desires or fears in our hearts, and *then* our minds bend reality to justify the desires and fears.

This is what the sluggard is doing. He deeply desires to stay at home and not work. There is no good reason to stay at home. So what does he do? Does he overcome his bad desire? No, his lazy heart exploits his mind to create unreal circumstances to justify his desire. He may even *believe* the creation of his mind. Deception can cross from moral depravity to mental derangement—from deceiving others to deceiving ourselves.

Thus Proverbs 26:16 says, "The sluggard is wiser in his own eyes than seven men who can give a discreet answer." Now why is that? Does laziness make people haughty? Not necessarily. But it does make them resistant to any truth that exposes their laziness. So when seven men say, "There is no lion in the street," the sluggard cannot concede. He must insist that his own answer is wiser: There *is* a lion in the street. Otherwise his laziness is exposed for what it is. Thus truth is sacrificed on the altar of self-justification.

It is an old tale. From Cain (Genesis 4:9) to American presidents, truth has been sacrificed to desire, and the mind has been shrewdly employed by the darkened heart to shroud its passions. This is the point of Romans 1:18: "They suppress the truth in unrighteousness." Truth is held hostage by the unrighteous commitments of the heart. The unrighteous heart then employs the mind to distract and deceive. As Jesus says, "Everyone who does evil hates the Light" (John 3:20). Doing the evil we love makes us hostile to the light of truth which will expose the evil and rob us of its fleeting pleasures. In this condition the mind becomes a factory of half-truths, equivocations, sophistries, evasions, and lies— anything to protect the evil desires of the heart from exposure and destruction.

We are *all* given to this. Our only hope is the transforming work of God in our hearts to free us from the bondage of a hardened heart that produces a futile mind. This is Paul's diagnosis of the "futile mind" and the "darkened understanding"—they are rooted in hardness of heart. "Walk no longer as the Gentiles…in the futility of their mind, being darkened in their understanding, excluded from the life of God because of the ignorance that is in them, *because of the hardness of their heart*" (Ephesians 4:17–18, emphasis added). The root cause is a heart cause, not a head cause. The mind is darkened and made futile by rebellion in the heart.

This does not mean that lovers of truth should stop speaking truth and explaining truth and defending truth. But it does mean that we should pray for God to change hearts so that they can see the beauty of truth and love it—even if it begins with: There is no lion in the street and you are lazy. This divine work is what Paul gives thanks for in Romans 6:17, "But *thanks be to God* that though you were slaves of sin, you became obedient from the heart to that form of teaching to which you were committed." Obedience came from the heart. Thanks be to God. And if thanks be to God, then let prayers be to God. He is our only hope—to escape our own delusions and deliver others.

6

EARLY MORNING AT THE MANSE

How a Father Fights for His Faith and His Family

> *This snapshot of my life in the early '80s*
> *is a favorite in the album of my memory.*
> *Things have changed. A different house.*
> *The boys have grown up. We have a daughter now.*
> *The radio station is different. But the passion*
> *to pray for my family and to begin the day*
> *with God is still strong. God has been kind to me.*

lick. KSJN plays softly. *Click.* I turn it off in three seconds. It is 6:00 a.m. I want Noël to sleep till 6:30. I slip out from under the sheet and quilt and tuck them in around her again. "God, I'm tired. Help me." I can hardly move. My eyelids are paralyzed. I can lift them with fingers. Not necessary. My blue energy boot slippers and terry cloth robe are in their usual spot on the floor by the bed. I could find them in my sleep.

I'm sitting on the edge of the bed. "Maybe I should sleep in this morning. Noël can get the boys off to school. I might get sick if I don't get more rest. I'll be more efficient. I spent half of my 'day off' at the hospital…. Get off of me, Satan! In the name of Jesus Christ, the Almighty, get off my back! God, I'm tired. Help me…. Those who wait upon the Lord will renew their strength. They will mount up with wings like eagles. They will run and not be weary" (Isaiah 40:31).

The slippers and robe are on now. The night-light in the bathroom spills out into the hall. I creep by the open door of the boys' bedroom on the way to the basement. "God, thank you for my sons. Oh, how I love my boys! Wake them up in righteousness, Jesus."

The basement has no heat, but one room is finished and has a carpet and a sofa and a desk. *Click.* I turn the three-way lamp on low. It is 6:05. The Bible is open on the couch from the day before. There is an orange pillow for my elbows. I throw the brown sweater Noël made over my head like a monk's habit (to keep off the draft from the window) and begin.

"God, I'm tired. Help me. Please, open my eyes so I can see wonders in your Word. Oh, God. Mighty God! Maker of heaven and earth and all the galaxies of the universe. That you should lend an ear to me in this little room half awake. That you should occupy yourself with me while millions of your people pray, and all the while you hold New York and Tokyo and Paris in the palm of your hand. That you should call this tempted flesh the temple of the Holy Spirit. That you speak to me from this page as personally and powerfully as though you sat here on the couch and talked. Oh, God, what condescension. What unutterable mercy to attend to a little ant like me. Help me believe, O God, and feel this truth: that all my hairs are numbered. 'Why are you cast down, O my soul, and why are you disquieted within me? Hope in God; for I shall again praise him, my help and my God' (Psalm 42:5–6, RSV).

"And now my wife, Lord. Thank you for her. Protect her from harm and from the evil one. Give her joy in the ministry with me. Waken her this morning with a song of praise in her heart and on her lips. Give her vision for service in this neighborhood. Incline her heart to the Word and not to getting gain. Fill her with your Spirit—of wisdom and joy and righteousness. Make her a wise and happy mother. Oh, bind our hearts together as you bind our hearts to yours.

"And finally, my sons. Even in their sleep, Lord, turn their hearts to you. And when I wake them with your Word, sow that seed in humble, open soil. And send its roots down to the inner heart and make an oak of faith. Oh, Christ, take my sons for your servants. Obliterate rebellion from their hearts. And may they grow to godly manhood, full of love to you and love to men. Let them not love the world, nor give a hoot for things or praise. But may your glory be their passion day and night until the Kingdom comes."

I meditate on Mark today and try to see the inner meaning of the miracle of the feeding of the five thousand. I think it means Jesus is the all-sufficient One. Little is much when he is in it. You can never give so much that you have nothing left over.

The grandfather clock sounds half the Westminster chime. It is 6:30. My heart is full. My eyes are open. My faith is alive. My joy is warm. My conscience is still. My hope is strong. I will awaken them all with love!

CRINILO

7

TEN LESSONS I LEARNED FROM MY FATHER

Honoring My Father in His Eightieth Year

When my father invited me to speak at his nonretirement "retirement" banquet at age eighty, I did not have to pray about it. There was no question about the Lord's will. A son will say yes and honor his father. I told the guests that these are the things I would say at my father's funeral, but now it is a high honor and joy to say them in his hearing. And now I get to publish them for others to read, even while he lives and ministers. May his honor spread. God has been good to me.

1. When things don't go the way they should, God always makes them turn for good.
Romans 8:28 was as prominent as John 3:16 in our home. I learned it from the lips of my father: God works all things together for good for those who love him and are called according to his purpose. This laid the foundation for my life. This is the way God is. Life is hard. God is sovereign. God is good.

2. God can be trusted.
My father never murmured at the providence of God, not even when God took my mother at age fifty-six. The loss was immense. The crying was long. But God was never doubted. "In God I have put my trust, I shall not be afraid. What can man do to me?" (Psalm 56:11).

3. People are lost and need to be saved through faith in Jesus.

My father was an evangelist. His traveling absence from two-thirds of my life carried one main message to me: Hell is real and terrible, and Jesus is a great Savior. Mother never hinted that the absence of my father was anything but a glorious privilege for us to support. It never entered my mind to resent it. Nor does it today.

4. Life is precarious, and life is precious. Don't presume that you will have it tomorrow, and don't waste it today.

"It is appointed unto men once to die, but after this the judgment" (Hebrews 9:27, KJV). I heard my father say these words many times while preaching. They were frightening words to me, and good for me. "Do not boast about tomorrow, for you do not know what a day may bring forth" (Proverbs 27:1). He knew—and therefore, I knew—too many stories of young people killed before they were ready to meet God. It was a serious world to grow up in.

5. A merry heart does good like a medicine, and Christ is the heart-satisfier.

My father was and is the happiest man I have ever known. In a sermon called "Saved, Safe and Satisfied," he said, "He is God. When you fully trust him you have all that God is and all that God has. You cannot be otherwise than satisfied with the perfect fullness of Christ." For all the passion of heaven and hell, it was the happiest home I have ever known.

6. A Christian is a great doer not a great don'ter.

We were fundamentalists—without the attitude. We had our lists of things. But that wasn't the main thing. God was the main thing. And God was worth everything.

7. The Christian life is supernatural.

Christian living is not possible without the Holy Spirit, and he comes in answer to prayer. There is not a night in my memory that my family did not pray together when I was growing up.

8. Bible doctrine is important, but don't beat people up with it.
He groaned over schools and grandmothers who split what the Bible holds together: Speak "the truth in love" (Ephesians 4:15). Truth and love. A good marriage. Keep it together, son.

9. Respect your mother.
If you wanted to see Daddy angry, let me sass my mother. "Honor her" is what God commands. And Daddy knew the price she paid to let him go away. Woe to the son who spoke a demeaning word to this great woman.

10. Be who God made you to be and not somebody else.
If you are short, form a ball team called "Little Potatoes but Hard to Peel." He never pressured me to be a pastor. Seek the will of God above all, son. And be what God made you to be.

I write with deepest affection. Thank you, Daddy.

⁂

8

LESSONS ON RETIREMENT FROM CHARLES SIMEON AND RAYMOND LULL

"He Who Loves Not, Lives Not;

He Who Lives by the Life Cannot Die"

In 1807, at the age of forty-eight, after twenty-five years of pastoral ministry at Trinity Church in Cambridge, the health of Charles Simeon broke. He became very weak and had to take an extended leave from his labor. In the next twelve years he learned an astonishing lesson about "retirement." Here is the way H. C. G. Moule tells the story.

[Simeon's] broken condition lasted with variations for thirteen years, till he was just sixty, and then it passed away quite suddenly and without any evident physical cause. He was on his last visit to Scotland, with Marsh, in 1819, and found himself, to his great surprise, just as he crossed the Border, "almost as perceptibly renewed in strength as the woman was after she had touched the hem of our Lord's garment." He saw in this revival no miracle, in the common sense of the word, yet as a distinct providence. He says that he had been promising himself, before he began to break down, a very active life up to sixty, and then a Sabbath evening; and that now he seemed to hear his Master saying: "I laid you aside, because you entertained with satisfaction the thought of resting from your labor; but now you have arrived at the very period when you had promised yourself that satisfaction, and have determined instead to spend your strength for me to the latest hour of your life, I have doubled, trebled, quadrupled your strength, that you may execute your desire on a more extended plan." *(Charles Simeon,* by Handley C. G. Moule [London: The InterVarsity Fellowship, 1948, orig. 1892], 125)

How many Christians set their sights on a "Sabbath evening" of life—resting, playing, traveling—the world's suggested substitute for heaven, since they do not believe that there will be one beyond the grave. We must reward ourselves in *this* life for the long years of labor, for who knows what the life beyond may hold if there is one at all. What a strange thing for a Christian to set his sights on—twenty years of play and puttering. What a tragic way to finish the last lap before entering the presence of the King who finished his race so differently!

Why not be like Raymond Lull?

He was born of an illustrious family at Palma in the island of Majorca off the west coast of Spain in 1235. By the time he was seventy-nine, the universities of Europe finally began to teach Oriental languages, for which he had labored. His pupils and friends naturally desired that he should end his days in the peaceful pursuit of learning and the comfort of companionship.

Such, however, was not Lull's wish. His ambition was to die as a missionary and not as a teacher of philosophy. In Lull's contemplations we read, "Men are wont to die, O Lord, from old age, the failure of natural warmth and excess of cold; but thus, if it be Thy will, Thy servant would not wish to die; he would prefer to die in the glow of love, even as Thou wast willing to die for him."

He had evangelized in the fanatical Muslim center of Tunis twice before and had been imprisoned and expelled. Now, in great old age, he longed not only for the martyr's crown, but also once more to see his little band of believers. Animated by these sentiments he crossed over to Bugia on August 14, 1314. For nearly a year he labored secretly among a little circle of converts.

At length, weary of seclusion and longing for martyrdom, he came forth into the open market and presented himself to the people as the same man whom they had once expelled from their town. He pleaded with love, but spoke plainly the whole truth. Filled with fanatic fury at his boldness, and unable to reply to his arguments, the populace seized him and dragged him out of the town. By the command, or at least the connivance, of the king, he was stoned on June 30, 1315 (quotes from *Raymond Lull: First Missionary to the Moslems,* by Samuel Zwemer [New York: Fleming H. Revell Company, 1902], 132–45).

We need not assume or follow all the bad theology surrounding the atoning effects of martyrdom taught in the Middle Ages. As a heart longs for the flowing streams, and longs the more as the brook approaches, and the smell sweetens and the thirst deepens, so longs the soul of the saint to see Christ and to glorify him in his dying (John 21:19; Psalm 42:1). It is beyond comprehension that soldiers of the cross would be satisfied in retiring from the battle just before the trumpet blast of victory—or just before admission to the coronation ceremony.

Rather let us embrace Lull's motto: "He who loves not, lives not; he who lives by the Life cannot die" (from Robert Glover, *The Progress of World-Wide Missions* [New York: Harper and Row, 1952], 37).

9

CAN CHRISTIANS BE HELD HOSTAGE BY THE SINS OF THE BELOVED?

When Is Mercy Merry and When Does It Mourn?

The sins of those we love can be as painful as the labor of childbearing. I have seen women who labored so long and hard that blood vessels broke in their faces, only to be relieved by a cesarean delivery. Paul groaned over the imperfections of his spiritual children. "My children, with whom I am again in labor until Christ is formed in you…I am perplexed about you" (Galatians 4:19–20).

Not only that, we know that Jesus himself wept over the sins of Jerusalem: "When He approached Jerusalem, He saw the city and wept over it" (Luke 19:41). Yes, and even the Holy Spirit can be grieved by our sinful speech: "Let no evil talk come out of your mouths…. Do not grieve the Holy Spirit of God, in whom you were sealed for the day of redemption" (Ephesians 4:29–30, RSV).

But here's a question: Should the sins of others hold us hostage in the prison of sorrow? In one sense, sorrow over another person's sins is a mark of compassion and love. We long for them to be holy and pure in heart, because "the pure in heart…will see God" (Matthew 5:8). So our sadness is evidence of longing that others would know the fullness of joy that comes with righteousness and peace: "The kingdom of God is…righteousness and peace and joy in the Holy Spirit" (Romans 14:17). Surely, then, this sadness of ours is a form of love.

On the other hand, there is something very wrong, it seems, if sinning people have power to steal our joy by their own sinful choices. This is, in fact, a kind of blackmail. "If you claim to love us, you must pay for our sin with a broken heart." Well, yes…and no. God does not put the strings of our hearts in the hands of sinners. He puts them in the hands of Jesus, who loves sinners. And this Jesus says, "These things I have spoken to you, that my joy may be in you, and that your joy may be made full" (John 15:11).

The same Jesus who wept over Jerusalem's sinfulness rejoiced over the sovereign hand of God in choosing who would see and who would remain blind: "[Jesus] rejoiced greatly in the Holy Spirit, and said, 'I praise You, O Father, Lord of heaven and earth, that You have hidden these things from the wise and intelligent and have revealed them to infants'" (Luke 10:21). In other words, even in his weeping over Jerusalem, there was an unshakable joy in the purposes of God being worked out in the world. Jerusalem could not blackmail Jesus with her backsliding.

Similarly, Jesus gives us that same unshakable joy: "Your hearts will rejoice, and no one will take your joy from you" (John 16:22, RSV). No one can take us hostage by sin and steal our joy, demanding a ransom of Christian misery. No one can blackmail the saints of God with bad behavior and threaten to nullify our love if we will not pay up with the sacrifice of our joy. If our joy is lost, Christ is belittled, and what then has love to offer the beloved sinner?

How then shall we love sinners? Shall we be indifferent to their sin and peril? No. Let us not be content with sins, but let us be content with *God* in relation to sinners. Can you distinguish between being content *in* circumstances but not being content *with* circumstances? Can you imagine weeping over a wayward son and resting in the sovereign goodness of God who does all things well (Mark 7:37)?

May God give us the solid joy of Christ, even as we mourn over those who will not share it but cannot steal it. For God "accomplishes all things according to the counsel of his will," and he is good (Ephesians 1:11, RSV; Psalm 100:5).

10

When "Want To" and "Ought To" Don't Match

Living Between Hypocrisy and License

If your "want to" does not conform to God's "ought to," what can you do to have peace? I see at least five possible strategies:

1. You can avoid thinking about the "ought to." This is the most common strategy in the world. Most people simply do not devote energy to pondering what they should be doing that they are not doing. It's easier just to keep the radio on.

2. You can reinterpret the "ought to" so that it sounds just like your "want to." This is a little more sophisticated and so not quite as common. It usually takes a college education to do this with credibility and a seminary degree to do it with finesse. (And I believe strongly in both college and seminary!)

3. You can muster the willpower to do a form of the "ought to" even though you don't have the heart of the "want to." This generally looks pretty good and is often mistaken as virtue, even by those who do it. In fact, there is a whole worldview that says doing "ought to's" without "want to's" is the essence of true virtue. The problem with this is that Paul said, "God loves a *cheerful* giver" (2 Corinthians 9:7, emphasis added), which puts the merely "ought-to givers" in a precarious position.

4. You can feel proper remorse that the "want to" is very small and weak—like a mustard seed—and then, if it lies within you, do the "ought to" by the exertion of will, while repenting that the "want to" is weak, and praying that the "want to" will soon be restored. Perhaps it will even be restored in doing the "ought to." This is not hypocrisy. Hypocrisy hides the absence of the "want to" and pretends it's there. Virtue confesses the defective desire in the hope that grace will forgive and restore.

5. You can seek, by the means of grace, to have God give the "want to" so that when the time to do the "ought to" comes, you will "want to." Ultimately the "want to" is a gift of God. "The mind of the flesh is hostile to God...*it is not able* to submit to the law of God" (Romans 8:7, author's translation, emphasis added). "The natural man *cannot* understand the things of the Spirit of God...because they are spiritually appraised" (1 Corinthians 2:14, author's translation). "Perhaps God may *grant* them repentance leading to the knowledge of the truth" (2 Timothy 2:25, emphasis added).

The biblical doctrine of original sin boils down to this (to borrow from St. Augustine): We are free to do what we like, but we are not free to like what we ought to like. "Through the one man's disobedience [Adam] the many were made sinners" (Romans 5:19). This is who we *are*. And yet we know from our own souls and from the Bible that we are accountable for the corruption of our bad "want to's." Indeed, the better you become, the more you feel ashamed of *being* bad and not just *doing* bad. As N. P. Williams said, "The ordinary man may feel ashamed of *doing* wrong: but the saint, endowed with a superior refinement of moral sensibility, and keener powers of introspection, is ashamed of *being* the kind of man who is liable to do wrong" (quoted in Edward Oakes, "Original Sin: A Disputation," *First Things,* No. 87, Nov. 1998, 24).

God's free and sovereign heart-changing work is our only hope. Therefore we must pray for a new heart. We must pray for the "want to"—*"Incline my heart* to Your testimonies" (Psalm 119:36, emphasis added). "Make glad the soul of Your servant, for to You, O Lord, I lift up my soul" (Psalm 86:4). He has promised to do it: "I will put My Spirit within you and cause you to walk in My statutes" (Ezekiel 36:27). This is the new covenant bought by the blood of Jesus (Hebrews 8:8–13; 9:15). "Therefore let us draw near with confidence to the throne of grace, so that we may receive mercy and find grace to help [us want to do what we ought to do] in time of need" (Hebrews 4:16).

11

THE ONLY ULTIMATE LOVE

Do People Go to the Grand Canyon to Enhance Their Self-Esteem?

God's loving *us* is a means to our joyfully glorifying *him*. In that sense, God's love is penultimate; God's glory is ultimate. You can see this in Romans 15:8–9. "Christ became *a servant…*in order that the Gentiles might *glorify God* for His mercy" (emphasis added). God has been merciful to us so that we would delight in glorifying him for his mercy. We see it again in Ephesians 1:4–6, "In *love* [God] predestined us to adoption…*to the praise of the glory of His grace*" (emphasis added). The goal of *loving us* through predestination is that we might have the everlasting joy of praising *his grace*. We see it again in Psalm 86:12–13, "I will *glorify* Your name forever. For Your *lovingkindness* toward me is great" (emphasis added). God's love is the ground. His glory is the goal.

Why is this important? It's important because unless we understand this, we will not know what love really is. The love of God is not God's making much of us, but God's saving us from self-centered sin so that we can enjoy making much of him forever. And our love to others is not our making much of them, but our helping them to find eternal satisfaction in making much of God. The only ultimate love is a love that aims at satisfying people in the glory of God. Any love that terminates on man is eventually destructive. It does not lead a person to the only lasting joy, namely, God. Love must be God-centered or it is not the greatest love; it leaves people without their deepest need and only hope.

Take the cross, for example. The death of Christ is the ultimate expression of divine love: "God demonstrates His own love toward us, in that while we were yet sinners, Christ died for us" (Romans 5:8). "In this is love…that He loved us and sent His Son to be the propitiation for our sins" (1 John 4:10). Yet in Romans 3:25 Paul says that the aim of the death of Christ was *to demonstrate [God's] righteousness,* because in the forbearance of God He passed over the sins previously committed" (emphasis added). Forgiving sins seems to create a huge problem for the righteousness of God. It makes him look like a judge who lets criminals go free without punishment. In other words, the mercy of God puts the justice of God in jeopardy.

So to vindicate his justice he does the unthinkable—he puts his Son to death as the penalty for our sins. The cross makes it plain to everyone that God does not sweep evil under the rug of the universe. He punishes it in Jesus for those who believe, and in hell for those who don't.

But notice that this ultimately loving act has at the center of it and at the bottom of it the demonstration and vindication of the glorious righteousness of God. Calvary love is a God-glorifying love. God exalts God at the cross. If he didn't, he could not rescue man from sin. But it is a mistake to say, "Well, if the aim was to rescue man, then man was the ultimate goal of the cross." No, man was rescued from sin in order that he might enjoy God's acts of glorifying God (see the first paragraph). If God values the glory of God so much in the rescuing of man, then the aim of that rescue would be to give man the ability and inclination to value God the way God does (see John 17:26). This is the ultimately loving aim of the cross. Christ did not die to make much of us, but to free us to enjoy, and participate in, God's making much of God forever.

It is profoundly wrong to turn the cross into a warrant for self-esteem as the root of mental health. If I stand before the love of God and do not feel a healthy, satisfying, freeing joy without turning that love into an echo of my self-esteem, then I am like a man who stands before the Grand Canyon and feels no satisfying wonder until he translates the canyon into a case for his own significance. That is not the presence of health but bondage to self. The only ultimate love is the sacrificial act of God saving me to share God's passion for the supremacy of God. Nothing glorifies him, or satisfies us, more.

12

"NO EVIL WILL BEFALL YOU." REALLY?

Beware of Satan's Use of Psalms

The beloved Psalm 91 seems out of sync with experience and other Scripture. What are we to make of its promises?

A thousand may fall at your side and ten thousand at your right hand, but it shall not approach you. (verse 7)

No evil will befall you, nor will any plague come near your tent. (verse 10)

With a long life I will satisfy him. (verse 16)

Do people of faith never perish in battle? Do they never succumb to plague? Do they always live long lives?

There are three ways to resolve this problem. 1) We could say that the person who wrote the psalm and those who included it in the Psalter and the Bible had their heads in the sand and got it wrong. 2) Or we could say that those who fall in battle and get a disease and don't live long did not make the Lord their refuge and walk by faith. In other words, the promise is absolute and everyone who fails to experience it must be unbelieving. 3) Or we could say that what the writer means is that God does in fact rule the flight of arrows and the spread of disease and the length of life; and he can and does give safety and health and life to whom he pleases, so that it is always a free gift of God. But he does not mean for us to presume upon these promises as guarantees that God will not permit us to fall by an arrow, succumb to disease, or die at age thirty-eight. In other words, the promises have exceptions or qualifications.

When he says, "Ten thousand may fall at your right hand, but it shall not approach you" (verse 7), he means for you to understand this unspoken qualification: "It will not approach you *without my permission and design*. And my design for those who are ever in my care is always good, even if I permit the arrow to take their life." Thus Derek Kidner says, "This is a statement of exact, sweeping providence, not a charm against adversity.... What it does assure us is that nothing can touch God's servant but by God's leave" *(Psalms 73–150* [London: InterVarsity Press, 1975], 333).

There are several reasons in the context of the Psalter and the Bible why I think this was intended by the psalmist. The first is that even in the psalms themselves there are predictions that "many are the afflictions of the righteous" (34:19). And though the Lord delivers us "out of them all," yet we *do* go into them and may come out only in heaven (Psalm 63:3, NIV, "Your love is better than life."). Moreover in Psalm 44:22 those who have not been false to God's covenant nevertheless confess, "For Your sake we are killed all day long; we are considered as sheep to be slaughtered," which is probably why Paul quotes this verse in Romans 8:36 about Christian martyrs, and then says, "But in all these things we are more than conquerors through Him who loved us" (8:37, NIV).

Perhaps most significant is the observation that Satan quotes Psalm 91:11–12 to Jesus in the wilderness (Matthew 4:6; Luke 4:10–11). How does Satan use this psalm? He uses it as though it had no qualifications. He takes Jesus to the pinnacle of the Temple and says to him, "If you are the Son of God, throw yourself down from here." And then he quotes Psalm 91: "For He will give His angels charge concerning you, to guard you in all your ways. They will bear you up in their hands, that you do not strike your foot against a stone" (verses 11–12). So Satan wants to exploit the very problem I am posing about this psalm. He is saying: "See! It is absolute. No qualifications. Use it. Prove the promise of God in your life! If it will apply to anyone, it will surely apply to you, the Son of God."

But Jesus rejects this use of the psalm and sets his face to prove that the psalm *does* have a qualification: He dies at a *young* age; he feels the *blow* of ripped flesh; and he is *pierced* by the nail and sword while ten thousand get off without a scratch. Jesus also teaches his disciples the paradoxical warning and promise: "They will put some of you to death…. Yet not a hair of your head will perish" (Luke 21:16–18). And Paul confirms this way of thinking, not only in Romans 8:28 and 8:35, but also in Philippians 4:19, where he says, "My God will supply all your needs," alongside the testimony, "I have learned the secret of…going hungry…and suffering need. I can do all things [including hungering and suffering need] through Him who strengthens me" (Philippians 4:12–13).

I urge you to follow Jesus' interpretation of Psalm 91, not Satan's. That is, in your Gethsemane of suffering, pray for deliverance according to God's sovereign power and mercy (twelve legions of angels could have rescued Jesus, Matthew 26:53). But then say, "Not my will but thine be done." And believe that what befalls will not, in the end, be evil for you, but good (Romans 8:28).

⟨⟩

13

WILL YOUR FAMILY DIG ITS OWN GRAVE?

Meditation on Martyrdom and Families

Most, though not all, of those who read this book are probably far removed from the threat of martyrdom. Yet the words of Jesus must be heard by all. The days will come when they are more relevant than they seem today. And even today they are immediately relevant for hundreds of thousands, as David Barrett makes plain in his annual statistical table which estimates that 164,000 Christians are dying as martyrs each year at the end of the twentieth century, probably the bloodiest of all centuries. Which should take no Christian by surprise. "Beloved, do not be surprised at the fiery ordeal which comes upon you to prove you, as though something strange were happening to you" (1 Peter 4:12, RSV). We must all hear the words of Jesus.

> They will lay their hands on you and will persecute you, delivering you to the synagogues and prisons, bringing you before kings and governors for My name's sake. It will lead to an opportunity for your testimony.... You will be betrayed even by parents and brothers and relatives and friends, and they will put some of you to death.... Yet not a hair of your head will perish. By your endurance you will gain your lives. (Luke 21:12–13, 16, 18–19)

This will be doubly hard—not only to die for Christ at the hands of unjust men, but to have our own family members, Judas-like, hand us over with a kiss. But there will also be other stories. Not all families will fail in that hour. Some will come forth as gold. Hearing of such families and such faith may help you be ready and help your friends and families to be ready. Let me tell you the story of the Haim family of Cambodia.

In the village of Siem Riep, Cambodia, Haim, a Christian teacher "knew that the youthful black-clad Khmer Rouge soldiers now heading across the field were coming this time for him.… Haim was determined that when his turn came, he would die with dignity and without complaint. Since "Liberation" on April 17, 1975, what Cambodian had not considered this day?… Haim's entire family was rounded up that afternoon. They were "the old dandruff!", "bad blood!", "enemies of the glorious revolution!", "CIA agents!" They were Christians.

The family spent a sleepless night comforting one another and praying for each other as they lay bound together in the dewy grass beneath a stand of friendly trees. Next morning the teenage soldiers returned and led them from their Gethsemane to their place of execution, to the nearby *viel somlap*, "the killing fields".…

The family were ordered to dig a large grave for themselves. Then, consenting to Haim's request for a moment to prepare themselves for death, father, mother, and children, hands linked, knelt together around the gaping pit. With loud cries to God, Haim began exhorting both the Khmer Rouge and all those looking on from afar to repent and believe the gospel.

Then in panic, one of Haim's youngest sons leapt to his feet, bolted into the surrounding bush and disappeared. Haim jumped up and with amazing coolness and authority prevailed upon the Khmer Rouge not to pursue the lad, but allow him to call the boy back. The knots of onlookers, peering around trees, the Khmer Rouge, and the stunned family still kneeling at the graveside, looked on in awe as Haim began calling his son, pleading with him to return and die together with his family. "What comparison, my son," he called out, "stealing a few more days of life in the wilderness, a fugitive, wretched and alone, to joining your family here momentarily around this grave but soon around the throne of God, free forever in Paradise?" After a few tense minutes the bushes parted, and the lad, weeping, walked slowly back to his place with the kneeling family. "Now we are ready to go," Haim told the Khmer Rouge.

Few of those watching doubted that as each of these Christians' bodies toppled silently into the earthen pit which the victims themselves had prepared, their souls soared heavenward to a place prepared by their Lord. (Don Cormack, *Killing Fields, Living Fields: An Unfinished Portrait of the Cambodian Church—the Church That Would Not Die* [Crowborough, England: Monarch Publications, 1997], 233–34).

Haim and his family will not have died in vain if you and I are moved to set our minds on things that are above, to love Christ more than this world, and to be so radically freed for love and witness and courage in the cause of truth that nothing can intimidate us.

⟨ΠΠΟ⟩

14

RIGHTEOUS JOB AND THE ROCK STAR

Pondering Power and Popular Influences on Youth

When Job lost his ten children to a windstorm that crushed them to death (like hurricanes that devastate and destroy today), he rent his robe, shaved his head, fell upon the ground and worshiped. And he said, "Naked I came from my mother's womb, and naked shall I return; the LORD gave, and the LORD has taken away; blessed be the name of the LORD" (Job 1:21, RSV). Then when he was struck with boils from head to toe, Job said to his God-cursing wife, "Shall we receive good at the hand of God and shall we not receive evil?" (Job 2:10, RSV). In both cases the author of the book of Job adds, "Job did not sin" in these bold assertions of God's sovereignty over wind and sickness and Satan (1:22; 2:10).

What are the main influences on young people today in this regard? What message is coming through concerning God's rule over all things, his rights as Creator to give and take, and his authority to govern the world? An alternative rock star and daughter of a North Carolina Methodist minister miscarried. To the idea that this painful event may have been in God's will she responded, "If it was, then I'm going to kick his ass because I'm not interested in 'thy will be done.' As a mother of this child, I wanted my will, not thy will" *(Foster's Sunday Citizen,* 15 November 1998).

Later Job speaks about people like his wife and this young woman. They are prosperous, not realizing that every breath they take is a gift of grace that they do not deserve (God is not "served by human hands, as though he needed anything, since he himself gives to all men life and breath and everything," Acts 17:25, RSV). They do not live lives of continual gratitude for God's patience and forbearance

("Do you presume upon the riches of his kindness and forbearance and patience? Do you not know that God's kindness is meant to lead you to repentance?" Romans 2:4, RSV). They take pleasure for granted and take pain as an occasion to blaspheme the Almighty. Thus Job says of them, "They say to God, 'Depart from us! We do not desire the knowledge of your ways. What is the Almighty, that we should serve him? And what profit do we get if we pray to him?'" (Job 21:15, RSV).

What is the Almighty that we should serve him?

Good question, depending on the tone of voice. Here's part of the answer.

- He is the reason you came into being. "By Him all things were created" (Colossians 1:16).
- He is the reason you stay in being. "He…upholds all things by the word of his power" (Hebrews 1:3).
- He decides why you have being and makes your being serve his aims. "All things have been created…*for* Him" (Colossians 1:16, emphasis added).
- He is the governor of all the authorities who seem so influential on the earth. "Jesus Christ…is…the ruler of the kings of the earth" (Revelation 1:5).
- He alone has authority to forgive sins. "Who can forgive sins but God alone?… The Son of Man has authority on earth to forgive sins" (Mark 2:7–10, NIV).
- It is utter folly to oppose God. "It is a terrifying thing to fall into the hands of the living God" (Hebrews 10:31).
- It is utter wisdom to love him and draw near to him. "In Your [God's] presence is fullness of joy; in Your right hand are pleasures forever" (Psalm 16:11). "Draw near to God and He will draw near to you" (James 4:8).

Let us then, with trembling joy, humble ourselves under the mighty hand of God. Weeping may last for the night, but joy comes in the morning (Psalm 30:5). God's ways are often strange. But when they are, Job is a better example for us than the rock star.

⟨∽∾⟩

15

HER BODY, HER SELF, AND HER GOD

Pondering Diaries from Yesterday, Today, and Tomorrow

The Minneapolis *Star-Tribune* (23 October 1997, A18) carried Mary McCarty's review of Joan Brumberg's book *The Body Project*. The book is about the difference between how girls saw themselves one hundred years ago and how they see themselves at the end of the twentieth century. Brumberg analyzes diaries of adolescent girls from the 1830s to the 1990s. Her conclusion, according to the reviewer: "In the nineteenth and early twentieth centuries, girls' diaries focused on 'good works' and perfecting the character. In the 1990s, the diaries are fixated on 'good looks,' on perfecting the body."

For example, one diary from 1892 says, "Resolved…to think before speaking. To work seriously. To be self-restrained in conversations and actions. To be dignified. Interesting myself more in others." Contrast this with an entry from 1982: "I will try to make myself better in any way I possibly can with the help of my budget and baby-sitting money. I will lose weight, get new lenses, already got new haircut, good makeup, new clothes and accessories."

What is remarkable about this shift from 1892 to 1982 is that it parallels exactly the shift, described in the Bible, away from what God wills for women. Consider the shift of focus from "good works" to "good looks."

Likewise, I want women to adorn themselves with proper clothing, modestly and discreetly, not with braided hair and gold or pearls or costly garments, but rather by means of *good works,* as is proper for women making a claim to godliness. (1 Timothy 2:9–10, emphasis added)

Your adornment must not be merely external—braiding the hair, and wearing gold jewelry, or putting on dresses; but let it be the hidden person of the heart, with the imperishable quality of a gentle and quiet spirit, which is precious in the sight of God.... You have become [Sarah's] children if you *do what is right* without being frightened by any fear. (1 Peter 3:3–4, 6, emphasis added)

Brumberg's diagnosis of the problem, however, seems to miss the mark. She writes, "Today, many young girls worry about the contours of their bodies...because they believe the body is the ultimate expression of the self." That may be true. But it is not helpful, because it gives the impression that *something else* besides the body is the ultimate expression of the self. In other words, Brumberg seems to assume that *self* is the starting point, and expressing the self is what life is all about. The problem, then, is just finding out what the "ultimate expression of the self" is.

The Bible has a radically different diagnosis of the problem. It has a radically different starting place. First Peter 3:5 (emphasis added) says, "In former times the holy women also, *who hoped in God,* used to adorn themselves, being submissive to their own husbands." The biblical starting point in dealing with the fear of looking unacceptable is God. Does a woman "hope in God," or hope in the approval of men (and other women)? This is the key to "not being frightened by any fear" (1 Peter 3:6). This is the key to being free from bondage to the mirror.

The biblical goal of a woman's life is not to find the ultimate expression of the self (neither "body" nor "character"). The biblical goal in life is to express the all-satisfying greatness and trustworthiness of God. Expressing God, not self, is what a godly woman wants to do. Excessive preoccupation with figure and hair and complexion is a sign that self, not God, has moved to the center. With God at the center—like the "sun," satisfying a woman's longings for beauty and greatness and truth and love—all the "planets" of food and dress and exercise and cosmetics and posture and countenance will stay in their proper orbit.

If this happens, the diaries of the next generation will probably go beyond looks *and* character and speak of the greatness of God and the triumphs of his grace. And they will more often be written from Calcutta than from the comfortable houses of America.

16

A LETTER TO MY WIFE SAYING YES TO ADOPTION

Monday, November 6, 1995, 11:12 P.M.

On December 15, 1995, Talitha Ruth
came into our lives. She was eight weeks
old and I was fifty years old. My wife Noël
had dreamed for years about this moment.
I had not been so sure that it was the wisest
thing to do. But that changed.
This is the public version of the (much longer)
letter I wrote to Noël to tell her that I was ready to
move ahead. I hope it encourages other couples to
entrust themselves to God's all-sufficient future
grace, and to do the same.

Dear Noël,

With confidence in the all-sufficient future grace of God, I am ready and eager to move ahead with the adoption of Talitha Ruth. I want to thank you that during these years, when your heart has yearned to adopt a daughter, you have not badgered me or coerced me. You have been wonderfully patient. You have modeled faith in the sufficiency of prayer. You have always expressed support of me and my ministry even if we should never adopt. You have been reasonable in all our discussions and have come forth with your rationale only when asked. You have honored my misgivings as worthy of serious consideration. God was good to put it in Phoebe's heart to call us about this child when she did and not before we were ready.

I realize more than ever that "the mind of man plans his way, but the LORD directs his steps" (Proverbs 16:9). This decision is not merely a tabulation of pros and cons. I would be deceiving myself to think that. Yet I am persuaded that this decision to adopt honors God more than not adopting. To my perspective, it seems to be the path that will "spread a passion for the supremacy of God in all things for the joy of all peoples." I believe it will bless Bethlehem and not hinder our work there. I believe it is the path of the greatest love for the greatest number. And therefore I have confidence that God is pleased with it.

I choose it, not under constraint or with any reservation of commitment. I relinquish every thought that because you initiated this idea, you will bear blame for the burdens it will bring. As with our choice to have children in the first place and with our choice to go to Germany and our choice to leave Bethel College and enter the pastorate, there is a common and united commitment to all that God will be for us in this path, including any "frowning providence" that he plans to sanctify to us. I believe our eyes are open, though we have learned that the toothache expected and the toothache experienced are not the same. We have come through enough to believe that God's future grace will be sufficient. His mercies are new every morning, and there will be mercies for every weight and wonder on this new path of our lives.

I thank God for you. I enter with you gladly on this path. Whether we live to see our daughter grown or not, we will have done well to welcome her. Life is very short, whether twelve hours like Ashley Hope Barrett or fifty years like me or seventy-six years like my father or ninety-four years like Crystal Anderson. What matters is not that we do all we might have done or all we dreamed of doing, but that, while we live, we live by faith in future grace and walk in the path of love. The times are in God's hands, not ours.

With this common conviction we will, God willing, embrace our new daughter and give ourselves, with all the might that God inspires in us, to love her into the kingdom. May the Lord establish the plans of our hearts and bring Talitha Ruth (and the future husband God already knows) into deep and lasting fellowship with Christ. May she be an ebony brooch of beauty around your aging neck and a crown of purity and joy on your graying head.

I love you,
Johnny

17

SKY RIDER, ETERNAL HOME, AND EVERLASTING ARMS

Meditation on the Uniqueness of God in Majestic Helpfulness

> *There is none like God, O [Israel],*
> *who rides through the heavens to your help,*
> *and in his majesty through the skies.*
> *The eternal God is your dwelling place,*
> *and underneath are the everlasting arms.*
>
> DEUTERONOMY 33:26–27, RSV

He "rides through the heavens…"
God is free to move where he wills and do what he pleases. God is not hindered, impeded, obstructed, or restrained in the fulfillment of his purposes. "I am God:..I work and who can hinder it?" (Isaiah 43:13, RSV). "I know that You can do all things, and that no purpose of yours can be thwarted" (Job 42:2).

"…to your help."
His freedom and unbounded success is in the service of his people. He rides through the heavens *to our* help. God is exuberant in his pursuit of ways to help us. "Goodness and mercy shall pursue me all the days of my life" (Psalm 23:6,

author's translation). "The eyes of the LORD run to and fro throughout the earth to show himself strong on [our] behalf" (2 Chronicles 16:9, NKJV). "The Son of Man also came not to be served but to serve" (Mark 10:45, RSV).

"There is none like God…"
The other gods want us to ride through the heavens to *their* help. They don't work for man; they need man to work for them. "Bel bows down, Nebo stoops, their idols are on beasts" (Isaiah 46:1, RSV). They need to be carried. But God carries his people. "From of old no one has heard or perceived by the ear, no eye has seen a God besides thee who works for those who wait for him" (Isaiah 64:4, RSV).

"…and in his majesty through the skies."
He shows his majesty in the act of helping his people. We get the help; he gets the majesty. "He exalts himself to show mercy to you" (Isaiah 30:18, RSV). He does not compromise his commitment to his own glory in serving us; he proves it.

"The eternal God is your dwelling place…"
He is help and he is home—eternal home. When you come home to him, you are home forever. He cannot be burned down, or blown down or broken into or foreclosed on. "In him we live and move and have our being" (Acts 17:28, RSV). Coming to him is coming home—forever.

> *O God, our help in ages past,*
> *our hope for years to come,*
> *be Thou our guide while life shall last*
> *and our eternal home.*
>
> ISAAC WATTS

"…and underneath are the everlasting arms."
He is not only around us like a home; he is under us like a Father's mighty arms. When he rides through the heavens to our help, and in his majesty

through the skies, he picks us up and holds us next to his heart with everlasting arms.

> *Leaning, leaning,*
> *Safe and secure from all alarms,*
> *Leaning, leaning,*
> *Leaning on the everlasting arms.*
>
> ELISHA HOFFMAN

"[Therefore] there is none like God, O [Israel]."
But don't demons and angels ride through the heavens? Yes, they do. Demons, though, do not ride "to our help," but only to our hurt. And, yes, angels ride through the heavens to our help (Hebrews 1:14), but they do not ride in divine "majesty." So the two things that set God apart in his riding through the heavens are the two things that make his riding infinitely precious: He comes to our help, and he comes to help, with unequaled majesty. "Trust in Him at all times, O people; pour out your heart before Him; God is a refuge for us" (Psalm 62:8).

෨෴෨

18

How to Pray for the Soul (Yours or Another's)

Praying in Sync with the Way God Works

For thoughtful people, how you pray for the soul is governed by how you believe God acts. So, for example, if you believe God changes people's souls so that they make new and right choices, then you will ask God to make those soul-changes through evangelism and nurture. But not everybody is thoughtful about the way they pray. They don't think about what view of God is behind their praying.

So what I suggest is that we learn to pray for the soul first *from the way the Bible prays for the soul*. If we do that, then our prayers will probably be good prayers, and in the process we will also learn about how God acts.

Here is the way I pray for my soul. I use these prayers over and over again—for myself and my children and wife and for our pastoral staff and elders and for all my church. This is the meat and potatoes of my prayer life.

1. The first thing my soul needs is an *inclination* to God and his Word. Without that, nothing else will happen of any value in my life. I must *want* to know God and read his Word and draw near to him. Where does that "want to" come from? It comes from God. So Psalm 119:36 teaches us to pray, *"Incline my heart* to Your testimonies and not to gain" (RSV, emphasis added).

2. Next I need to have *the eyes of my heart opened* so that when my inclination leads me to the Word, I see what is really there and not just my own ideas. Who opens the eyes of the heart? God does. So Psalm 119:18 teaches us to pray, *"Open my eyes,* that I may behold wonderful things from Your law" (emphasis added).

3. Then I need for my *heart to be enlightened* with these "wonders." I need to perceive glory in them and not just interesting facts. Who enlightens the heart? God does. So Ephesians 1:18 teaches us to pray "that the *eyes of your heart may be enlightened"* (emphasis added).

4. Then I am concerned that my heart is badly fragmented and that parts of it might remain in the dark while other parts are enlightened. So I *long for my heart to be united* for God. Where does that wholeness and unity come from? From God. So Psalm 86:11 teaches us to pray, "O LORD, I will walk in Your truth; *unite my heart* to fear Your name" (emphasis added).

5. What I really want from all this engagement with the Word of God and the work of his Spirit in answer to my prayers is *that my heart will be satisfied with God* and not with the world. Where does that satisfaction come from? It comes from God. So Psalm 90:14 teaches us to pray, *"Satisfy us in the morning with Thy steadfast love,* that we may rejoice and be glad all our days" (RSV, emphasis added).

6. But I don't want my happiness to be fragile or weak, but to be strong and durable in the face of the worst adversities. I want to be *strong in joy,* and persevering during the dark seasons. Where does that strength and durability come from? It comes from God. So Ephesians 3:16 teaches us to pray, "That [God] would grant you, according to the riches of His glory, *to be strengthened with power through His Spirit in the inner man"* (emphasis added).

7. I do not want my strength in Christ to simply be fruitful for me, but for others. Clearly "it is more blessed to give than to receive" (Acts 20:35). So I want to *produce good deeds and works of love* for others, so that the glory of God will be seen in my life, and others will taste and see that the Lord is good. Who produces these good deeds of love? God does. So Colossians 1:10 teaches us to pray, "That [we] will *walk in a manner worthy of the Lord...bearing fruit in every good work"* (emphasis added).

8. Finally, lest the ultimate aim of it all be missed, I pray day after day—as a kind of banner flying over all my prayers—"Hallowed be Thy name" (Matthew 6:9). Lord, cause your name to be known and feared and loved and cherished and admired and praised and trusted because of my life and ministry.

All this I pray "in Jesus' name," because God gives these things only on the basis of Jesus' death. He died for me and removed the wrath of God so that the Father might freely give me all things (Romans 8:32).

Lord, teach us to pray, from beginning to end, in a biblical way with a biblical view of how you act in the world. Show us yourself and how you work so that we might pray as we ought. And teach us to pray as we ought so that we might see how you work.

19

Beware of Common Sense!

"Command What You Wish, and Give What You Command"

Second Chronicles 30 tells how King Hezekiah recovered the Passover for Israel. It had fallen into neglect, and he was broken by this disobedience. So he sent couriers throughout the land calling the people to repentance and obedience.

The message of the king brimmed with conditional statements. For example: *"If* you return to the LORD,1... *[then]* he will not turn His face from you" (verse 9, NKJV, emphasis added). These conditional statements show that God really responds to our choices. That is, *if* we make a certain choice, God does one thing, and *if* we make a different choice, God does something different. So Hezekiah calls the people to return to the Lord *so that* he will return to them.

This responsiveness of God to the choices we make causes some people to jump to a very unwarranted "common sense" conclusion. They say: "Well, if God responds to our choices, then what we choose and what God does in response must depend ultimately on us." This is what I call "philosophical" interpretation rather than "exegetical" interpretation. In other words, this way of understanding conditional statements in the Bible comes from commonsense human reasoning rather than careful attention to the *un*common ways of God revealed in the text.

Let me illustrate from 2 Chronicles 30 (emphasis added). Here are the exhortations Hezekiah sends to the people. They are laden with conditions.

- Verse 6: "O sons of Israel, return to the LORD God of Abraham, Isaac, and Israel, *that* He may return to those of you who escaped and are left from the hand of the kings of Assyria." In other words, if you return to the Lord, he will return to you.
- Verse 7: "Do not be like your fathers and your brothers, who were unfaithful to the LORD God of their fathers, *so that* He made them a horror, as you see." God's action to "make them a horror" was the result of the fathers being unfaithful to the Lord.
- Verse 8: "Now do not stiffen your neck like your fathers, but yield to the LORD and enter His sanctuary which He has consecrated forever, and serve the LORD your God, *that* His burning anger may turn away from you." God's burning anger will turn away from you, if you serve the Lord your God.
- Verse 9: "For *if* you return to the LORD, *[then]* your brothers and your sons will find compassion before those who led them captive and will return to this land. For the LORD your God is gracious and compassionate, and will not turn His face away from you *if* you return to Him." Returning to the Lord is a condition that the people must meet if they are going to receive the compassion of the Lord in not turning his face away from them.

What was the response to Hezekiah's couriers who carried these messages of conditional hope? Verse 10 says that some people "laughed them to scorn." But others from "Asher, Manasseh, and Zebulun humbled themselves and came to Jerusalem" (verse 11). The same humble choice was made in Judah (verse 12). What made the difference in how these people responded? Verse 12 gives the uncommonsense answer: "The hand of God was also on Judah *to give them one heart to do what the king and the princes commanded* by the word of the LORD."

Don't read this too quickly. Think about the stunning implications. They are enormous. What verse 12 teaches, in the light of the preceding context, is that God commanded, "Return to me and I will return to you." Some people did return. Why did they? Verse 12 gives the deepest reason: *God gave them a heart to do what he had commanded.* "The hand of God was also on Judah *to give them one heart to do what the king and the princes commanded.*"

Is this a contradiction? To say: "If you do what the king commanded, God will turn his anger away from you," and then to say, "God gave them a heart to do what the king commanded"? Is it a contradiction to state a condition that people must meet, and then say that God enables them to meet the condition? No, it is not a contradiction. Only a philosophical prejudice against what this text teaches would call it so.

This sheds light on dozens of biblical texts. Indeed on the whole structure of biblical thought. When we read sentences like, "If you return to God, he will return to you," we dare not jump to the conclusion that what we choose, and what God does in response, depends ultimately on us. Verse 12 teaches explicitly: What God commands, God may also give. It is the closest biblical parallel to St. Augustine's famous prayer, "Command what you wish, but give what you command" *(Confessions,* X, xxix, 40).

The lesson for us is a warning and an exhortation. Beware of interpreting with commonsense inferences, rather than giving heed to the text. Rather, be glad for the grace of God beneath your response to the grace of God. If grace did not awaken us to grace, we would sleep through the revolution. "For from him and through him and to him are all things. To him be glory for ever" (Romans 11:36, RSV).

20

CLYDE KILBY'S RESOLUTIONS FOR MENTAL HEALTH

Awakening Amazement at the Strange Glory of Ordinary Things

At the First Covenant Church on October 22, 1976, Clyde Kilby, who is now with Christ in heaven, gave an unforgettable lecture. I went to hear him that night because I loved him. He had been one of my professors in English literature at Wheaton College. He opened my eyes to more of life than I knew could be seen. Oh, what eyes he had! He was like his hero C. S. Lewis in this regard. When he spoke of the tree he saw on the way to class in the morning, you wondered why you had been so blind all your life. Since those days in classes with Clyde Kilby, Psalm 19:1 has been central to my life: The sky is telling the glory of God.

That night Dr. Kilby had a pastoral heart and a poet's eye. He pled with us to stop seeking mental health in the mirror of self-analysis, but instead to drink in the remedies of God in nature. He was not naive. He knew of sin. He knew of the necessity of redemption in Christ. But he would have said that Christ purchased new eyes for us as well as new hearts. His plea was that we stop being unamazed by the strange glory of ordinary things. He ended that lecture with a list of resolutions. As a tribute to my teacher and a blessing to your soul, I offer them for your joy.

1. At least once every day I shall look steadily up at the sky and remember that I, a consciousness with a conscience, am on a planet traveling in space with wonderfully mysterious things above and about me.

2. Instead of the accustomed idea of a mindless and endless evolutionary change to which we can neither add nor subtract, I shall suppose the universe guided by an Intelligence which, as Aristotle said of Greek drama, requires a beginning, a middle, and an end. I think this will save me from the cynicism expressed by Bertrand Russell before his death, when he said: "There is darkness without, and when I die there will be darkness within. There is no splendor, no vastness anywhere, only triviality for a moment, and then nothing."

3. I shall not fall into the falsehood that this day, or any day, is merely another ambiguous and plodding twenty-four hours, but rather a unique event, filled, if I so wish, with worthy potentialities. I shall not be fool enough to suppose that trouble and pain are wholly evil parentheses in my existence, but just as likely ladders to be climbed toward moral and spiritual manhood.

4. I shall not turn my life into a thin, straight line which prefers abstractions to reality. I shall know what I am doing when I abstract, which of course I shall often have to do.

5. I shall not demean my own uniqueness by envy of others. I shall stop boring into myself to discover what psychological or social categories I might belong to. Mostly I shall simply forget about myself and do my work.

6. I shall open my eyes and ears. Once every day I shall simply stare at a tree, a flower, a cloud, or a person. I shall not then be concerned at all to ask what they are but simply be glad that they are. I shall joyfully allow them the mystery of what Lewis calls their "divine, magical, terrifying and ecstatic" existence.

7. I shall sometimes look back at the freshness of vision I had in childhood and try, at least for a little while, to be, in the words of Lewis Carroll, the "child of the pure unclouded brow, and dreaming eyes of wonder."

8. I shall follow Darwin's advice and turn frequently to imaginative things such as good literature and good music, preferably, as C. S. Lewis suggests, an old book and timeless music.

9. I shall not allow the devilish onrush of this century to usurp all my energies but will instead, as Charles Williams suggested, "fulfill the moment as the moment." I shall try to live well just now because the only time that exists is now.

10. Even if I turn out to be wrong, I shall bet my life on the assumption that this world is not idiotic, neither run by an absentee landlord, but that today, this very day, some stroke is being added to the cosmic canvas that in due course I shall understand with joy as a stroke made by the architect who calls himself Alpha and Omega.

21

THE MISSING NOTE OF SOVEREIGN JOY

A Lesson on Love from Augustine

Few people in the history of the church have surpassed St. Augustine in portraying the greatness and beauty and desirability of God. He is utterly persuaded by Scripture and experience "that he is happy who possesses God" (Thomas A. Hand, *Augustine On Prayer* [New York: Catholic Book Publishing Co., 1986], 17). "You made us for yourself, and our hearts find no peace till they rest in you" (Augustine, *Confessions*, I, 1). He will labor with all his might to make this God of sovereign grace and sovereign joy known and loved in the world.

> You are ever active, yet always at rest. You gather all things to yourself, though you suffer no need.... You grieve for wrong, but suffer no pain. You can be angry and yet serene. Your works are varied, but your purpose is one and the same.... You welcome those who come to you, though you never lost them. You are never in need yet are glad to gain, never covetous yet you exact a return for your gifts.... You release us from our debts, but you lose nothing thereby. You are my God, my Life, my holy Delight, but is this enough to say of you? Can any man say enough when he speaks of you? Yet woe betide those who are silent about you! (Augustine, *Confessions*, I, 4)

If it is true, as R. C. Sproul says, that today "we have not broken free from the Pelagian captivity of the church" ("Augustine and Pelagius," in *Tabletalk*, June 1996, 52), then we should pray and preach and write and teach and labor with all our might to break the chain that holds us captive. Pelagius, a monk from Britain, was a popular preacher in Rome in AD 401–409. He was an archenemy of Augustine because he rejected the notion that the human will was enslaved by sin and needed special grace to trust Christ and do good. He recoiled at Augustine's prayer, "Give me the grace [O Lord] to do as you command, and command me to do what you will!" *(Confessions,* X, 31). R. C. Sproul says, "We need an Augustine or a Luther to speak to us anew lest the light of God's grace be not only overshadowed but be obliterated in our time" ("Augustine and Pelagius," 52).

Yes, we do. But we also need tens of thousands of ordinary pastors, who are ravished with the extraordinary sovereignty of joy that belongs to and comes from God alone. And we need to rediscover Augustine's peculiar slant—a very biblical slant—on grace as the free gift of sovereign joy in God that frees us from the bondage of sin. We need to rethink our Reformed view of salvation so that every limb and every branch in the tree is coursing with the sap of Augustinian delight.

We need to make plain that *total depravity* is not just badness, but blindness to beauty and deadness to joy; and *unconditional election* means that the completeness of our joy in Jesus was planned for us before we ever existed; and that *limited atonement* is the assurance that indestructible joy in God is infallibly secured for us by the blood of the covenant; and *irresistible grace* is the commitment and power of God's love to make sure we don't hold on to suicidal pleasures, and to set us free by the sovereign power of superior delights; and that the *perseverance of the saints* is the almighty work of God to keep us, through all affliction and suffering, for an inheritance of pleasures at God's right hand forever.

This note of sovereign, triumphant joy is a missing element in too much Reformed theology and Reformed worship. And it may be that the question we should pose ourselves is whether this is so because we have not experienced the triumph of sovereign joy in our own lives. Can we say the following with Augustine?

How sweet all at once it was for me to be rid of *those fruitless joys* which I had once feared to lose!... *You drove them from me,* you who are the true, the *sovereign joy.* You drove them from me and took their place.... O Lord my God, my Light, my Wealth, and my Salvation. *(Confessions, IX, 1)*

Or are we in bondage to the pleasures of this world so that, for all our talk about the glory of God, we love television and food and sleep and sex and money and human praise just like everybody else? If so, let us repent and fix our faces like flint toward the Word of God in prayer: Oh, Lord, open my eyes to see the sovereign sight that in your presence is fullness of joy and at your right hand are pleasures for evermore (Psalm 16:11).

22

How to Be Filled with the Holy Spirit

How Do You Drink the Wine of God?

Meditation on Ephesians 5:18—21, RSV

> *And do not get drunk with wine,*
> *for that is debauchery; but be filled*
> *with the Spirit, addressing one another*
> *in psalms and hymns and spiritual songs,*
> *singing and making melody to the Lord*
> *with all your heart, always and for everything*
> *giving thanks in the name of our Lord Jesus*
> *Christ to God the Father. Be subject to one*
> *another out of reverence for Christ.*

Ephesians 5:18 says, "Do not get drunk with wine, for that is debauchery; but be filled with the Spirit." There are at least four effects of being filled with the Spirit. First, in verse 19 the effect is very musical: "…addressing one another in psalms and hymns and spiritual songs, singing and making melody to the Lord with all your heart." Clearly, joy in Christ is the mark of being filled with the Spirit.

But not only joy. Also gratitude in verse 20: "…always and for everything giving thanks in the name of our Lord Jesus Christ to God the Father." Perpetual gratitude, gratitude for everything, comes from being filled with the Spirit—which obviously aims at overcoming grumbling and pouting and self-pity and bitterness and scowling and murmuring and depression and worry and discouragement and gloominess and pessimism!

But not only musical joy and universal gratitude—also, loving submission to each other's needs: "Be subject to one another out of reverence for Christ" (verse 21). Joy, gratitude, and humble love—these are some of the marks of being filled with the Spirit.

To this should also be added a fourth effect: boldness in witness. You see this most clearly from Acts 4:31: "They were all filled with the Holy Spirit, and began to speak the word of God with boldness." No one can fail to be bold and eager in witness when the Spirit is producing in him overflowing joy, perpetual gratitude, and humble love. Oh, how we need to be filled with the Spirit! Let's seek it! Pursue it!

But the crucial question is, how? Start with the closest parallel: Don't be drunk with wine, be filled with the Spirit! (verse 18). How do you get drunk with wine? You drink it. Lots of it. So how then shall we get drunk (filled) with the Spirit? Drink it! Lots of it. Paul said in 1 Corinthians 12:13, "We were all made to drink of one Spirit." Jesus said, "If anyone thirst, let him come to me and drink. He who believes in me, as the scripture has said, 'Out of his heart shall flow rivers of living water.' Now this he said about the Spirit" (John 7:37–39, RSV).

How can you drink the Spirit? Paul said, "Those who live according to the Spirit set their minds on the things of the Spirit" (Romans 8:5, RSV). We drink the Spirit by setting our minds on the things of the Spirit. What does "setting the mind on" mean? Colossians 3:1–2 (RSV) says, "Seek the things that are above...set your minds on things that are above." "Setting the mind on" means seeking, directing your attention toward, being very concerned about (Philippians 3:19). It means being devoted to and taken up with. So drinking the Spirit means seeking the things of the Spirit, directing your attention to the things of the Spirit, being devoted to the things of the Spirit.

What are the "things of the Spirit"? When Paul said in 1 Corinthians 2:14,

"The natural man does not [welcome] *the things of the Spirit"* (emphasis added), he was referring to his own Spirit-inspired teachings (2:13)—specifically his teaching about the thoughts and ways and plans of God (2:8–10). Therefore, "the things of the Spirit" are the teachings of the apostles about God. Jesus also said, "The words that I have spoken to you are Spirit and life" (John 6:63). Therefore, the teachings of Jesus are also the "things of the Spirit."

So drinking the Spirit means setting our minds on the things of the Spirit. And setting our minds on the things of the Spirit means directing our eager attention to the teachings of the apostles about God and to the words of Jesus. If we do this long enough, we will get drunk with the Spirit. In fact, we will get addicted to the Spirit. Instead of having chemical dependencies, we will develop a wonderful Spirit dependency.

One more thing: The Holy Spirit is not like wine, because he is a person and is free to come and go anywhere he wills (John 3:8). Therefore Luke 11:13 (RSV) must be added. Jesus said to his disciples, "If you then, who are evil, know how to give good gifts to your children, how much more will the heavenly Father give the Holy Spirit to those who ask him!" If we want to be filled with the Spirit we must ask our heavenly Father for it. And that is just what Paul does for the Ephesians in Ephesians 3:19 (RSV). He asks his Father in heaven (verse 19) that the believers "might be filled with all the fulness of God." Drink and pray. Drink and pray. Drink and pray.

23

WHAT IS COMMUNION WITH GOD?
WISDOM FROM JOHN OWEN

Thoughts on Hebrews 10:22

> *Let us draw near with a true*
> *heart in full assurance of faith.*

The old Puritans called this *drawing near* "communion with God." We need to learn from them. J. I. Packer says that the Puritans differ from evangelicals today because for them:

> Communion with God was a *great* thing; to evangelicals today it is a comparatively *small* thing. The Puritans were concerned about communion with God in a way we are not. The measure of our unconcern is the little that we say about it. When Christians meet, they talk to each other about their Christian work and Christian interests, their Christian acquaintances, the state of the churches, and the problems of theology—but rarely of their daily experience of God. (*A Quest for Godliness* [Wheaton, Ill.: Crossway Books], 215)

According to Packer the greatest of the Puritans was John Owen (1616–1683). Owen's experience of communion with God is a great example for us. God saw to it that Owen and the suffering Puritans of his day lived on God in a way that makes most of our experience look shallow. Writing a letter during an illness in 1674 he said to a friend, "Christ is our best friend and ere long will be our only friend. I pray God with all my heart that I may be weary of everything else but converse and communion with Him" (Peter Toon, *God's Statesman* [Greenwood, S.C.: The Attic Press], 153). God used illness and all the other pressures of Owen's life to drive him into communion with God and not away from it.

But Owen was also very intentional about his communion with God. He said, "Friendship is most maintained and kept up by visits; and these, the more free and less occasioned by urgent business...." (John Owen, *Works,* VII [Edinburgh: Banner of Truth Trust, 1965], 197). In other words, in the midst of all his academic and political and ecclesiastical labors, he made many visits to God.

And when he made these visits, he did not go only with petitions for things or even for deliverance from his many hardships. He went to see his glorious Friend and to contemplate his greatness. The last book he wrote—he was finishing it as he died—is called *Meditations on the Glory of Christ.* That says a great deal about the focus and outcome of Owen's life. In it he said:

> The revelation...of Christ...deserves the severest of our thoughts, the best of our meditations and our utmost diligence in them.... What better preparation can there be for [our future enjoyment of the glory of Christ] than in a constant previous contemplation of that glory in the revelation that is made in the Gospel? *(Works,* I, 275)

The contemplation Owen has in mind is made up of at least two things: On the one hand there is what he called his "severest thoughts" and "best meditations" or, in another place, "assiduous meditations," and, on the other hand, relentless prayer. The two are illustrated in his work on Hebrews.

One of his greatest achievements was his seven-volume commentary on Hebrews. When he finished it near the end of his life, he said, "Now my work is done: it is time for me to die" *(God's Statesman,* 168). How did he accomplish this great work and remain close to God? We get a glimpse from the preface:

I must now say, that, after all my searching and reading, *prayer and assiduous meditation* have been my only resort, and by far the most useful means of light and assistance. By these have my thoughts been freed from many an entanglement." *(Works* I, lxxxv, emphasis added)

Thus Owen drew near to God by prayer and assiduous meditation and found light and freedom. This was a zeal for communion with God that accords with knowledge. This is the kind of zeal that we want. This is the sweet personal knowledge that keeps our zeal in bounds and makes it burn the more brightly. With this knowledge and zeal, let us draw near day by day and hour by hour.

24

WHAT IF OUR DYING IS DISCIPLINE?

Meditation on 1 Corinthians 11:29–32

Next to living for Christ, dying for him is the hardest thing to do. We need all the help we can get. The issue is faith. Will we trust him to the end? Will we rest in his grace and not panic that we are hell-bound? Will we be able to handle the fear that our dying is punishment and the prelude to perishing? Oh, how many are the doubts sown by the devil! We must learn how to drive him off with the sword of the Spirit, the Word of God. So here is another part of our necessary defense.

Let's assume that we have indeed sinned in a reckless way, and that God is displeased. And let's suppose that we are "disciplined" or "judged" for this by the Lord with some sickness. Be careful. I do not say *"punished"* in the sense of bearing the penalty for sin. Christ bore the penalty for all our sins: "He Himself bore our sins in His body on the cross" (1 Peter 2:24). Rather, I say *"disciplined"* in the sense of rebuke and correction and purification and preservation from worse sinning. "The Lord disciplines him whom he loves, and chastises every son whom he receives" (Hebrews 12:6, RSV).

But what about death? Would God actually take us away in death as part of such a discipline? The apostle Paul says he sometimes does this. In dealing with sins at the Lord's Supper he writes:

He who eats and drinks, eats and drinks judgment to himself if he does not judge the body rightly. For this reason many among you are weak and sick, *and a number sleep* [that is, have died]. But if we judged ourselves rightly, we would not be judged. But when we are judged, we are disciplined by the Lord *so that we will not be condemned* along with the world. (1 Corinthians 11:29–32, emphasis added)

In other words, sometimes getting weak and sick and even dying are the discipline of the Lord. And the aim is not condemnation. That happened on the cross. For us, there is now *no condemnation* (Romans 8:1, emphasis added). The aim, rather, is that we "not be condemned along with the world" (1 Corinthians 11:32). In other words, sometimes death is a disciplinary deliverance to save us from condemnation. "A number [have died]…so that [they] will not be condemned along with the world."

Of course, this is not the reason for *every* death of God's precious saints. Don't jump to the conclusion that your sickness or your death is owing to a trajectory of sinning from which you have to be rescued. But suppose that this is indeed what is happening?

Is that encouraging? Will thinking about this help you die more peacefully and with greater faith and hope? My answer is that *everything* in the Bible is meant to help you die and to be encouraging for your faith in the light of truth (Romans 15:4).

How then would this truth strengthen us for a hope-filled death? It would happen like this. Is it not a great threat to our peace, the thought that we are sinners? Does not the thought that God is sovereign and could lift this sickness if he willed, threaten us with fearful feelings that if the sickness stays, he must be against us? And how shall we handle these fears when we know that we are indeed sinners and corruption indeed remains in us? In those moments, we look for some encouragement from the Bible that God is willing to save believers who have sinned and are very imperfect.

Yet we know that God is holy and hates sin, even sin committed by his children. We also know that God disciplines his children with sorrowful experiences (Hebrews 12:11). We are not among those who say God has nothing to do with the painful experiences of life. So we look for help and hope from God's utterly realistic Word. And we find it in 1 Corinthians 11:32; namely, that the death of saints—even a death which is "discipline" and "judgment"—is *not* condemnation, but salvation. God is taking the life of this sinning saint because he loves him so much he will not let him go on in sin.

This is solid encouragement. Not easy. And not commonly taught. But rock solid. What it says to all of us is this: We do not need to be certain whether the time of our death is owing to our sinning or to the devil's cruelty (Revelation 2:10) or to God's other purposes. What we need is the deep assurance that *even if* our dying comes from our own folly and sin, we can rest peacefully in the love of God. At such a moment these words will be precious beyond measure: "We are disciplined by the Lord *so that we will not be condemned*" (emphasis added). In this way we learn to die well.

25

"The Greatest Thing in the World Is to Be Saved"

Thinking About the Greatness of What
We Are Saved For

Not long before his death on September 27, 1982, I visited Dr. Wilford Widen in the hospital. He looked up at me from his bed with a smile and said, "Pastor John, the greatest thing in the world is to be saved." Those words are the abiding legacy of a great saint who gave oversight to the Sunday school at our church for forty years and led the building campaign for one of our buildings.

Do you feel this? If not, perhaps the reason is that you never really felt very lost and desperate before the judgment of God or threatened by an eternity of conscious torment in hell. Oh, how we love being saved after we have just come close to being killed. Perhaps by a powerful ocean undertow. Or by getting a finger caught in the drain at the bottom of a swimming pool. (Yes, filled with water! I remember it well.) Or almost walking out in front of a car that speeds by just three feet from you at forty miles an hour, but your wife's voice catches you in the split second before you step into death. Or a remission from a long battle with cancer. Or release from a prison camp in the Gulag after sixteen years of expecting death. Or after surviving a plane crash when others perished.

Oh, how we love life at those moments and cleave to everything precious. So it is when you taste the preciousness of being saved from sin. Not just the words. Not just a fact learned from the Bible, but really feeling that you are justly damned and hopelessly lost and cut off from God and life and joy. Then to learn that God has made a way. That he will forgive you. That he will accept you and love you and work all things for your good. That *all* your sins can be forgiven and cast into the deepest sea and never brought up against you anymore. Oh, the preciousness of being saved from sin and judgment and hell!

But is it biblical to say that the greatest thing in the world is to be saved? Well, of course, the greatest thing in the world is *God*. But Dr. Widen did not mean to compare our experience of being saved with God. He meant to compare it to all other experiences. The reason that being saved is the greatest experience in the world is because GOD is the greatest Person in the world, and being saved means being rescued from sin and damnation so that we can know and enjoy God forever. If God were not the greatest Reality in the universe, being saved to be with him would not be the greatest experience in the universe.

Yes, but is it *biblical* to say this? Well, here is the text that I have in mind as I say it. Jesus said to the seventy disciples in Luke 10:20, "Do not rejoice in this, that the spirits are subject to you, but *rejoice that your names are recorded in heaven*" (emphasis added). In other words, you have just had great ministerial success. Demons have fallen before you. People have been delivered. This is wonderful. This is what you have been sent to do. Praise God for this triumph.

But. Let this not be your first joy or your root joy or your indispensable joy. Rather, "rejoice in this, that your names are written in heaven." That is, rejoice that you are enrolled in the redeemed. Rejoice that you will go to heaven when you die. Rejoice that God has written you among the elect. Rejoice that you are saved. This is the greatest thing. Not ministry. But knowing God, seeing God, enjoying God. The greatest thing in the world is to be saved. Because it is being saved to enjoy *God* forever.

CRILLO

26

THE AGONIZING PROBLEM OF THE ASSURANCE OF SALVATION

Where to Look When Looking In Is Fearful

The most agonizing problem about the assurance of salvation is not the problem of whether the objective facts of Christianity are true (God exists, Christ is God, Christ died for sinners, Christ rose from the dead, Christ saves forever all who believe, etc.). Those facts are the utterly crucial bedrock of our faith. But the really agonizing problem of assurance is whether I personally am saved by those facts.

This boils down to whether I have saving faith. What makes this agonizing—for many in the history of the church and today—is that there are people who think they have saving faith, but don't. For example, in Matthew 7:21–23 Jesus says, "Not everyone who says to Me, 'Lord, Lord,' will enter the kingdom of heaven, but he who does the will of My Father who is in heaven. Many will say to Me on that day, 'Lord, Lord, did we not prophesy in Your name, and in Your name cast out demons, and in Your name perform many miracles?' And then I will declare to them, 'I never knew you; depart from me, you who practice lawlessness.'"

So the agonizing question for many is: Do I really have saving faith? Is my faith real? Am I deceiving myself? Some well-intentioned people try to lessen the problem by making faith a mere decision to affirm certain truths, such as: Jesus is God, and he died for my sins. Some also try to make the problem of assurance less agonizing by denying that any kind of life change is really necessary to demonstrate the reality of faith. So they find a way to make James 2:17 mean something other than what it seems to mean: "Even so faith, if it has no works, is dead." But these strategies to help assurance backfire. They deny some Scripture; and even the minimal faith they preserve can be agonized over and doubted by the tormented soul. They don't solve the problem, and they lose truth. And, perhaps worst of all, they sometimes give assurance to people who should not have it.

Instead of minimizing the miraculous, deep, transforming nature of faith, and instead of denying that there are necessary life changes that show the reality of faith, we should tackle the problem of assurance another way. We should begin by realizing that there is an *objective* warrant for resting in God's forgiveness of our sins, and there is a *subjective* warrant for assurance that our sins are forgiven. The objective warrant is the finished work of Christ on the *cross* that "has perfected for all time those who are being sanctified" (Hebrews 10:14). The subjective warrant is our *faith* which bears fruit in "being sanctified."

Next we should realize that saving faith has two parts. First, faith is a spiritual sight of glory (or beauty) in the Christ of the gospel. In other words, when you hear or read what God has done for sinners in the cross and the resurrection of Jesus, this appears to your heart as a great and glorious thing in and of itself, even before you are sure you are saved by it. I get this from 2 Corinthians 4:4 where Paul says that what Satan hinders in the minds of unbelievers is seeing "the light of the gospel of the glory of Christ, who is the image of God." For faith to be real there must be a supernatural "light" that God shines into the heart to show us that Christ is glorious and wonderful (2 Corinthians 4:6). This happens as a work of the Spirit of God through the preaching of the gospel.

Second, faith is a warranted resting in this glorious gospel for our own salvation. I say "warranted resting" because there is an "*un*warranted resting"—people who think they are saved who are not, because they have never come to see the glory of Christ as compellingly glorious. These people believe only on the basis of wanting rescue from harm, not because they see Christ as more beautiful and desirable than all else. But for those who "see the light of the gospel of the glory of Christ," their resting is warranted.

What this means practically, is, first, that we should continually look to the cross and the work of God in Christ because this is where God makes the light of the gospel shine. If we become excessively introspective and analyze our emotions too much, we will sink into hopeless doubt because the self-authenticating light shines not from within us, but from Christ in the gospel. We must look outside ourselves to Christ and his work if we hope to have assurance sustained inside ourselves.

Second, we should continually pray for God to enlighten the eyes of our hearts (Ephesians 1:18). Third, we should express our trust in Christ by loving each other; because, as John said, "We *know* that we have passed out of death into life, because we love the brethren" (1 John 3:14, emphasis added). In the end, assurance is a precious gift of God. Let us pray for each other that it will abound among us.

27

ARE YOU A DESCENDANT OF KING DAVID?

Meditation on Psalm 18:50 and Isaiah 55:3

> *He gives great deliverance to His king,*
> *and shows lovingkindness to His anointed,*
> *to David and his descendants forever.*

> *I will make with you an everlasting*
> *covenant, my steadfast, sure love for David.*

Take a deep breath and ponder your place on the throne of David, the great Jewish king of old. Are Christians really heirs of the promises to David and his descendants? In Psalm 18:50, David said, "He gives great deliverance to His king, and shows lovingkindness to His anointed, to David and his descendants forever." Can ordinary Christians, three thousand years later, read this and know that we are included in the promise of deliverance and lovingkindness?

Consider Isaiah 55. It begins with a very broad invitation, "Ho! Every one who thirsts, come to the waters; and you who have no money come, buy and eat. Come, buy wine and milk without money and without cost" (verse 1). This invitation includes everyone who will come to God hungry and thirsty and bankrupt, ready to be satisfied by grace instead of world and wages. Then in verse 3, speaking to the same group, Isaiah says, "Incline your ear, and come to me; hear, that your soul may live; and *I will make with you an everlasting covenant, my steadfast, sure love for David"* (RSV, emphasis added). Notice: This covenant is promised to *all* who will come to God for satisfaction, hungry and thirsty. And yet this covenant is God's "steadfast, sure love *for David."*

Therefore, it is true that humble, hungry saints are beneficiaries of the promises made to King David. How can this be, especially three thousand years later?

Well, the way God planned for the promises to David to be fulfilled was through a "Son of David" who would be God's final "Anointed One," that is, his Messiah (Psalm 18:50, see above). The throne of David would be the throne of the universe, and the government flowing from it would be eternal: "For to us a child is born, to us a son is given; and the government will be upon his shoulder, and his name will be called 'Wonderful Counselor, Mighty God, Everlasting Father, Prince of Peace'" (Isaiah 9:6, RSV). God's word to David through the prophet Nathan had been, "I will be his father and he shall be My son; and I will not take My lovingkindness away from him…. But I will settle him in My house and in My kingdom forever, and his throne shall be established forever" (1 Chronicles 17:13–14).

The New Testament proclaims that Jesus is this Messiah, this "Son of David." "I, Jesus…I am the root and the descendant of David, the bright morning star" (Revelation 22:16). This was at the heart of apostolic preaching: "Saul kept increasing in strength and confounding the Jews who lived at Damascus by proving that *this Jesus is the Christ [Messiah]"* (Acts 9:22).

How then do we Christians relate to this "Son of David," this final King on whom the everlasting government of the world now rests? In a rare statement, Hebrews 2:13 quotes the Messiah as saying of his people, "Behold, I and the *children* whom God has given me." In other words, the followers of Jesus, the Messiah, the "Son of David," the everlasting King, are his *children,* his descendants. This is similar to Galatians 3:7, where Paul says, "It is those who are of faith who are sons of Abraham." That is, faith unites us to Christ, the seed of Abraham (Galatians 3:16), and by that union we become the children of Abraham and beneficiaries of the promises God made to him. In the same way, faith unites us to the "Son of David" so that we become children of David and beneficiaries of his promises.

This, then, means that Psalm 18:50 is indeed ours. "He gives great deliverance to His king, and shows lovingkindness to His anointed, to David and his *descendants* forever." We are his descendants in Christ. The deliverance is ours. The lovingkindness is ours. The "steadfast, sure love for David" (Isaiah 55:3) is ours. And, to completely take our breath away, the King himself promises, "He who overcomes, I will grant to him to sit down with Me on My throne, as I also overcame and sat down with My Father on His throne" (Revelation 3:21).

28

THERE IS NO SALVATION
OUTSIDE ISRAEL

*Did the Old Testament Teach That
Gentiles Could Be True Jews?*

If you are a Christian, you are a Jew. If you are not a Jew, you are not a Christian. There is no salvation outside Israel. These are bold claims. But that is what the apostle Paul teaches in the books of Romans, Ephesians, and Galatians.

For example, he says in Romans 2:29, "But he is a Jew who is one inwardly; and circumcision is that which is of the heart, by the Spirit, not by the letter." Then he says that the way Gentiles find God is by becoming "fellow citizens" in the "commonwealth of Israel" (Ephesians 2:11–19) and by being "grafted into" Israel (Romans 11:17–25). Another way to put it is that "if you belong to Christ, then you are Abraham's descendants, heirs according to promise" (Galatians 3:29). The reason for this is that Christ himself is "the seed" of Abraham (Galatians 3:16), so that being in Christ means being Abraham's "seed," and, therefore, heirs of the promise (Galatians 3:29, 16).

Now the question is, did Paul reinterpret the Old Testament? Or is that kind of teaching really there? Did the Old Testament itself teach that a Gentile could be a "true Jew," and that one who is a Jew by birth might *not* be a "true Jew"? For Paul, the validity of our salvation hangs on the validity of our attachment to Israel. Therefore, a lot is at stake if Paul misinterpreted the Old Testament. Here is why I think he didn't.

In Genesis 17:18–25, Ishmael, Abraham's son, was circumcised, and Abraham pleaded with God that Ishmael might be his heir: "'Oh that Ishmael might live before You!' But God said, 'No, but Sarah your wife will bear you a son, and you shall call his name Isaac; and I will establish My covenant with him for an everlasting covenant for his descendants after him'" (verses 18–19). This shows that mere descendancy from Abraham is no guarantee of being an heir of the promise (a "true Jew"). Similarly Rebekah gave birth to twins by Isaac, but only one of them, Jacob, not Esau, was the heir of the promise (Genesis 25:23; Romans 9:10–13). Thus, as Paul says, "it is not the children of the flesh who are children of God ["true Jews"] but the children of promise are regarded as descendants" (Romans 9:8).

In Leviticus 26:41–42, many Jews are pictured as "uncircumcised in heart." "If their uncircumcised heart becomes humbled so that they then make amends for their iniquity, then I will remember My covenant with Jacob." Thus, even though they are physical Jews, they will not inherit the covenant if they do not change inside, similar to what Paul says in Romans 2:29.

In Deuteronomy 10:16–17, Moses commands the people, "Circumcise your heart, and stiffen your neck no longer. For the LORD your God is the God of gods and the Lord of lords…who does not show partiality…." This means that heart-circumcision, not physical, external Jewishness is essential with God. Similarly, Jeremiah 4:4 says, "Circumcise yourselves to the LORD and remove the foreskins of your heart, men of Judah and inhabitants of Jerusalem, or else My wrath will go forth like fire and burn with none to quench it, because of the evil of your deeds." Without inward love to God and trust in God, the same wrath comes on Jews as on Gentiles. Thus, as Paul said in Romans 2:25, without heart-circumcision "your circumcision has become uncircumcision."

Jeremiah 9:25–26 says, "'Behold, the days are coming,' declares the LORD, 'that I will punish all who are circumcised and yet uncircumcised—Egypt and Judah, and Edom and the sons of Ammon, and Moab and all those inhabiting the desert who clip the hair on their temples; for all the nations are uncircumcised, and all the house of Israel are uncircumcised of heart.'" These nations clip hair instead of foreskin. Thus they have a form of "circumcision." Jeremiah, amazingly, puts Israel in the same category as these nations under the wrath of

God because the mark of their Jewishness is no more valuable than the clipping of pagan hair if they are "uncircumcised in heart." Again, as Paul said, "your circumcision has become uncircumcision."

This is perhaps enough to show that in Romans 2:25–29 Paul is not reinterpreting the Old Testament. He is drawing out a lesson about true Jewishness that was taught by the law and the prophets. True Jews are not those with external marks of Jewishness, but those with circumcised hearts which love the God of Abraham (Deuteronomy 30:6). Therefore Gentiles with faith in Christ are "in Christ," who is the seed of Abraham, and so are the children of Abraham, heirs of the promise (Galatians 3:7, 29).

Now what shall we do with this truth? Paul did not teach this for mere intellectual interest or historical information. He taught it for the sake of humility and hope. He was especially concerned that non-Jews see themselves properly in relation to God's work in Israel. So he said to them: "Do not boast over the [Jewish] branches. If you do boast, remember it is not you that support the root [the promises to Abraham], but the root that supports you" (Romans 11:18, RSV).

So knowing that we non-Jews are "latecomers" to the covenant of Abraham and that we are nevertheless loved as full fellow-heirs should humble us and give us hope. Humble hope in the Messiah, Jesus Christ, is the aim of all redemption. For humility puts us in our lowly place of happy dependence, and hope puts God in his exalted place of glorious mercy.

29

JUSTIFIED, BUT NOT FORGIVEN?

Pondering the Difference Between Judicial Wrath and Fatherly Displeasure

How can we be justified by faith, once for all, and yet need to go on confessing our daily sins so that we will be forgiven? On the one hand, the New Testament teaches that, when we trust Christ, our faith is reckoned to us as righteousness (Romans 4:3, 5–6); the righteousness of God is imputed to us (Philippians 3:9). We stand before God "in Christ" as righteous and accepted, yes, even "forgiven," as Paul says, "David [in Psalm 32:1] pronounces a blessing upon the man to whom God reckons righteousness apart from works: 'Blessed are those whose iniquities are forgiven, and whose sins are covered'" (Romans 4:6–7, RSV). Thus justification, in Paul's mind, embraces the reality of forgiveness.

But, on the other hand, the New Testament also teaches that our ongoing forgiveness depends on confession of sins. "If we confess our sins, he is faithful and just, and will forgive our sins and cleanse us from all unrighteousness" (1 John 1:9, RSV). Confessing sins is part of "walking in the light," which is what we must do if the blood of Jesus is to go on cleansing us from our sins: *"If we walk in the light as He Himself is in the light…the blood of Jesus His Son cleanses us from all sin"* (1 John 1:7, emphasis added). And Jesus taught us to pray daily, "Forgive us our debts, as we also have forgiven our debtors" (Matthew 6:12).

How then shall we see ourselves in relation to God? Are all our sins already forgiven, or are they forgiven day by day as we confess them? Does justification

95

mean that all sins are forgiven—past, present, and future—for those who are justified? Or is there another way to see our sin in relation to God?

Let's listen first to a pastor and theologian from 350 years ago, Thomas Watson.

> When I say God forgives all sins, I understand it of sins past, for sins to come are not forgiven till they are repented of. Indeed God has decreed to pardon them; and when he forgives one sin, he will in time forgive all; but sins future are not actually pardoned till they are repented of. It is absurd to think sin should be forgiven before it is committed....
>
> The opinion that sins to come, as well as past, are forgiven, takes away and makes void Christ's intercession. He is an advocate to intercede for daily sin (1 John 2:1). But if sin be forgiven before it be committed, what need is there of his daily intercession? What need have I of an advocate, if sin be pardoned before it be committed? So that, though God forgives all sins past to a believer, yet sins to come are not forgiven till repentance be renewed. *(Body of Divinity* [Grand Rapids: Baker Book House, 1979], 558)

Is Watson right?

It depends. Yes, I think one can talk this way about forgiveness if one keeps firmly in mind that the purchase and ground and securing of *all* (past, present, and future) was the death of Jesus, once for all. The ambiguity comes in the question, When do we *obtain* forgiveness for all the sins we will ever commit? Does this question mean, When was our forgiveness purchased and secured for us? Or does it mean, When will our forgiveness be applied to each transgression so as to remove God's displeasure for it? The answer to the first question would be, at the death of Christ. And the answer to the second question would be, at the renewal of our repentance.

Which raises another question: Does God feel displeasure toward his justified children? If so, what kind of displeasure is this? Is it the same kind of displeasure he has toward the sins of unbelievers? How does God see our daily sins? He sees them as breaches of his will that grieve him and anger him. This grief and anger, however, while prompted by real blameworthiness and real guilt, is not "judicial wrath," to use Thomas Watson's phrase. "Though a child of God, after pardon, may incur his fatherly displeasure, yet his judicial wrath is removed. Though he may lay on the rod, yet he has taken away the curse. Corrections may befall the saints, but not destruction" *(Body of Divinity,* 556).

God also sees our sins as "covered" and "not reckoned" because of the blood of Christ (Romans 4:7–8). Thus, paradoxically, he sees our sins as both *guilt-bringing* (and thus producing grief and anger) and *guaranteed-of-pardon* (though not yet pardoned in the sense of his response to confession and the actual removal of his fatherly displeasure). What is it that distinguishes God's *judicial wrath* toward the unbeliever's unconfessed sin from God's *fatherly displeasure* toward the believer's unconfessed sin? The difference is that the believer is united to God in Christ by a new covenant. The promise of this covenant is that God will never turn away from doing good to us and will never let us turn away from him, but will always bring us back to confession and repentance. "I will make with them an everlasting covenant, that *I will not turn away from doing good to them;* and I will put the fear of me in their hearts, *that they may not turn from me"* (Jeremiah 32:40, RSV, emphasis added).

This new covenant commitment was purchased by Christ for us (Luke 22:20) and applied to us through faith so that, though we incur our Father's displeasure, we, who are justified believers, never incur the judicial wrath of God to all eternity. Or to put it another way, since the forgiveness of all our sins is purchased and secured by the death of Christ, therefore God is totally committed to bring us back to confession and repentance as often as necessary so that we may receive and enjoy that forgiveness in the removal of his fatherly displeasure. It is our Father's pleasure to restore us to his pleasure until such restorings are needed no more.

30

IMPERFECTION: THE MARK OF ALL THE PERFECTED

Meditation on Hebrews 10:14

> *For by one offering He has perfected*
> *for all time those who are being sanctified.*

Two things here are mightily encouraging for us in our imperfect condition as saved sinners.

First, notice that Christ has perfected his people, and it is already complete. "For by one offering *He has perfected for all time* those who are being sanctified." He *has* done it. And he has done it *for all time*. The perfecting of his people is complete and it is complete forever. Does this mean that Christians don't sin? Don't get sick? Don't make mathematical errors in school? That we are already perfect in our behavior and attitudes?

There is one clear reason in this very verse for knowing that is not the case. What is it? It's the last phrase. Who are the people that have been perfected for all time? It is those who "are *being* sanctified" (emphasis added). The ongoing continuous action of the Greek present tense is important. "Those who *are being* sanctified" (emphasis added) are not yet fully sanctified in the sense of committing no more sin. Otherwise they would not need to go on being sanctified.

So here we have the shocking combination: The very people who *"have been* perfected" are the ones who *"are being* sanctified." We can also think back to chapters 5 and 6 to recall that these Christians are anything but perfect. For example, in Hebrews 5:11 he says, "You have become dull of hearing." So we may safely say that "perfected" in Hebrews 10:14 does not mean that we are sinlessly perfect in this life.

Well, what does it mean? The answer is given in the next verses (15–18). The writer explains what he means by quoting Jeremiah on the new covenant, namely, that in the new covenant which Christ has sealed by his blood, there is total forgiveness for all our sins. Verses 17–18: "Their sins and their lawless deeds I will remember no more. Now where there is forgiveness of these things, there is no longer any offering for sin." So he explains the present perfection in terms (at least) of forgiveness.

Christ's people are perfected now in the sense that God puts away all our sins (9:26), forgives them, and never brings them to mind again as a ground of condemnation. In this sense, we stand before him perfected. When he looks on us he does not impute any of our sins to us—past, present, or future. He does not count our sins against us.

Now notice, second, for whom Christ has done this perfecting work on the cross. Hebrews 10:14 tells us plainly: "By one offering He has perfected for all time *those who are being sanctified*" (emphasis added). You can put it provocatively like this: Christ *has* perfected once and for all those who *are being* perfected. Or you could say, Christ *has fully* sanctified those who *are now being* sanctified—which the writer does, in fact, say in verse 10, "By this will *we have been sanctified* through the offering of the body of Jesus Christ once for all." Thus verse 10 says, we *"have been* sanctified." Verse 14 says, we *"are being* sanctified."

What this means is that you can know that you stand perfect in the eyes of your heavenly Father, if you are moving away from your present imperfection toward more and more holiness by faith in his future grace. Let me say that again, because it is full of encouragement for imperfect sinners like us and full of motivation for holiness. Hebrews 10:14 means that you can have assurance that you stand perfected and completed in the eyes of your heavenly Father, not because you are perfect now, but precisely because you are *not* perfect now but are "being sanctified"—"being made holy."

You may have assurance of your perfect standing with God because by faith in God's promises, you are moving away from your lingering imperfections toward more and more holiness. Our remaining imperfection is not a sign of our disqualification, but a mark of all whom God "has perfected for all time"—if we are in the process of "being changed" (2 Corinthians 3:18).

So take heart. Fix your eyes on the once-for-all, perfecting work of Christ. And set your face against all known sin.

⌇⌇⌇

31

TEN REASONS TO LOVE THE TRUTH

The Perils of Vulgar Relativism

> *...who perish, because they did not*
> *receive the love of the truth so as to be saved.*
>
> 2 THESSALONIANS 2:10

On May 5, 1994, Michael Novak received the twenty-fourth Templeton Prize for Progress in Religion and addressed the assembly at Westminster Abbey with a message titled "Awakening from Nihilism" (printed in *First Things,* No. 45, August/September, 1994). It is a scathing attack on the horrific effects of relativism in the twentieth century. Of all the lessons that can be learned from the past hundred years the first is this: "Truth matters." His assessment of the fundamental problem today:

> One principle that today's intellectuals most passionately disseminate is vulgar relativism, "Nihilism with a happy face." For them it is certain that there is no truth, only opinion: my opinion, your opinion. They abandon the defense of the intellect.... Those who surrender the domain of the intellect make straight the road to fascism. Totalitarianism...is the will-to-power unchecked by any regard for truth. To surrender the claims of truth upon humans is to surrender Earth to thugs.... Vulgar relativism is an invisible gas, odorless, deadly, that is now polluting every free society on earth. It is a gas that attacks

the central nervous system of moral striving.… "There is no such thing as truth," they teach even the little ones. "Truth is bondage. Believe what seems right to you. There are as many truths as there are individuals. Follow your feelings. Do as you please. Get in touch with yourself.…" Those who speak in this way prepare the jails of the twenty-first century. They do the work of tyrants. (20–21)

When you come to the Bible with those words ringing in your ears, it is not surprising or oppressive, but sobering and thrilling to find that truth is central. Why? For the simple reason that God is central, and God is the ground of all truth. Here is what we find. Cherish this.

1. Biblical truth saves.

Take heed to yourself and to your teaching; hold to that, for by so doing you will save both yourself and your hearers. (1 Timothy 4:16, RSV; see also Acts 20:26–27; 2 Thessalonians 2:10)

2. Biblical truth frees from Satan.

You shall know the truth, and the truth shall make you free. (John 8:32; see also 2 Timothy 2:24–26)

3. Biblical truth imparts grace and peace.

May grace and peace be multiplied to you in the knowledge of God and of Jesus our Lord. (2 Peter 1:2, RSV)

4. Biblical truth sanctifies.

Sanctify them in the truth; Your word is truth. (John 17:17; see also 2 Peter 1:3, 5, 12; 2 Timothy 3:16–17)

5. *Biblical truth serves love.*

It is my prayer that your love may abound more and more, with knowledge and all discernment. (Philippians 1:9, RSV)

6. *Biblical truth protects from error.*

Attain to the unity of the faith and of the knowledge of the Son of God…so that we may no longer be…tossed to and fro…by every wind of doctrine. (Ephesians 4:13–14, RSV)

7. *Biblical truth is the hope of heaven.*

Now I know in part; then I shall understand fully, even as I have been fully understood. (1 Corinthians 13:12, RSV)

8. *Biblical truth will be resisted by some.*

The time is coming when people will not endure sound teaching, but having itching ears they will accumulate for themselves teachers to suit their own likings. (2 Timothy 4:3, RSV)

9. *Biblical truth, rightly handled, is approved by God.*

Do your best to present yourself to God as one approved, a workman who has no need to be ashamed, rightly handling the word of truth. (2 Timothy 2:15, RSV)

10. *Biblical truth: Continue to grow in it!*

Grow in the grace and the knowledge of our Lord and Savior Jesus Christ. (2 Peter 3:18)

I pray that the effect of these biblical words will be a strong conviction that there is such a thing as truth in a world of "vulgar relativism," and that the Bible itself is the all-decisive Word of the One who is Truth. If that conviction would take root and spread, we would not be among the number who "prepare the jails of the twenty-first century." We would, in fact, be the true liberators: "You will know the truth, and the truth will make you free" (John 8:32).

32

SHOULD CHRISTIAN COLLEGES INDOCTRINATE?

The Other Alternative to the Adolescent Academia

James Davison Hunter is a sociologist teaching at the University of Virginia. He published a book in 1987 titled *Evangelicalism: The Coming Generation* (Chicago: University Press). It was based on research he had done in American Christian Colleges. Here is one of his conclusions:

> We can see the multiple ironies of Christian higher education. On the one hand, Christian higher education historically evolved into precisely the opposite of what it was supposed to be, that is, into bastions of secularity if not anti-Christian sentiment. Contemporary Christian higher education, on the other hand, produces the unintended consequences of being counterproductive to its own objectives, that is, it produces individual Christians who are either less certain of their attachments to the traditions of their faith or altogether disaffected from them. Education, to the degree that it is not indoctrination, weakens the tenacity with which Evangelicals hold on to their worldview. In sum, Evangelical education creates its own contaminating effects. And the more Christian higher education professionalizes and bureaucratizes (that is, the more it models itself institutionally after secular higher education), the more likely this process will intensify. (178)

All of us know wonderful exceptions to this claim—people who are stronger in their faith and deeper in their grasp of biblical truth and more capable of defending it than if they had not gone to a Christian college. I put myself in that number.

But surely Hunter was not whistling in the wind. He has no fundamentalist ax to grind. To the degree that he is right, what are we to say? What I want to say is this: "Indoctrination" is not the only alternative to faith-weakening education. In our day, the word "indoctrination" usually refers to unthinking transmission of tradition. But I would affirm strongly that this is not the only alternative to the secularizing effect of Christian higher education.

The real alternative is a faculty made up of great Christian thinkers who are great lovers of God with profound allegiance to the truth of God's Word and razor-sharp discernment of all the subtle idols of our age. What is needed is great teachers with great hearts for the great old verities of the faith—verities that they hold because there are great reasons for holding them—reasons that will stand up to hard questions.

Faith is destroyed when little academic minds and little hearts for God niggle away at magnificent and precious realities with no remorse…when there is no great love for God and his Word and no great passion to see the truth of God magnified and defended with profound credibility and authenticity…when faculty demonstrate their academic standing not in the really great and difficult task of constructive explication and justification of truth, but in the simple and adolescent task of deconstruction and cynicism.

I have sat under Ph.D.s who never grew up. It never even occurred to them that they might bear the responsibility of being the elders and fathers in Israel. Or the mothers in Israel. Instead, they were the homeboys who still thought it was cool to call mother "my old lady" and who were embarrassed if the evidence pointed to the truth and beauty of something traditional.

Our problem is not that "indoctrination" is the only alternative to education. It isn't. Our problem is that so few people have ever tasted great Christian education or seen great Christian thinking going on from a profoundly God-centered perspective in an atmosphere where students can feel that the faculty would gladly die for Jesus.

ⲟⲙⲙⲟ

33

LUTHER, BUNYAN, BIBLE, AND PAIN

Meditation on Psalm 119:71

> *It is good for me that I was afflicted,*
> *that I may learn Your statutes.*

From 1660 to 1672, John Bunyan, the English Baptist preacher and author of *Pilgrim's Progress,* was in the Bedford jail. He could have been released if he had agreed not to preach. He did not know which was worse, the pain of the conditions or the torment of freely choosing it in view of what it cost his wife and four children. His daughter, Mary, was blind. She was ten when he was put in jail in 1660.

> The parting with my Wife and poor children hath often been to me in this place as the pulling of the Flesh from my bones...not only because I am somewhat too fond of these great Mercies, but also because I...often brought to my mind the many hardships, miseries and wants that my poor Family was like to meet with should I be taken from them, especially my poor blind child, who lay nearer my heart than all I had besides; Oh the thoughts of the hardship I thought my Blind one might go under, would break my heart to pieces. *(Grace Abounding to the Chief of Sinners* [Hertfordshire: Evangelical Press, 1978], 123)

But this broken Bunyan was seeing treasures in the Word of God because of this suffering that he would probably not have seen any other way. He was discovering the meaning of Psalm 119:71, "It is good for me that I was afflicted, that I may learn Your statutes."

I never had in all my life so great an inlet into the Word of God as now [in prison]. The Scriptures that I saw nothing in before are made in this place to shine upon me. Jesus Christ also was never more real and apparent than now. Here I have seen him and felt him indeed.... I have seen [such things] here that I am persuaded I shall never while in this world be able to express.... Being very tender of me, [God] hath not suffered me to be molested, but would with one scripture and another strengthen me against all; insomuch that I have often said, were it lawful I could pray for greater trouble for the greater comfort's sake. (*Grace Abounding*, 123)

In other words, one of God's gifts to us in suffering is that we are granted to see and experience depths of his Word that a life of ease would never yield.

Martin Luther had discovered the same "method" of seeing God in his Word. He said there are three rules for understanding Scripture: praying, meditating, and suffering. The trials, he said, are supremely valuable: They "teach you not only to know and understand but also to experience how right, how true, how sweet, how lovely, how mighty, how comforting God's Word is: It is wisdom supreme." Therefore the devil himself becomes the unwitting teacher of God's Word:

The devil will afflict you [and] will make a real doctor of you, and will teach you by his temptations to seek and to love God's Word. For I myself...owe my papists many thanks for so beating, pressing, and frightening me through the devil's raging that they have turned me into a fairly good theologian, driving me to a goal I should never have reached. (Ewald M. Plass, *What Luther Says*, vol. 3 [St. Louis: Concordia Publishing House, 1959], 1360)

I testify from my small experience that this is true. Disappointment, loss, sickness, and fear send me deeper than ever into God and his Word. Clouds of trifling are blown away, and the glory of unseen things shines in the heart's eye. Let Bunyan and Luther encourage us to lean on God's Word in times of affliction as never before. I know that there are seasons when we cannot think or read, the pain is so great. But God grants spaces of some relief between these terrible times. Turn your gaze on the Word and prove the truth of Psalm 119:71, "It is good for me that I was afflicted, that I may learn Your statutes."

34

DOES GOD REALLY WANT YOU TO BE ENCOURAGED?

On Seizing the Gift of Hope

Meditation on Hebrews 6:17–18

Holidays are dangerous times of discouragement. The expectations for gladness are higher, so realities of sadness are heavier. You're *supposed* to be gloomy in February—at least, in Minnesota—so it's more tolerable then. But Thanksgiving and Christmas—and birthdays and anniversaries and homecomings—are supposed to be festive. Hence, the doubly dangerous threat of discouragement at holidays and celebrations. May I offer some preventative medicine?

> When *God desired to show more convincingly* to the heirs of the promise the unchangeable character of his purpose, he added an oath, so that through two unchangeable things [the promise and the oath], in which it is impossible that God should prove false, we who have fled for refuge might have *strong encouragement to seize the hope set before us.* (Hebrews 6:17–18, author's translation, emphasis added)

"God desired to show more convincingly..."
This text assumes that God had *already* said enough to give us encouragement. But God is not a God of minimums. His aim is not to speak as few encouraging words as possible. He speaks some words to give us hope. Then, being the

effusive God he is, he says to himself, "This is good. I like doing this. I think that I shall do this again." And so he speaks some more words of encouragement.

But not just *more.* They are *better.* He moves from simple promises (which are infallible and infinitely trustworthy!) to oaths. And not just any oaths, but the best and highest kind—oaths based on himself. Why? Not because his word is weak. But because we are weak, and he is patient.

He desires to show—prove...demonstrate...point out...represent...display...reveal...drive home—the hopefulness of our future. He really wants us to feel this. He goes the second (and third and fourth) mile to help us feel encouraged. This is what he wants. This is what he *really* wants. "When God *desired* to show more convincingly..." He is not coerced. He "desires."

"...that we might have strong encouragement..."
How encouraged does God want us to feel? Hebrews 6:18 says, "Strong encouragement!" Note the word! He might have said, "great encouragement" or "big encouragement" or "deep encouragement." They would all be true. But the word is really "strong." Encouragement that stands against seasonal downers. Preach this to yourself. "God desires me to have strong encouragement!" "God really desires me to have *strong* encouragement!"

"...to seize the hope set before us..."
There are good times in this life. But let's face it: The days are evil; our imperfections frustrate us; and we are getting older and moving toward the grave. If in this life only we have hoped in Christ we are of all people most to be pitied (1 Corinthians 15:19). There are good times yet to come in this life. But fewer. And even these are rubbish, compared to the surpassing worth of gaining Christ in death (Philippians 1:21). Even here we can rejoice with joy unspeakable and full of glory. But only because there is a "hope set before us." Reach out and seize it. God encourages you to. Take it now. Enjoy it now. Be encouraged by it now. Be strongly encouraged. Because your hope is secured with double infiniteness: the promise of God and the oath of God.

35

THEY GAVE IT THEIR BEST
SHOT IN VAIN

If They Don't Knock You Down,
They Can't Let You Up

When Jesus was dead and buried, with a big stone rolled against the tomb, the Pharisees came to Pilate and asked for permission to seal the stone and guard the tomb. Pilate said, "You have a guard of soldiers; go, make it as secure as you can" (Matthew 27:65, RSV). So they did. They gave it their best shot—in vain.

It was hopeless then; it is hopeless today; and it will always be hopeless. Try as they may, people can't keep Jesus down. They can't keep him buried. They may use physical force or academic scorn or media blackout or political harassment or religious caricature. For a season they will think the tomb is finally sealed. But it never works. He breaks out.

It's not hard to figure out: He can break out because he wasn't forced in. He *lets* himself be libeled and harassed and blackballed and scorned and shoved around and killed. "I lay down my life, that I may take it again. No one takes it from me, but I lay it down of my own accord. I have power to lay it down, and I have power to take it again" (John 10:17–18, RSV). No one can keep him down because no one ever knocked him down. He lay down when he was ready.

If China was closed for forty years to Western missionaries, it's not because Jesus slipped and fell into the tomb. He stepped in. And when it was sealed over, he saved fifty million Chinese from inside—without Western missionaries. And when it was time, he pushed the stone away so we could see what he had done.

When it looks like he is buried for good, Jesus is doing something awesome in the dark. "The kingdom of God is as if a man who scattered seed on the ground, and should sleep and rise night and day, and the seed should sprout and grow, he knows not how" (Mark 4:26–27, RSV). The world thinks Jesus is done for—out of the way. They think his Word is buried for good in the dust of irrelevant antiquity.

But Jesus is at work in the dark places: "Unless a grain of wheat falls into the earth and dies, it remains alone; but if it dies, it bears much fruit" (John 12:24). He let himself be buried ("no one takes my life from me"), and he will come out in power when and where he pleases ("I have power to take it again"). And his hands will be full of fruit made in the dark.

"God raised him up, having loosed the pangs of death because *it was not possible for him to be held by it*" (Acts 2:24, RSV, emphasis added). Jesus has his priesthood today "by the power of an *indestructible life*" (Hebrews 7:16, RSV, emphasis added).

For twenty centuries the world has given it their best shot—in vain. They can't bury him. They can't hold him in. They can't silence him or limit him. Jesus is alive and utterly free to go and come wherever he pleases. "All authority in heaven and on earth has been given to me" (Matthew 28:18, RSV). All things were made through him and for him and he is absolutely supreme over all other powers (Colossians 1:16–17).

Trust him and go with him, no matter what. You cannot lose in the end. Stand in awe of his freedom and quiet, invincible power.

の〜

36

DISCERNMENT BY DESIRE

Finding God's Will by the Fragrance of the Holy

Most of the choices we make in a day are not made after consciously weighing a list of criteria. We dress and eat and sit and walk and a hundred other things without consciously asking: Is this the will of God? I think this is inevitable and good. It reveals our true inner nature. If we are going to do what pleases God, most of the time it will be by reflex, not reflection.

This means that one faculty of discernment is deeper than reflective reason. What faculty is that? Perhaps we should call it *the discerning faculty of desire*. If choices are being made, moment by moment, without reflection, then the faculty of desire is not merely following the dictates of reason; it is following its own nose. Desire, or something closely connected to it, "smells" the preferred choice and embraces it before reflection.

Though I have thought about this a long time since reading about it in Jonathan Edwards, what I see more clearly now is that this same method of choosing seems to apply to choices we make even after very long reflection. Suppose you are a part of choosing a new pastor for your church. One step would be to reflect on the nature of God, the ways of God, and the commandments of God in the Bible. Another step would be to extrapolate from the Bible certain guidelines that are not explicitly addressed by Scripture. This takes "wisdom" and we are to pray for it, according to James 1:5.

Of course, this assumes that alongside biblical reflection we are observing all the relevant facts of the situation. In the case of the new pastor, for example, you would be observing his character, spiritual life, preaching ability, pastoral skills, background, personality, reputation, and so on. This is the raw material that the biblical principles have to work with.

But it seems to me that there comes a point when all the biblical teaching has been applied and all the observation has been performed and all the wisdom has been prayed for and many choices (many candidates) have been ruled out. The circle of possible remaining choices is small. But inside it there are still several good choices, not just one. Our finite minds do not know all that God knows and we are at the limit of what we can discern by prayerful, spiritual reflection on the Bible and the person and the circumstances.

God could speak to us in a dream or a prophetic word or some other revelatory way as he did to Philip in Acts 8:26 or to Paul in Acts 16:9. But he may not do this. And it does not appear that this is his normal way of leading us. What then are we to do?

The new thing that I am seeing more clearly these days is this: We are to do what we do 90 percent of the time when being led by the Spirit of God. We are to let our Spirit-shaped desires be our guide. We are to *discern by desire*. In other words, when we have narrowed down the choices into a small circle enclosed by biblical principle and spiritual wisdom and careful observation, then inside that circle we prayerfully ask: In which choice do we *delight?* According to Psalm 1:1–2, the alternative to walking in the counsel of the ungodly is to *"delight* in the law of the Lord." Our faculty of delight is crucial in keeping us from folly.

The assumption here is that our faculty of delighting or desiring is healthy and God-saturated. And that is the great challenge of the Christian life: Be transformed in the renewing of your mind that you may *approve* [not just prove, but approve, that is, test and then delight in] the will of God (Romans 12:2). Our great need is to be people whose delights are the very delights of God.

⌒〜〜〜⌒

37

You Are About to Change Your Job

Thinking About How God Shakes Us Loose and Leads in a New Way

God is calling many of you who read this book to rethink your life goals. And your life work. These are exciting days. Unsettling days. But you are yearning deep inside to live and work closer to the brink of eternity. You are dissatisfied with working just to make money. You are questioning the point of a job that has little significance for eternity. The thought of doing something risky and radical and out of step with the American dream keeps coming back to you.

What should you do?

Don't suffocate the dream. Don't drown it in busyness. Don't rush past the beckoning pull-off. Do what God's servants have done for centuries. Spend an extended time alone in prayer and fasting.

Jesus began his ministry by fasting forty days alone (Matthew 4:1–11). And just before choosing the twelve apostles, he spent a whole night in prayer (Luke 6:12).

Wesley Duewel, a former missionary to India under OMS International, discovered that the world and busyness can so fill the mind with godless thoughts, that he needed a prayer retreat in which he read at least fifty chapters of the Bible before he was again really in tune with God. "I have at times read as many as fifty chapters from God's Word before I was completely alone with God. But on some of those occasions I received such unexpected guidance that my life has been greatly benefited" *(Let God Guide You Daily* [Grand Rapids: Zondervan Publishing House, 1988], 77).

Elijah was sent by the Spirit forty days into the wilderness to Mount Horeb to hear the "still small voice" of God and get guidance about the kings of Syria and Israel and about his successor Elisha (1 Kings 19:11–18).

The Bible says not to get drunk with wine but to be filled with the Spirit (Ephesians 5:18). But how do you get drunk with wine? By drinking *a lot* of it. So how do you get filled with the Spirit? One way is by drinking a lot of him. How do you do that? We receive the Spirit by hearing with faith (Galatians 3:2). Hearing what? The Word of God. I am convinced we will not be filled with the Spirit of truth until we drink ourselves drunk with the Word of God. That's what a day of prayer and fasting is for.

If we are filled with the Spirit, all our faculties will be more sensitive to God's leading in all the ways that he leads. Most of us do not give ourselves the soaking in God that can penetrate to the deep preferences that really govern our choices without our even knowing it. There is a kind of tuning in to the mind of God in his Word that comes with lingering in his Word-saturated presence. This is the fullness that could make all the difference in whether your heart resonates with the new music God is playing in your life.

David Brainerd frequently set aside days of prayer and fasting. On Thursday, November 3, 1743, he fasted and read 1 Kings 17–19; 2 Kings 2–4; Exodus 3–20; "the story of Abraham," and "the story of Joseph's sufferings." He prayed as he read, and then God met his need. "I had for many months entirely lost all hopes of…doing any special service for God in the world. It has appeared entirely impossible that one so black and vile should be thus improved for God! But at this time God was pleased to revive this hope" *(The Life of David Brainerd,* ed. Norman Pettit, in *The Works of Jonathan Edwards* [New Haven: Yale University Press, 1985], 225f).

So it may be for many of you. If the Spirit is causing you to think about a turn in the road, don't keep your foot on the accelerator of your life. Slow down. Take a detour to the place of quietness called prayer and fasting. Get alone for a day with God and his Word. Believe it or not, he would love to meet you (2 Corinthians 6:16–17).

38

WHAT IS A "ROOT OF BITTERNESS"?

The Price of Presumption

Meditation on Hebrews 12:15

> *See to it that no one comes short of the*
> *grace of God; that no root of bitterness*
> *springing up causes trouble,*
> *and by it many be defiled.*

Bitterness is usually associated with anger and grudges. But is that what it means in Hebrews 12:15? I don't think so. Let's ask a few questions. First of all, does "root *of* bitterness" mean that the root *is* bitterness (like block *of* wood)? Or does it mean that the root grows up into a plant and bears the bitter fruit? So *"of* bitterness" then would mean "giving rise to bitterness," as in the phrase, "news *of* great joy." Second, does "bitterness," in Hebrews 12:15, mean "festering anger," or does it mean "poisonous and foul"? Third, where did this image of a "root of bitterness" come from?

Let's start with the last question. Answer: It came from Deuteronomy 29:18. "Beware lest there be among you a man or woman or family or tribe, whose heart turns away this day from the LORD our God to go and serve the gods of those nations; lest there be among you *a root bearing poisonous and bitter fruit*" (RSV, emphasis added). This background also helps us answer the first two questions: The root is not itself bitterness, but rather bears the fruit of bitterness. And the bitterness it bears is something poisonous. This bitter fruit *may* be festering anger, or it may be something else. The point seems to be that it is deadly.

The key question is, What is this root that causes deadly, bitter fruit to sprout in the church? The next verse in Deuteronomy 29 gives the surprising answer, and it fits perfectly with the book of Hebrews. Verse 18 ends: "…lest there be among you *a root bearing poisonous and bitter fruit."* Then verse 19 begins by defining this root: "One who, when he hears the words of this sworn covenant, blesses himself in his heart, saying, *'I shall be safe, though I walk in the stubbornness of my heart.'* This would lead to the sweeping away of moist and dry alike" (RSV, emphasis added).

What then is the root that brings forth the bitter fruit? It is a person who has a wrong view of eternal security. He feels secure when he is not secure. He says, "I shall be safe [secure], though I walk in the stubbornness of my heart." He misunderstands the covenant God makes. He thinks that because he is part of the covenant people, he is secure from God's judgment.

This kind of presumption is what the book of Hebrews deals with repeatedly—professing Christians who think they are secure because of some past spiritual experience or some present association with Christian people. The aim of Hebrews is to cure Christians of presumption and to cultivate earnest perseverance in the full assurance of faith and holiness. At least four times it warns us that we must not neglect our great salvation but rather be vigilant to fight the fight of faith every day lest we become hardened and fall away and prove that we had no share in Christ (2:3; 3:12–14; 6:4–7; 10:23–29).

This is also the very point of the context of the term "root of bitterness" in Hebrews 12:15. "Pursue peace with all men, and the sanctification without which no one will see the Lord. See to it that no one comes short of the grace of God; that no *root of bitterness* springing up causes trouble, and by it many be defiled" (12:14–15). This is a warning not to let the attitude of Deuteronomy 29:19 take root, "I shall be safe, though I walk in the stubbornness of my heart" (RSV). It is a warning not to treat holiness lightly or to presume upon more grace.

Therefore a "root of bitterness" is a person or a doctrine in the church which encourages people to act presumptuously and treats salvation as an automatic thing that does not require a life of vigilance in the fight of faith and the pursuit

of holiness. Such a person or a doctrine defiles many and can lead to the experience of Esau, who played fast and loose with his inheritance and could not
repent in the end. "[Let] there be no immoral or godless person like Esau, who
sold his own birthright for a single meal. For you know that even afterwards,
when he desired to inherit the blessing, he was rejected, for he found no place
for repentance, though he sought for it [the repentance] with tears" (Hebrews
12:16–17). That would be bitter indeed. Don't let a root grow up in the church
or in your life that would spread such cavalier treatment of our great inheritance.

39

WHEN GOD'S WILL IS THAT HIS WILL NOT BE DONE

Meditation on 1 Samuel 2:22–25

> *Now Eli was very old; and he heard all that*
> *his sons were doing to all Israel, and how*
> *they lay with the women who served at the*
> *doorway of the tent of meeting. And he said*
> *to them, "Why do you do such things, the*
> *evil things that I hear from all these*
> *people? No, my sons; for the report is not*
> *good which I hear the LORD's people*
> *circulating. If one man sins against another,*
> *God will mediate for him; but if a man sins*
> *against the LORD, who can intercede for*
> *him?" But they would not listen to the voice*
> *of their father, for the LORD desired to put*
> *them to death.*

It was too late for Eli's sons. They had crossed the line of no return. The sentence had been given by the Lord. They were to be slain by the Lord. And they were slain, according to 1 Samuel 4:11. "And the ark of God was taken; and the two sons of Eli, Hophni and Phinehas, died."

There are three implications of this text for our lives.

1. It is possible to sin so long and so grievously that the Lord will not grant repentance.

That is why Paul said that after all our pleading and teaching, "God may grant them repentance"—not "will grant them repentance" (2 Timothy 2:25). "With gentleness correcting those who are in opposition, if perhaps God may grant them repentance leading to the knowledge of the truth…" (emphasis added). There is a "too late" in the life of sin. As it says of Esau in Hebrews 12:17, "He found no place for repentance, though he sought for it with tears." He was forsaken; he could not truly repent. His heart was too hard.

This does not mean that those who truly repent even after a whole lifetime of sinning cannot be saved. They certainly can be and will be! God is staggeringly merciful. Witness the thief on the cross: "Today you will be with Me in paradise" (Luke 23:43). Jesus had said, "The one who comes to Me I will certainly not cast out" (John 6:37). And so it proved to be for the thief on the cross in the eleventh hour. But no one knows where the point of no return is. The deciding factor is not a set number of years of sinning or a particular kind of sin. God alone knows in the case of each person where the line is crossed. This is a call for making haste to reconcile with God (Hebrews 3:15) and a call to be vigilant against willful and protracted sinning (Hebrews 10:26).

2. God may not permit a sinning person to do what is right.

"But they would not listen to the voice of their father, for the LORD desired to put them to death." Listening to the voice of their father was the right thing to do. But they would not. Why? "For the LORD desired to put them to death." The reason given for why they did not obey their father was that God had other purposes for them and had given them up to sinning and death. This shows that there are times when the *will of God's decree* is different from *the will of God's command.* God commanded, "Children, obey your parents" (Ephesians 6:1). But in this case he willed that, instead of obedience, they persist in their sin and be slain. It was judgment. God is not sinning in this will of decree. He is ordering things so that sin continues for holy and just purposes. But willing that sin be in such cases is not sin.

3. Sometimes our prayers for God's revealed will to be done will not be done because God has decreed something different to bring about his holy and wise purposes.

I suppose that Eli prayed for his sons to be changed. That surely is how he should have prayed. God *commanded* that children obey their parents. So we should pray that they obey. But God had decreed that Hophni and Phinehas not obey, but rather be slain. When something like this happens (which we do not ordinarily know ahead of time) while we are crying out to God for change, the answer of God is not: "I don't love you." Nor is it, "I don't hear you." Nor is it even, "I don't approve of your prayer." Rather the answer is (even when we can't hear it): "I have wise and holy purposes in not overcoming this sin and not granting repentance. You do not see these purposes now. Trust me. I know what I am doing. I love you."

These are the hardest times of submission to the will of God. We cry. We ache. We plead for change in our children or spouse or parents or colleague or neighbor. We make our case with God that his revealed will of holiness and faith and love come forth in their lives. But year after year we see no change. Oh, the test to faith this is! But let us not join the rebellion. Let us put our hands on our mouths and unclench our fists and prostrate ourselves before the Lord of infinite wisdom and justice and love. And let us say, when all our tears are spent, May the Lord do what seems good to him (1 Samuel 3:18).

40

THE ROOT OF MENTAL HEALTH:
BEING HEALED BY KNOWING GOD

On Not Helping People Be Happy on Their Way to Hell

The most common remedy for most behavioral and mental disorders today is some form of self-worth enhancement. It pervades our educational institutions, the psychotherapeutic and counseling system, the personnel and motivational industry, advertising, and even the church. I think the remedy is flawed. Here is a letter I wrote to a man to clarify the sentence, "It is profoundly wrong to turn the cross of Christ into a warrant for self-esteem as the root of mental health." Call him Aquila.

Dear Aquila,

1. The operative phrase in my sentence, "It is profoundly wrong to turn the cross of Christ into a warrant for self-esteem as the root of mental health," is "the root of mental health." I believe that it is profoundly wrong to say that being loved by God brings mental health if what is meant by "being loved" is mainly that I should now have self-esteem—if "being loved"

means "I am loveable." Or "I am worth loving." Or "God don't love junk."

This makes two mistakes. One is that it misses the reality and glory and wonder and freedom of grace, which is God's absolutely free choice to set his love on whomever he pleases and raise up from stones children to Abraham if he wants to show us that stones will do fine. The other mistake is to belittle the immeasurably great experience of the love of God in and of itself, not for its signing off on my worth. In my way of seeing things, the love of God is God's gift of enabling me to see him and be with him and enjoy him forever. If I try to take that divine, treasured gift of God to me and say that it makes me happy because it helps me feel good about me, something is profoundly wrong.

2. However, in saying that the root of mental health is *not* self-esteem, but rather the enjoyment of God as God and his free grace as grace, I did not say that there is no truth in the concept of human value (though I choke on the phrase "self-worth" since the word "self" in front of the word "worth" seems to really push the issue beyond where the Bible takes it). Jesus said, you are of more value than the birds (Matthew 6:26). I take that to mean ultimately that humans have the unique capacity to enjoy God as God and reflect his worth and glory as no other creature can. Thus the worth of the human being is our God-given potential to make much of God by enjoying him and valuing him and cherishing him and his ways.

3. Must we believe that we are "perfectible" in order to hope in heaven as we ought? Yes. And everything hangs on what "perfect" would mean and who is doing the perfecting. *God* does it ("May the God of peace Himself sanctify you entirely," 1 Thessalonians 5:23), and perfect means perfectly suited and fitted and completed to delight in God with the very energy and purity with which he delights in himself ("The love with which You [Father] loved Me [your Son] [will] be in them, and I in them," John 17:26).

4. Should we tell an abandoned person that they have great "self-worth" when they feel like a failure and a piece of junk? (First, let's chuck the phrase "self-worth" because it is so loaded with a psychologized, man-centered worldview that it probably will not help communicate what a feeling of God-centered significance really is.) As you pointed out so well, the issue is trust. Has God blown it in this relationship? Has he made a mistake in making that person homely or nervous or blind or short or plump or average or unathletic? I think

that the quick retreat to self-esteem therapy is hopelessly misleading and leaves the real problem unresolved, while perhaps helping people feel good because they are somebody (which our use of God just happens to serve to support). *The issue is*: Do they love God as God in a way that satisfies them enough to pick up and go on? Do they trust his goodness and wisdom and power and riches to help them do what they must do? Do they rejoice in him because they are granted the ten-billion-dollar privilege of knowing him and being loved by him? Or must they have that vision of glory echo their own worth before they get any help from it?

I do not deny or hide that it is wonderfully significant to know God and to be used by God to make him known and loved by others. So there comes a time that I will say this, and say it in a way that makes it plain that the wonder of it lies in the preciousness of knowing God and mirroring him well enough by my delight in him that others can see his worth in me and join me in enjoying him. Now that would be real significance!

I hope you can see and feel the world in which my thoughts orbit. The issue is: What is the *root* of mental health? My answer is, God. Or seeing God as God and enjoying him as God, which involves being forgiven by God and welcomed with utterly free grace. I personally believe that these truths are hijacked when they are used to make self-esteem the root of mental health. The minor evangelical adjustments to the world's way of making people happy on the way to hell are not radical enough for me.

You have served me well. Thanks.

Pastor John

41

THE SIMULTANEOUS SOUND OF LAUGHTER AND WEEPING

Living in the Real World of Constant Pain and Pleasure (Somewhere)

How can you laugh when so many are weeping? Or how can you weep when so many are shouting with joy? Real life pulls us one way and the other all at the same time. I find help from how the Bible describes this experience.

In the book of Ezra the people of Israel return from exile in Babylon to Jerusalem to rebuild the temple of God. After seventy years of captivity, Jeremiah's prophecy is fulfilled and the people can go home. They begin work on the temple. According to Ezra 3:10–11, "when the builders had laid the foundation of the temple of the LORD...all the people shouted with a great shout when they praised the LORD because the foundation of the house of the LORD was laid." This makes sense. It is a great day of gladness. A new beginning.

But the next verses (Ezra 3:12–13) say, "Yet many of the priests and Levites and heads of fathers' households, the old men who had seen the first temple, wept with a loud voice when the foundation of this house was laid before their eyes, while many shouted aloud for joy; so that the people could not distinguish the sound of the shout of joy from the sound of the weeping of the people."

Some wept and some shouted for joy.

Why did the old men weep? They wept because they "had seen the first temple." In other words, what they were able to build now was not going to be anywhere near the size and greatness of the former temple. This is what Haggai

2:3 says: "Who is left among you who saw this temple in its former glory? And how do you see it now? Does it not seem to you like nothing in comparison?"

So some wept because they compared the new temple with the glory of what once was. Others rejoiced because the new temple was so much greater than captivity in Babylon and no temple at all. Both of these perspectives are true. Both emotions are valid. This is the way life is. In families and churches—and even in our own hearts—both perspectives and both emotions rise and fall.

Take health, for example. You lose your health, perhaps your eyes or your kidneys or your memory or your ability to walk. There is a season of "Babylonian captivity." But then, perhaps after years, there is an answer to prayer—a miracle or a God-sent treatment—and some of your former health is restored. Do you shout for joy, or do you weep? Probably you will do both. You will remember "the former glory" and the loss will hurt. But then you will see that a respite is given. A new day. A new beginning. Not the same. But new and good and full of possibilities and hope. And you will rejoice.

Or consider the unexpected byways of marriage or the painful choices of grown children or the sporadic setback and progress of vocation. In any day, are there not reasons to weep and reasons to rejoice? So much depends on where you fix your mind. Do you dwell on what might have been (for example, what if my mother had not been killed when I was twenty-eight, but instead had been here for her grandchildren as they grew up)? Or do you dwell on what new things God has done (and will do!) to show the sufficiency of his grace (like another good wife for my dad and all my children on a heavenly trajectory!)?

On this side of the resurrection of Jesus, and on this side of the final fulfillment of the promise to work it all for good (Romans 8:28–32), there will still be grief. Yes, but, as Paul says in 1 Thessalonians 4:13, not as those who have no hope. Our weeping will be weeping on the rock of hope.

My prayer for myself and all of you is that our weeping might be deep but not prolonged. And while it lasts, let us weep with those who weep. And when joy comes in the morning, let us rejoice with those who rejoice (Psalm 30:5; Romans 12:15).

42

THANK GOD FOR DIARIES, JOURNALS, AND BIOGRAPHIES!

Meditation on the Life of David Brainerd

Oh, the refreshing, liberating, exhilarating experience of living for several days with the saints in another century! In preparing for the Bethlehem Conference for Pastors, I immersed myself in the diaries and journals of David Brainerd. He was a missionary to the American Indians of New York, Pennsylvania, and New Jersey. For several days I lived most of my waking hours in the years 1718 to 1747—the years this flaming young man lived. It was a short life. But, oh, what a life! What an agonizing, burdened, painful life. But what a testimony to the long-suffering, severe mercy of God.

His father died when he was nine. His mother died when he was fourteen. He died of tuberculosis when he was twenty-nine. Virtually the whole of his missionary life he coughed up blood with painful spasms. There was no cure. And God did not heal. He suffered almost relentless attacks of depression which they called "melancholy" in those days. It was like a death, and when it lifted it was glorious: "Tuesday, May 6, 1746. Enjoyed some spirit and courage in my work: was in a good measure free from melancholy: Blessed be God for freedom from this death" (Jonathan Edwards, *The Life of David Brainerd, The Works of Jonathan Edwards,* vol. 7, Norman Pettit, ed. [New Haven: Yale University Press, 1985], 390).

He was expelled from Yale a year before graduation and was never allowed to have his degree. He had said that one of the tutors "had no more grace than a chair." That was ground for expulsion in those days. So he was bumped from the normal ministerial route, became a missionary, and changed the face of history.

He never married and felt keenly the loneliness of the wilderness. "Wednesday, May 18, 1743. I have no fellow Christian to whom I might unbosom myself and lay open my spiritual sorrows and with whom I might take sweet counsel in conversation about heavenly things and join in social prayer" (207). "Tuesday, May 8, 1744. My heart sometimes was ready to sink with the thought of my work, and going alone in the wilderness. I knew not where" (248).

Life in the wilderness was hard. "Most of my diet consists of boiled corn, hasty pudding, etc. I lodge on a bundle of straw, and my labor is extremely difficult: I have little appearance of success to comfort me.... I have taken many considerable journeys...and yet God has never suffered one of my bones to be broken...though I have often been exposed to cold and hunger in the wilderness...have frequently been lost in the woods.... Blessed be God that has preserved me" (484).

But in it all was the relentless pursuit of God and holiness. "When I really enjoy God, I feel my desires of him the more insatiable, and my thirstings after holiness the more unquenchable.... Oh, for holiness! Oh, for more of God in my soul! Oh, this pleasing pain! It makes my soul press after God.... Oh, that I might not loiter on my heavenly journey!" (186).

Why is David Brainerd so encouraging to me? Because God took this pain-wracked, moody, lonely, compulsive, struggling young lover of God and used him to lead several hundred Indians to eternal glory, to spark the founding of Princeton and Dartmouth colleges, and to inflame two hundred years of missionaries with his radically dedicated four-year missionary life. William Carey had Brainerd's *Life* with him in India; Henry Martyn in Persia; Robert M'Cheyne in Scotland; David Livingstone in Africa; and Jim Elliot in Ecuador.

And I venture to say that none of this would have come about without his heartbreaking expulsion from college. Oh, let us sing, brothers and sisters:

> *Judge not the Lord by feeble sense*
> *But trust him for his grace.*
> *Behind a frowning providence*
> *he hides a smiling face.*

GOD MOVES IN A MYSTERIOUS WAY, WILLIAM COWPER

43

WE ARE NOT CONTENT JUST TO SOW
Pondering Ordinary and Extraordinary Seasons of Ministry

R T. Kendall, pastor of Westminster Chapel in London, tells the story of a missionary to Africa who preached for twenty years without much success, though he often invited his hearers to come forward and confess Christ. Then one day, genuine revival broke out. To his amazement he witnessed people walking forward under great conviction even while he was preaching! What he had failed to get people to do for twenty years was now happening spontaneously.

The lesson: When the Holy Spirit is poured out in an extraordinary way, more people are converted in a day than in years and years of faithful labor. Note: I said "faithful" labor, not "failing" labor! The absence of manifest conversions does not mean that a person has been faithless in labor. Only God knows how long a minister must sow before the reaping comes—or if the faithful minister himself will have the privilege of doing the reaping. But if he sows and another reaps, still the sower has not sowed in vain.

Jesus said to the disciples in John 4:37–38, "One sows, and another reaps. I sent you to reap that for which you have not labored; others have labored, and you have entered into their labor."

But should I be content to say, "I am a sower, another will reap"? No, not until my life is over. Then, if the reaping has not come, I will rest my life on this: One sows, another reaps.

But until then, I would be unfaithful to the command of Christ if I were content with merely sowing. He said, "Make disciples!" Not only that, I would be untrue to love. Love for people doesn't merely say, "Here's the seed, take it or leave it." Love pleads, love persuades, and love prays. Love prays until its dying breath for that wonderful, ordinary work of the Spirit to save one here and one there, month after faithful month. And love prays for that extraordinary outpouring of the Spirit that we call revival.

At Pentecost, three thousand people were converted in one day. Why? Because the Holy Spirit was present with extraordinary power ("They were all filled with the Holy Spirit," Acts 2:4), and Christ was preached with penetrating truthfulness. "When they heard this they were cut to the heart, and said to Peter and the rest of the apostles, 'Brethren, what shall we do?'" (Acts 2:37, RSV).

The suddenness and size of revival events are wonderful but not without flaws. We must not put all our prayer eggs in that basket. Every day holds the promise of reaping with eternal significance as well as sowing in patience for the appointed day of harvest. Historian Mark Noll cautions us with a balanced word on revival:

> As a historian, three things increasingly impress me about awakenings in church history: first, that they really do occur, and—from medieval, monastic revivals through classic evangelical awakenings to modern pentecostal renewal—they really have brought great benefit to the church. Second, revivals tend to exaggerate, so that along with real benefit often come increased problems like exalted opinions of one's self in God's general design. Third, most of the circumstances that have made a permanent difference in spreading the gospel and deepening the church's understanding of the gospel have taken place in ordinary church settings rather than revivals. ("What Christian Leaders Are Saying About Spiritual Renewal," *Vocatio,* vol. 11, no. 1, Winter 1999, 6)

Therefore, let us not idealize the steady-state life of faithful sowing as if there can be nothing more of God's extraordinary blessing. Nor let us be overly effusive about the hope of revival as the answer to all our needs. Rather let us pray without ceasing and labor without sparing for the greatest blessing on this day's sowing, that it would be blessed with reaping, and that it would be a part of God's plan to bring extraordinary seasons of harvest and holiness to the church and to the nations.

CIIIIO

44

NEWS! NEWS! NEWS!

Getting the Gospel and Theology in Right Order

There are preachers and not just teachers for the same reason there are reporters and not just commentators. The reason is that there is news and not merely comment. News begs to be heralded, at least if it's good news. Later it may need to be explained and argued about.

Ordinary Christians need to remember this. Christianity is *news* before it is theology. Picture the scene: There is a horrible situation with many people trapped, their lives in peril. There seems to be no way of rescue or escape. It is terrifying. Behind closed doors authorities plan a daring assault and deliverance. Suddenly, there is a breakthrough. Rescuers succeed, with incredible loss, in making a way out. Countless people begin to escape. The news spreads like wildfire: "There is a way out! There is a way out! Come to the coded house. There is a tunnel to freedom."

Christianity is first news. Then theology.

J. Gresham Machen loved to stress this sixty years ago because he was utterly committed to the factuality of Christianity. News is about facts, not mere ideas. Christianity is about something that happened, not merely about somebody's ideas. There were real events: a child born of a virgin, a few years of teaching and healing, a trial, a crucifixion, a death, a resurrection, an ascension into heaven. And then there was an explosion of news telling.

In his book *God Transcendent* (Edinburgh: Banner of Truth Trust, 1982, 39), Machen says:

We could not hope to be listened to if we had merely our own thoughts; there are so many others in the world wiser and more learned than we. But in a time of peril in a beleaguered city the humblest of day-laborers is more worth listening to than the greatest of orators, if he has news.

In times of peril, a bringer of news is better than great philosophers. Nor does it matter if his accent is good. Or his grammar. Or his looks. If he has good news for beleaguered people, he will be more treasured than ten thousand theologians. Plain people who have heard the news and been saved by it should take heart from this. People need news first. Hard questions can be answered later. We need joyful, breathless news bringers, not just intelligent news commentators.

Yes, yes, I hear the caution. We need both. Yes, sometimes the news is unintelligible without comment. Yes, it is good news that the good news is intellectually compelling. Yes, yes, yes. I love all that. But what I think needs to be stressed for some people is that *we have news!* And it is better news than the discovery of a cure for cancer. Infinitely better. We need to believe this and to feel this, and then to go about newscasting.

It really is a joyful thing to bring good news. I know that many people do not feel they are in peril. That complicates newscasting. But if you really believe the peril and really believe the news, it is still a thrilling thing to tell people about the events that have made a way to safety and hope and everlasting joy.

What we need to do often is ponder the news-ness of Christianity. It is news, not just ideas or arguments. It is those too. But first and powerfully and joyfully, it is news. "Do not be afraid; for behold, I bring you *good news* of a great joy which shall be for all the people" (Luke 2:10, emphasis added).

What's the news? It's this. Although sin is great and universal and deadly (Romans 3:23; 6:23), Jesus, the Son of God, has come into the world to save sinners (1 Timothy 1:15). He saves us from eternal punishment (Matthew 25:46). Christ died for our sins (1 Corinthians 15:3). God made him to be sin who knew no sin so that we might become the righteousness of God in him (2 Corinthians 5:21). We are justified by his blood and reconciled to God (Romans 5:9–10). There is no condemnation to those who are in Christ Jesus (Romans 8:1). The just has died for the unjust, to bring us into fellowship with God (1 Peter 3:18). This Jesus, Lord of the universe, has been raised indestructibly from the dead and cannot die or be defeated (Romans 6:9; Hebrews 7:16). The way to be saved by him is not works of merit, but faith in the God who justifies the ungodly (Romans 4:5; 5:1; Ephesians 2:8–9). No human has ever conceived the greatness of what God has prepared for those who love him (1 Corinthians 2:9).

Is it any wonder that this message—this news—spread triumphantly across the Roman world in those early days, even in the context of paganism, pluralism, occultism, and persecution (days like ours)? The news was just too good to contain. And all history exclaims: "How beautiful are the feet of those who preach good news!" (Romans 10:15, RSV).

✒

45

THE DANGERS OF COMPUTER UNREALITY

Five Resolutions

Is there a biblical warrant for personal resolutions? Something very close is the biblical concept of making and keeping vows. "Make your *vows* to the LORD your God, and perform them" (Psalm 76:11, RSV, emphasis added). Like everything else valuable, this can be abused and turned into presumptuous negotiation with the Almighty. But it does not have to be that.

One can look into one's own heart and see the weaknesses of the flesh and say to God: "I know that, left to myself, I will make a mess of my life. I do not presume to have the ability in myself to keep promises or vows that I make to you. I thank you for the biblical promise that you will put reverence in my heart to keep me from leaving you (Jeremiah 32:40), and that you will work in me what is pleasing in your sight (Hebrews 13:21). I believe that one small means you have ordained to keep me from sin is the making of vows. Please, show me when this would be fitting, and grant me the grace to do what I promise."

Here are five computer dangers and five resolutions (or vows) that we all might do well to make.

1. DANGER: *The hook of constant curiosity*
Personal computers offer a neverending possibility for discovery. Even the basic environment of Windows can consume hours and days and weeks of curious punching and experimenting. Color schemes, layouts, screensavers, shortcuts,

icons, file-managing, calculators, clocks, calendars. Then there are the endless software applications consuming weeks of your time as they lure you into their intricacies. All this is very deceptive, giving the illusion of power and effectiveness, but leaving you with a feeling of emptiness and nervousness at the end of the day.

RESOLUTION: I will strictly limit my experimental time on the computer and devote myself more to truth than to technique.

2. DANGER: *The empty world of virtual (un)reality*

How sad to see brilliant, creative people pouring hours and days of their lives into creating cities and armies and adventures that have no connection with reality. We have one life to live. All our powers are given to us by the real God for the real world leading to a real heaven and real hell.

RESOLUTION: I will spend my constructive, creative energy not in the unreality of "virtual reality," but in the reality of the real world.

3. DANGER: *"Personal" relations with my PC*

Like no other invention, the personal computer comes closest to being like a person. You can play games with it. There are programs that will dialogue with you about your personality. It will talk to you. It will always be there for you. It is smarter than your dog. The great danger here is that we really become comfortable with this manageable electronic "person," and gradually drift away from the unpredictable, frustrating, sometimes painful dealings with human persons.

RESOLUTION: I will not replace the risk of personal relationships with impersonal electronic safety.

4. DANGER: *The risk of tryst*

"Tryst \ trist \ noun: an agreement (as between lovers) to meet." Sexual affairs begin in private time together, extended conversation, and the sharing of soul. It can now be done in the absolute seclusion of your private e-mail screen name. It can be immediate and "live," or delayed and "recorded." You can think that "it's just nothing"—until he or she shows up in town. It has happened already too many times.

RESOLUTION: I will not cultivate a one-on-one relationship with a person of the opposite sex other than my spouse. If I am single, I will not cultivate such a relationship with another person's spouse.

5. DANGER: *PC Porn*

More insidious than X-rated videos, we can now not only watch, but join the perversity in the privacy of our own den. Interactive porn will allow you to "do it" or make them "do it" with your mouse. I have never seen it. Nor do I ever intend to. It kills the spirit. It drives God away. It depersonalizes people. It quenches prayer. It blanks out the Bible. It cheapens the soul. It destroys spiritual power. It defiles everything.

RESOLUTION: I will never open any program for sexual stimulation, nor purchase or download anything pornographic.

Computers and the Internet and e-mail are remarkable gifts of God. Yes, they are threats to our schedules and hearts and families—as is the telephone and television and radio and a hundred handheld electronic games. All God's gifts can be made idols and even weapons of rebellion against the Giver. But they need not be.

Instead we should ask with the psalmist, "What shall I render to the LORD for all His benefits toward me?" (Psalm 116:12). And we should answer, as he does, "I shall lift up the cup of salvation and call upon the name of the LORD. I shall pay my vows to the LORD" (Psalm 116:13–14). In other words, when God helps us—as he does every moment of every day—we will not repay him with wage-labor to even our accounts; but we will (again and again) lift up an empty cup of need and call on him to fill it. And with that fresh gift of grace we will keep our resolutions. Not in our strength. But in the "cup-filling" strength of God. Sit before your computer. Make your vows. And lift your cup.

⟊⟊⟊

46

DARWINISM ON MY FRONT PORCH

Are You a Tick-Tock in the Timeline of Evolution?

Side by side on my front porch were the newspaper article carrying one worldview and a magazine carrying the other. The magazine article quoted Philip Johnson, law professor at Berkeley:

> If we say, "Did a bacterium by gradual steps turn into a lobster or an insect or a worm…" most people ask "Is it possible God could have done it that way?" That's a boring question. Of course it is possible. But if God is in the picture at all, then what's the evidence that he did change a bacterium by gradual steps into a worm? There's no evidence. It is not recorded in the fossils. It's not testable in the laboratories. It's something that if anybody believes it, they believe it on faith, faith in evolution. *(World,* 22 November 1997, 13)

Here at the turn of the century, Johnson has been leading a remarkable crusade that specializes in *Defeating Darwinism by Opening Minds,* which is the title of one of his books. His first book on evolution was *Darwin on Trial.* As a law professor, Johnson is an expert in handling evidence. Though he is a Christian, he does not generally start arguing from the Bible since his audiences don't usually share that starting point. He simply argues from the evidence that evolutionists use—which he shows will not bear the weight of the worldview put on it. Accepting Darwinism, or naturalistic evolution, is a leap of faith.

The same day I read *World* magazine, I also read in the Minneapolis *Star-Tribune* an incredibly forthright statement of Darwinian faith by Renee Twombly. Here is her unvarnished affirmation of faith:

> As a human do you feel, shall we say, a bit superior to everything else breathing around you? You can't help it if *Homo sapiens* can move mountains while ants prefer little hills, right? *Well, truth is, that you are just a tick-tock in the time line of evolution on Earth, a little twig in the developmental tree of life....* Biological and environmental adaptation, along with the ability of a new species' offspring to survive and thrive, determines whether or not that species lives or dies.
>
> Evolution, in this view, is not a predictable process, *but more the luck of the draw without a higher guiding principle.* Life is not inherently progressive, moving step by step up a ladder of improvement to reach a perfect being, which many assume is human. Moral of the story? Check back after the next evolutionary tick-tock. (26 November 1997, A16, emphasis added)

Not everybody has the time or ability to grapple with all the evidence as Philip Johnson does. God knows that. Therefore he designed the world so that *"since the creation of the world His invisible attributes, His eternal power and divine nature, have been clearly seen, being understood through what has been made, so that they [those who deny it] are without excuse"* (Romans 1:20, emphasis added). Evolutionists will give an account as to whether the leap of faith they make from bacteria to lobsters is as reasonable as the step of faith Christians make from this ordered universe to God.

In addition to the universe, there is Jesus Christ. Ms. Twombly, with a casual stroke of the keys, claims that the difference between Jesus and an ant is a tick-tock on the clock of evolution. That is a very big, and very dangerous, claim. When humans celebrate Christmas, it is essentially the same as ants doing some instinctual dance. It's just a matter of substance plus energy plus time. Nothing essential has changed.

Please realize what is going on here. With the wave of an imaginary wand, the Darwinists sweep God out of heaven and Christ off the earth. Then they go to the classrooms of the nation and say, "Respect each other and do good"—and wonder why kids kill each other like animals.

To such "believers" in evolution I will happily say: The origins of species are more explainable on biblical assumptions than the Jesus of the New Testament is on Darwinian assumptions. Creation and Christ reveal the God who creates the cosmos and saves from sin. If you do not see this, keep looking. The link is more accessible than the one between an ant and a human.

47

DOES GOD HAVE CIVIL RIGHTS?

Urban Injustice, the Fourteenth Amendment, and God

God has all the rights of the universe. This is part of his glory that we are commanded to declare to the white and black and brown and yellow and red nations of America. To mention a few:

- He has the right to forgive sin. "The Son of Man has authority on earth to forgive sins." (Matthew 9:6)
- He has the right to command unclean spirits. "What is this? A new teaching with authority! He commands even the unclean spirits, and they obey him." (Mark 1:27)
- He has the right to take his life back from the grave. "No one has taken [my life] away from Me, but I lay it down on My own initiative. I have authority to lay it down, and I have authority to take it up again." (John 10:18)
- He has the right to execute judgment. "[God] gave Him authority to execute judgment, because He is the Son of Man." (John 5:27)
- He has the right to give eternal life. "You [God] gave Him authority over all flesh, that to all whom You have given Him, He may give eternal life." (John 17:2)
- He has the right to cast into hell. "Fear the One who, after He has killed, has authority to cast into hell; yes, I tell you, fear Him!" (Luke 12:5)
- He has the right to fix times and seasons. "It is not for you to know times or epochs which the Father has fixed by His own authority." (Acts 1:7)

- He has the right to create any kind of person. "Or does not the potter have a right over the clay, to make from the same lump one vessel for honorable use and another for common use?" (Romans 9:21)
- He has the right to control plagues. "Men were scorched with fierce heat; and they blasphemed the name of God who has the power over these plagues." (Revelation 16:9)
- Every right in the universe has been given to Jesus. "All authority has been given to Me in heaven and on earth." (Matthew 28:18)

Rights are rooted in being. Humans have rights because human being is different from animal being. Humans are created in the image of God. Therefore we possess a dignity of being that animals and plants do not have. "Whoever sheds man's blood, by man his blood shall be shed, *for in the image of God He made man"* (Genesis 9:6, emphasis added).

The fourteenth amendment says that "no State shall deprive *any person* of life, liberty, or property, without due process of law." Thus these fundamental rights are rooted in *personhood*—personal being. We may deprive bugs of life, liberty, and property because they do not have personal being. Humans are *persons* because we are created in the image of God who is a Person.

Therefore God has absolute rights, because he has absolute being. "God said to Moses, 'I am who I am;' and He said, 'Thus you shall say to the sons of Israel, "I am has sent me to you"'" (Exodus 3:14). As the source and original of all personal being, he has all the rights that persons have who are created in his image. If beings beneath God have rights because they are nearer to God in their being, then God has infinitely greater rights than all human persons.

So why are we not outraged that God's rights are not acknowledged in America? Why do cities burn over the denial of a man's rights but not over the denial of God's rights? Not that cities should burn to show God's rights. That is not the way of Jesus. We establish God's rights by the Word, not the sword—or the torch. "My kingdom is not of this world. If My kingdom were of this world, then My servants would be fighting so that I would not be handed over to the Jews; but as it is, My kingdom is not of this realm" (John 18:36).

"The earth is the LORD's and everything in it" (Psalm 24:1, NIV). So everything that exists is God's property. It exists for his purposes. But, contrary to the fourteenth amendment, he is deprived of this property without due process of law. People take houses and cars and businesses and parks and schools and theaters and newspapers and TV stations and use them without any consultation with the Owner at all. They deny his ownership and act against his stated purposes for these things. His rights are violated every day. Where is the outrage?

The root of all injustice in our urban centers, or anywhere else, is the pervasive human injustice against God. Where the rights of our Creator and Savior are daily denied, we should not be surprised that the rights of persons created in his image are denied in a cavalier and selfish way. Until God is given his rights, no human rights will have much significance beyond convenience. And when they are no longer convenient, they will be ignored, whether by violent police, traffic violators, looters, or murderers. The end of godlessness is anarchy.

> Then let us adore and give him his right,
> All glory and power, all wisdom and might:
> All honor and blessing, with angels above,
> And thanks never ceasing and infinite love.

"YE SERVANTS OF GOD, YOUR MASTER PROCLAIM," CHARLES WESLEY

48

CAN JOY INCREASE FOREVER?

Meditation on Ephesians 2:7

> *In the ages to come He [will] show*
> *the surpassing riches of His grace in*
> *kindness toward us in Christ Jesus.*

Jonathan Edwards knows heaven perhaps even better than hell. Which is saying a lot in view of his reputation as one who knows hell well. I have believed this for some time because of reading his sermons on heaven (for example, "The Portion of the Righteous," "The Pure in Heart Blessed," "Praise, One of the Chief Employments of Heaven"). In addition, reading Edwards's *Miscellanies* on heaven and reading John Gerstner's book, *Jonathan Edwards on Heaven and Hell* (Grand Rapids: Baker Book House, 1980), shows how Edwards soared in his meditations on heaven.

But only when I took up Edwards's book, *The End for Which God Created the World,* did I see the remarkable insight that heaven will be a neverending, ever-increasing discovery of more and more of God's glory with greater and ever greater joy in him.

As a child I feared heaven. Neverendingness seemed to me like frozenness. Doesn't 1 Corinthians 13:12 say, "Then I will know fully just as I also have been fully known"? And wouldn't that mean that the moment we get to heaven we will know all we are going to know and that the rest of eternity will be neverending sameness? Which strikes the fear of boredom into our hearts.

Edwards says no. All this text must mean is that our knowledge will be accurate in heaven and no longer "through a glass darkly." It does not have to mean that we know, all at once, all that can be known. Rather, he reasons, God is infinite and wills to reveal himself to us for the enjoyment of his fullness forever. Yet we are finite and cannot at any time, or in any finite duration of time, comprehend the limitless, infinite fullness of God's glory. Yet God wills to lavish this fullness on us for our pleasure in him (Ephesians 2:7).

Therefore the implication is that our union with God, in the all-satisfying experience of his glory, can never be complete, but must be increasing with intimacy and intensity forever and ever. The perfection of heaven is not static. Nor do we see at once all there is to see—for the finite cannot take in all of the infinite. It is not our destiny to become God. Therefore, there will always be more for a finite creature to know and enjoy of God. The end of increasing pleasure in God will never come. God is inexhaustible, infinite.

Here is the way Edwards puts it: "I suppose it will not be denied by any, that God, in glorifying the saints in heaven with eternal felicity, aims to satisfy his infinite grace or benevolence, by the bestowment of a good [which is] infinitely valuable, because eternal: and yet there never will come the moment, when it can be said, that *now* this infinitely valuable good has been actually bestowed" *(The End for Which God Created the World,* ¶285, in *God's Passion for His Glory* [Wheaton: Crossway, 1998], 251).

Moreover, he says, our eternal rising into more and more of God will be a "rising higher and higher through that infinite duration, and…not with constantly diminishing (but perhaps an increasing) [velocity] …[to an] infinite height; though there never will be any particular time when it can be said already to have come to such a height" *(God's Passion for His Glory,* 279). It will take an infinite number of ages for God to be done glorifying the wealth of his grace to us—which is to say he will never be done. And our joy will increase forever and ever. Boredom is absolutely excluded in the presence of an infinitely glorious God.

49

PRISON PROFANITY: WHERE DOES IT COME FROM?

Meditation on Ephesians 4:29 and 5:4

While spending two days in jail for trespassing to save life, I read Paul's prison epistles. This helped me understand what I was hearing from the other cells. What I heard around me and above me was raunchy. Almost all the talk was dirty and harsh. "Out of the abundance of the heart the mouth speaks" (Matthew 12:34, RSV). Which means that these men's hearts were overflowing with filth and venom.

I sat there in Cell 143 trying to figure out why the only form of discourse was nasty, lewd, and lecherous. Even in "friendly" conversation, the mood was mean spirited. Why? Why was everything from wives to waffles labeled with a four-letter word?

Of course, this is habit now for most of these men—like saying "um" when you talk. But where did the habit come from? If a husband beats his wife, nobody would be content with the explanation: "Oh, that's just a habit. It doesn't mean anything." This habitual filth begs for an answer.

Here's one suggestion: There is a kind of macho ego-satisfaction that comes from pointless swearing and foul, sacrilegious talk. The thing that makes it macho is that offensive language feels assertive and virile. So if you are weak and insecure, one way to camouflage it is to pepper your conversation with social no-no's. Using no-no's is like playing with switchblades and brass knuckles. It feels tough and gutsy. It gives an insecure person a sense of swagger. It's the verbal form of in-your-face countercultural clothing and hairstyles.

Now why is there this bondage to braggadocio?

Interestingly, in Ephesians the alternative to "foul talk" is not "clean talk," but talk that builds up and ministers grace to those who hear. "Let no unwholesome word proceed from your mouth, but only such a word as is good for edification according to the need of the moment, so that it will give grace to those who hear" (Ephesians 4:29). Another name for that is love.

Moreover, in the same section of Scripture the alternative to "coarse joking" is not "clean joking" but thanksgiving. "There must be no filthiness and silly talk, or coarse jesting, which are not fitting, but rather giving of thanks" (Ephesians 5:4). A spirit of thankfulness is so at odds with a spirit of coarse jesting that when one rises, the other falls. And a spirit that yearns to edify is so at odds with foul talk that when one rises, the other falls.

What hit me as I sat there and listened, was that the "foul talk" and the "coarse jesting" were a pitiful attempt to fill a void which God meant to be filled with gratitude to him and love to others.

Both of these vacancies relate to the bondage to braggadocio. 1) *Gratitude to God* is a response to being cared for by a great God. It signifies that God is the source of our safety and meaning in life. It's the mark of a secure, healthy, mature person. Thus bragging is excluded because our strength and security come from God, not ourselves. 2) *Love for others* is the overflow of God-given security for the good of others. It signifies that we have the resources to care about others because God cares about us. Thus bragging is excluded from love because this overflow comes from God, not ourselves, and because bragging calls attention to oneself and not to God.

Which means, in the end, that the crying need at Hennepin County Correctional Facility is for God. It is not first a need for language change or attitude change or social change. Behind foul talk is a gaping void where God's grace belongs, and behind coarse jesting is the gaping void where joyful gratitude belongs. It is a God issue. Let the disease determine the remedy.

Lord, grant your people, with all boldness, to open their mouths and declare the supremacy of God, the glory of Christ in the gospel, and the all-satisfying taste of grace in the face of foul talk and coarse jesting.

꩜

50

HOW CAN ELSIE RUN?

How to Run and Box When You Are Over Eighty

Elsie Viren was for sixty-two years (1929 to 1991) on the staff at Bethlehem Baptist Church in various capacities generally called "church missionary." She was a rock of persevering faithfulness to Christ and his church.

Near the end she lay with a slowly mending hip in the Augustana Home near the church. Her memory was limited and her eyes were dim. But she knew when we came, and she talked with customary spunk and courtesy and gratitude.

During her final illness, I preached two messages at the church under the theme "Olympic Spirituality" (because the Olympics were on everyone's mind). The Bible speaks of "running the race" (Hebrews 12:1), and "not boxing the air" (1 Corinthians 9:26), and "fighting the fight" (2 Timothy 4:7), and "pommeling the body" in athletic discipline (1 Corinthians 9:27). I asked the question: How can Elsie run? She does not look like an Olympic marathoner these days. How can Elsie box? Or does she even have to? Are running and boxing only for the fit and hardy?

The answer is that we all must run, whether old or young, whether sick or healthy. And this is possible for the sick and senile because the race is run with the heart, not the legs, and the fight is fought with the heart, not the fists. It is a race and a fight not against other athletes, but against unbelief. It is possible for the aged and weak to win this fight because the fight is a fight against lost hope, not against lost health.

Here's the biblical evidence for this. In 1 Timothy 6:12 Paul says to Timothy: *"Fight the good fight of faith;* take hold of the eternal life to which you were called when you made the good confession" (RSV, emphasis added). The fight is a "fight of faith." It is not a fight to get out of bed, but to rest in God.

It is not a fight to keep all the powers of youth, but to trust in the power of God. The race is run against temptations that would make us doubt God's goodness. It is a fight to stay satisfied in God through broken hips and lost sight and failed memory. The race can and may be run flat on your back. In fact, it may be run and fought better by the paralyzed than by the able and seemingly self-sufficient.

Again Paul said in 2 Timothy 4:7, "I have fought the good fight, I have finished the race, *I have kept the faith"* (RSV, emphasis added). Finishing the race means keeping faith. It is a race against unbelief, not against aging.

Another way to put it is that the fight is a fight to keep hoping in God. "[Christ will] present you holy and blameless and irreproachable before [God], provided that you continue in the faith, stable and steadfast, *not shifting from the hope of the gospel"* (Colossians 1:22–23, RSV, emphasis added). Finishing the race means *not giving up the hope of the gospel.* It is a race against hopelessness, not against flawlessness.

When we cheer on the diseased or aging runners who run their final laps in hospital beds, what we are really saying is, "Do not throw away your confidence which has a great reward" (Hebrews 10:35). The finish line is crossed in the end, not by a burst of human energy, but by collapsing into the arms of God. And let us not forget: In the Christian race, we do not finish alone. We finish together. It is part of the rules. "Encourage one another day after day, as long as it is still called 'Today,' so that none of you will be hardened by the deceitfulness of sin" (Hebrews 3:13). The more difficult it becomes for an older person to use the mind and the memory, the more we must fight with him and for him, wielding the sword of the Spirit where his own hand is weak. If any strays, we bring him back with mercy and meekness (Galatians 6:1; James 5:20). We encourage the fainthearted and help the weak (1 Thessalonians 5:14). We "visit the widows in their affliction" (James 1:27)—whatever it takes to help them fight the fight and finish the race.

Do you know an Elsie? Don't leave her (or him) to fight alone. Remember that you too are in the body, and one day you will lie on your back alone, unable to read the Bible and barely able to think clearly to pray. Who will hold up your arm? Who will put the sword in your hand? Who will help you run?

51

THE UNASHAMED GOD

Meditation on Hebrews 11:16

> *But as it is, they desire a better country,*
> *that is, a heavenly one.*
> *Therefore God is not ashamed to*
> *be called their God;*
> *for he has prepared for them a city.*

I want very much for God to say of me what he said of Abraham and the other heroes of faith in Hebrews 11: "I am not ashamed to be called your God" (Hebrews 11:16). As risky as it sounds, does this not really mean God might actually be "proud" to be called my God? Maybe he would say, "Not only am I *not ashamed* to be called your God, I am *proud* to be called your God." Possibly "not ashamed" might only mean, "I am *pleased* to be called your God." But it seems that "not ashamed" is really an understatement for "proud."

So I would really like to know what would make God proud to be called my God. Fortunately this wonderful possibility is surrounded (in Hebrews 11:16) by reasons: one before and one after.

Take the one behind first: "God is not ashamed to be called their God, *[for]* he has prepared for them a city." The first reason he gives why he is not ashamed to be called their God is that *he has done something for them.* He made them a city—the heavenly city "whose architect and builder is God" (verse 10). So the first reason he is not ashamed to be called their God is that *he has worked for them.* Not the other way around. He did *not* say: "I am not ashamed to be called their God because *they made for me* a city." He made something for them. That's the starting point. The pride of God in being our God is rooted first in something he has done for us, not vice versa.

Now consider the reason he gives in front—in the first part of Hebrews 11:16. It goes like this: "They desire a better country, that is, a heavenly one. *Therefore* God is not ashamed to be called their God" (emphasis added). The word "therefore" signals that a reason has just been given for why he is not ashamed. The reason is *their desire.* They desire a better country—that is, a better country than the earthly one they live in; namely, a heavenly one. This is the same as saying they desire heaven, or they desire the city God has made for them.

So two things make God unashamed to be called our God. He has prepared something great for us, and we desire it above all that is on the earth. So why is he proud to be the God of people who desire his city more than all the world? Because our desire calls attention to the superior worth of what God offers over what the world offers.

In other words, the reason God is proud to be our God is *not* because *we* have accomplished something so great. But because he has accomplished something great, and we *desire* it. There is nothing to brag about in desiring. It's like getting hungry when you are shown a delicious meal. That is what the city of God is like.

What a city it is! No pollution, no graffiti, no trash, no peeling paint or rotting garages, no dead grass or broken bottles, no harsh street talk, no in-your-face confrontations, no domestic strife or violence, no dangers in the night, no arson or lying or stealing or killing, no vandalism, and no ugliness. The city of God will be perfect because God will be in it. He will walk in it and talk in it and manifest himself in every part of it. All that is good and beautiful and holy and peaceful and true and happy will be there because God will be there. Perfect justice will be there, and recompense a thousandfold for every pain suffered in obedience to Christ. And it will never deteriorate. In fact, it will shine brighter and brighter as eternity stretches out into unending ages of increasing joy.

When we desire this city more than we desire all that this world can give, God is not ashamed to be called our God. When we make much of all he promises to be for us, he is proud to be our God. This is good news. God loves to magnify *his work for us,* not ours for him. Granted, it's humbling. But if you want mercy more than you want merit, it's good news.

So open your eyes to the better country and the city of God, and let yourself desire it with all your heart. God will not be ashamed to be called your God.

52

GOD DOES NOT REPENT LIKE A MAN

Meditation on 1 Samuel 15:11, 29

> *I regret that I have made Saul king,*
> *for he has turned back from following Me*
> *and has not carried out My commands.*

> *The Strength of Israel will not lie nor repent;*
> *for he is not a man, that he should repent. (KJV)*

After Saul disobeys Samuel, God says, "I regret [repent] that I have made Saul king, for he has turned back from following Me and has not carried out My commands" (1 Samuel 15:11). Some have argued that since God "repents" of things he has done, therefore he could not have foreseen what was coming. Else why would he repent or regret if he knew in advance the consequence of his decision?

This is not, however, a compelling argument against God's foreknowledge. First of all, the argument assumes that God could not, or would not, lament over a state of affairs he himself chose to bring about. Not only is that not true to *human* experience; more importantly, *God's* heart is capable of complex combinations of emotions infinitely more remarkable than ours. He may well be capable of lamenting over something he chose to bring about.

Not only that, God may also be capable of looking back on the very act of bringing it about, lamenting that act in one regard, while affirming it as best in another regard. For example, if I discipline my son for blatant disobedience and he runs away from home because I disciplined him, I may feel some remorse over the discipline—not in the sense that I disapprove of what I did, but in the sense that I feel some sorrow that the disciplinary action was a necessary part of a wise way of dealing with this situation, and that it led to his running away. If I had it to do over again, I would still discipline him. It was the right thing to do. Even knowing that one consequence would be alienation for a season, I approve the disciplinary action and at the same time regret the same action. If such a combination of emotions can accompany my own decisions, it is not hard to imagine that God's infinite mind may be capable of something similar.

Now the question is: Does the Bible teach that God laments some of his decisions in the sense that I have described above (which does not imply that He is ignorant of their future consequences), or does the Bible teach that God laments some of his decisions because he did not see what was coming?

The answer is given later in 1 Samuel 15. After God says in verse 11, "I repent that I have made Saul king," Samuel says in verse 29, as if to clarify, "The Strength of Israel will not lie nor repent: for he is not a man, that he should repent." The point of this verse seems to be that, even though there is a sense in which God does repent (verse 11), there is another sense in which he does not repent (verse 29). What's the difference? The clue is in the words, "He is not a man." That is, when he repents, it is *not* marked by the limitations common to man. The difference would naturally be that God's repentance happens *in spite of* perfect foreknowledge, while most human repentance happens *because we lack* foreknowledge. God's way of "repenting" is unique to God: "God is not a man that he should repent" (the way a man repents in his ignorance of the future).

For God to say, "I feel sorrow that I made Saul king," is not the same as saying, "I would not make him king if I had it to do over." God is able to feel sorrow for an act that he does in view of foreknown evil and pain, and yet go ahead and will to do it for wise reasons. And so later, when he looks back on his act, he can feel sorrow for the act that led to the sad conditions, such as Saul's disobedience.

Hence we have our precious assurance of Numbers 23:19, "God is not a man, that He should lie, nor a son of man, that He should repent; has He said, and will He not do it? Or has He spoken, and will He not make it good?" I say it is *precious* because, as this verse makes more plain than 1 Samuel 15:29, God's commitment to his promises hangs on his not repenting like a man. In other words, God's promises are not in jeopardy, because God can foresee all circumstances. He knows that nothing will occur that will cause him to take back his promises. That is our soul's rest.

53

DEVIL PRAYERS AND DIVINE PLEASURES

Meditation on Being Real

A great incentive to be authentic in our love to God is to recognize our best religious efforts duplicated in hell. Consider the "piety" of the demoniac in Luke 8:28 (author's translation).

- When he saw Jesus, he cried out and fell down before him, and said with a loud voice, "What have you to do with me, Jesus, Son of the Most High God? I beseech you, do not torment me."
- The devil has religious insight: he recognizes Jesus as the Son of God.
- The devil has a form of piety; he prays to Christ and entreats his benevolence: "Do not torment me!"
- The devil prays in a humble, contrite posture: "He fell down before him."
- The devil prays earnestly and with expressions of deep feeling: "He cried out...and said with a loud voice."
- The devil uses humble expressions in his prayer: "I beseech you!"
- The devil uses respectful and honorable designations for Christ: "Jesus, Son of the Most High God!"

What is missing here? One thing: *love to Christ.*

Oh, how many who go under the banner of the saints render their religion to God out of constraint and not love! But how miserable must be such a life!

So much self-deceit! So much burdensome duplicity! So much unnaturalness!

Away with it! Let us be pure! Or let us be pagan!

But mark this: "Blessed are the pure in heart, for they shall see God" (Matthew 5:8). To see God is to sing (Psalm 135:3)! And we were made to sing. We were made for sacred pleasures and for songs of purity. We were made to be real. Through and through. Oh, the joy of being genuine with God and man!

James marveled that professing Christians could be so far from true, saving faith. To shock them he reminded them that the devil is a pretty orthodox person. "You believe that God is one. You do well; the demons also believe, and shudder" (James 2:19). Not only are they fairly orthodox in their theology; they have better religious responses to what they believe than some professing Christians, for they tremble at the reality of God.

The point for James was that right doctrine without a demonstrative, heartfelt delight in God and reliance on God is spiritually worthless. Devils realize it and sell their souls to do as much damage as they can before they are bound and cast into the lake of fire (Matthew 25:41). But religious humans seem to be unaware of it. This is what is so pitiful—people with no real love to God pronouncing truths about God. People in love with themselves and with the praise that comes with religious performance, but who have not tasted the true glory of God himself.

Oh, let us shudder at this possibility in our lives. And let us "taste and see that the LORD is good!" (Psalm 34:8). Compared to his excellencies, all the world is an uncooked egg white. But the honey of heaven makes the eyes glow. "Come, buy wine and milk without money and without price" (Isaiah 55:1, RSV).

54

A WORD ON POETRY

*Pondering the Implication of Rock-Solid
Reality for Creative Art*

> Sound words, I know, Timothy is to use,
>
> And old Wives' Fables he is to refuse;
>
> But yet grave Paul him nowhere doth forbid
>
> The use of Parables; in which lay hid
>
> That Gold, those Pearls, and precious stones that were
>
> Worth digging for, and that with greatest care.
>
> JOHN BUNYAN
> "THE AUTHOR'S APOLOGY FOR HIS BOOK"
> THE PILGRIM'S PROGRESS

Good poetry speaks truth. Not that each line is naked fact, but lines, when taken all together, tell what really is in spite of what may seem to be. There is no doubt that "now we see through a glass darkly" (1 Corinthians 13:12). Finite and fallen as we are, we need much help to see the light. To us there are dark places in the truth. But who can say, in this brief vapor's breath of life, what light might break upon the soul that looks, unwavering, and long enough at some dark spot, with prayer and pondering and hope that it may turn into a portal for the sun?

So quickly do we pass over hard words and painful stories in the Bible. The poet lingers. And looks. And looks. And looks at this dark spot. Until he weeps and rages and then, perhaps, sees. Then, all too imperfectly, he tries with words to make the needle point of light more visible for others—to bore the point more wide or press the doubting face against the tiny perforation in the wall of pain. He writes a poem.

Like Jeremiah staring at the ruins of Jerusalem, where dying mothers boiled their children for a meal. When all the beard is plucked, and clothes are rent, and voice is hoarse from screaming, then what? A poem—called *Lamentations*. A long, long labor, first to see, and then to say that even here God's mercies are new every morning, and His faithfulness is great. Five chapters: the first, the second, and the fourth divided into twenty-two stanzas, each beginning with a different letter of the Hebrew alphabet. Three agonizing acrostics. Then chapter three, the most personally intense of all, is still more tightly structured: Again twenty-two stanzas, but now each stanza has exactly three lines, and all three in each stanza begin with the same letter—one stanza for each letter of the Hebrew alphabet. And finally chapter five, not an acrostic, but again twenty-two lines long.

Why? Why this form? Why do poets do these things to themselves? Surely, if there is any place for authentic, unencumbered spontaneity, it is here in the overflow of agony. Why bind the heart with such a severe discipline of poetic form? Why labor for weeks to give such shape to suffering?

It is a testimony, written on the heart, that reality has contours. Being is one way and not another. There are hard, unbending facts. God said, "I am who I am." Not what we feel him to be, or wish him to be, or make him to be. He simply is. We must write the verse of our lives within the constraints of unbending, ultimate fact. Therefore, laboring to look and look and look at what is really there, until we feel what we are meant to feel, and then to say what we have seen and felt in some exacting poetic form is a testimony to the truth that we are not God.

Christ is the great, granite, Objective Fact. He is the anchor that keeps poetry from floating away on the waves of emotion into the never-never land of saying anything we please any way we please. He is the lens which lets us see if the modern, creative king really has any clothes on. He is the hard, immovable, unshapable, intractable Reality that banks the sea of emotion into a river that has to flow this way and not that, deep and not shallow. When he died for our sins, it became evident, once and for all, that our fallen spontaneity needs the fine, sharp, painful control of a severe Calvary-like discipline before going public in poetry—or even prose. He is the difference between artsy gamesmanship and lasting glory.

55

PRAYERFULLY RANSACK THE BIBLE

Pondering the Both-And of Prayer and Study

In order to understand the Word of God, and delight in the God of the Word, and to be changed from the inside out, we must pray, "Open my eyes that I may see wonderful things in your Law" (Psalm 119:18, NIV). But when we pray for eyes to see, we must not shift our minds into neutral. Don't assume that the indispensability of prayer means the dispensability of focused thought on the Word of God. When you pray to see the glory of Christ, don't drift or coast mentally. This is a huge mistake that comes from Eastern spirituality, not the Bible.

What then?

1. Pray and Read

Read the Word! What a privilege! And what an obligation! And what a potential for seeing God! Consider Ephesians 3:3–4. "By revelation there was made known to me the mystery, as I wrote before in brief. By referring to this, *when you read* you can understand my insight into the mystery of Christ" (emphasis added). When you *read!* God willed that the greatest mysteries of life be revealed through reading.

Yes, Ephesians 1:18 shows the importance of prayer ("I pray that the eyes of your heart may be enlightened"). But praying cannot replace reading. Praying may turn reading into seeing. But if we don't read, we will not see. The Holy Spirit is sent to glorify Jesus, and the glory of Jesus is portrayed in the Word. So read.

2. Pray and Study

Second Timothy 2:15: "Be diligent (or "study") to present yourself approved to God as a workman who does not need to be ashamed, accurately handling the word of truth." God gave us a book about himself, not so that we might read in any old careless way we wish. Paul says, "Be diligent to…accurately handle the word of truth." That means work at the Word if you want the most from it.

The pendulum swings back and forth. Some say *pray* and don't lean on the unspiritual, human work of study. Others say *study* because God is not going to tell you the meaning of a word in prayer. But the Bible will not have anything to do with this dichotomy. We must study and accurately handle the Word of God, and we must pray or we will not see in the Word the one thing needful, the glory of God in the face of Christ (2 Corinthians 4:4, 6).

Benjamin Warfield, a great studier of the Bible, wrote in 1911, "Sometimes we hear it said that ten minutes on your knees will give you a truer, deeper, more operative knowledge of God than ten hours over your books. 'What!' is the appropriate response, 'than ten hours over your books, on your knees?'" ("The Religious Life of Theological Students," in Mark Noll, ed., *The Princeton Theology* [Grand Rapids: Baker Book House, 1983], 263).

3. Pray and Ransack

Our approach to the Bible should be like a miser in the gold rush, or a fiancée who has lost her engagement ring somewhere in the house. She ransacks the house. That is the way we seek God in the Bible.

> *If you cry for discernment,*
> *Lift your voice for understanding;*
> *If you seek her as silver,*
> *And search for her as for hidden treasures;*
> *Then you will discern the fear of the LORD*
> *And discover the knowledge of God.*
>
> PROVERBS 2:3–5

Seek as for silver, search as for hidden treasures. This is ransacking the Bible for all that it is worth. If there are hidden treasures, act like it. God ordains that he will give to those who seek with all their heart (Jeremiah 29:13).

4. Pray and Think

In 2 Timothy 2:7 (author's translation), Paul tells Timothy how to read his letter: *"Think over what I say,* for the Lord will give you understanding in everything." Yes, the Lord "gives" understanding. But not without thinking. Don't replace thinking with praying. Think *and* pray. Read and study and ransack and think. But all is in vain without prayer. Both-and, not either-or.

So we have seen again and again: Prayer is indispensable if we would see the glory of God in the Word of God. But we have also seen that *reading* and *studying* and *ransacking* and *thinking* the Word is also necessary. God has ordained that the *eye-opening work of his Spirit* always be combined with the *mind-informing work of his Word.* His aim is that we see the glory of God and that we reflect the glory of God. And so he opens our eyes when we are looking at the glory of God in the Word.

So… Read! Study! Ransack! Think!—and pray, "Open my eyes that I may see wonderful things in your Law" (Psalm 119:18).

⌒ɱɱↄ

56

HOW CAN ETERNAL LIFE BE
A FREE GIFT AND YET
"ACCORDING TO WORKS"?

Meditation on Romans 2:6–8

> *God will render to every man according to his*
> *works: to those who by patience in well-doing*
> *seek for glory and honor and immortality, he*
> *will give eternal life; but for those who are*
> *factious and do not obey the truth, but obey*
> *wickedness, there will be wrath and fury. (RSV)*

One of the questions raised about death is whether Christians face a divine judgment and, if so, why and what kind. It is a good question because, on the one hand, we believe that our acceptance with God is based on free grace purchased by the substitutionary sacrifice of Christ and that this acceptance is attained though faith not earned through meritorious works. But, on the other hand, the New Testament frequently teaches that believers will be judged by God along with all men and that both our eternal life and our varied rewards will be "according to works."

For example, Romans 2:6–8 says, "God will render to every man according to his works: to those who by patience in well-doing seek for glory and honor and immortality, he will give eternal life; but for those who are factious and do not obey the truth, but obey wickedness, there will be wrath and fury" (RSV).

This passage teaches that eternal life will be "according to works." To those who seek glory by patience in well-doing, God will render eternal life. The same thing is taught clearly to believers in Galatians 6:8–9, "The one who sows to his own flesh will from the flesh reap corruption, but the one who sows to the Spirit will from the Spirit reap *eternal life*. Let us not lose heart in doing good, for in due time we will reap [eternal life] if we do not grow weary" (emphasis added). So in both Romans 2 and Galatians 6, eternal life is rendered in accord with patience in well-doing.

But this does *not* mean that it will be *earned by works* instead of obtained by faith. In Romans 6:23 Paul says, "The *free gift* of God is eternal life in Christ Jesus our Lord." Eternal life is not earned. It is free. *"By grace* are you saved *through faith,* and this is not your own doing, it is the *gift of God, not of works* lest any man should boast" (Ephesians 2:8–9, emphasis added). Faith receives eternal life freely as a gift. There is no way it can be earned as a wage through works.

But eternal life *is* rendered *according to our works.* This is made plain not only in Romans 2:6–8 and Galatians 6:8–9, but also in 1 Corinthians 6:9–11; Galatians 5:6, 21; Ephesians 5:5; James 2:14–26; Hebrews 12:14; Matthew 7:24–27; Luke 10:25–28; and many other places that teach the necessity of obedience (which is the fruit of faith) in the inheritance of eternal life.

So we must learn to make the biblical distinction between *earning* eternal life *on the basis of works* (which the Bible does *not* teach!) and *receiving* eternal life *according to works* (which the Bible does teach!). Believers in Christ will stand before the judgment seat of God and will be accepted into eternal life on the basis of the shed blood of Jesus covering our sin (Ephesians 1:7) and the righteousness of God reckoned to our account through faith (Romans 3:22; 4:5; Philippians 3:9). But our free acceptance by grace through faith will be *according to works.*

"According to works" means that God will take the fruit of the Spirit (Galatians 5:22) and the "good deeds" by which the light of our faith shines (Matthew 5:16), and he will accept them as *corroborating evidence* of our faith.

His sentence of acquittal will not be because we are not guilty. It will be because Christ bore our guilt. The place of our works at the judgment is to serve as corroborating public evidence that we did indeed put our trust in Christ. "We know that we have passed out of death into life, because we love the brethren" (1 John 3:14). "By this we know that we have come to know Him, if we keep His commandments" (1 John 2:3). Therefore when we are acquitted and welcomed into the kingdom, it will not be *earned* by works but it will be *according to* works. There will be an "accord" or an agreement between our salvation and our works. (See *A Godward Life,* Book One, reading #90.)

If these things are so, two practical effects emerge. One is a sense of peace with God that Christ has died for us and lives again to intercede for us with an all-sufficient sacrifice and a perfect obedience. "We have peace with God through our Lord Jesus Christ" (Romans 5:1). This is precious beyond words in the times of assailing doubt. The other effect is a sense of urgency and seriousness about the demand that we be real and not phony in our faith. If a changed life of love (the sum of good works) is the evidence of our faith, then oh, how vigilant and earnest and passionate we should be about the things of God and the fight of faith. Lord, let us heed 1 Timothy 6:12, "Fight the good fight of faith; take hold of the eternal life to which you were called."

57

JESUS AND THE CHILDREN

Pondering Children as Pride Detectors

One thing to watch for when assessing a person's spiritual fitness for ministry is how he or she relates to children. Put a child in the room and watch. This is what Jesus did to make his point. Children are the litmus paper to expose the presence of pride.

You might think that the main thing Jesus would do is to say, "Don't be proud, become like children." He did say essentially that in Matthew 18:3, "Truly, I say to you, unless you turn and become like children, you will never enter the kingdom of heaven" (RSV). But he said something else even more striking. When Jesus saw that his disciples were arguing over which of them was the greatest, "He called the twelve and...taking a child, He set him before them, and taking him in His arms, He said to them, 'Whoever receives one child like this in My name receives Me; and whoever receives Me does not receive Me, but Him who sent Me'" (Mark 9:34–37).

Receiving a child into your arms in the name of Jesus is a way to receive Jesus. And receiving Jesus is a way to receive God. Therefore how we deal with children is a signal of our fellowship with God. Something is deeply amiss in the soul that does not descend (or is it really *ascend?*) to love and hold a child.

Therefore, it may be good to call to mind the ways Jesus related to children. Ponder these and let them stir in you the longings of Christ. What could be more significant than receiving Christ and receiving God the Creator in him? Amazingly, Jesus says we may do this in ministry to children.

1. Jesus was a child.

For to us a child is born, to us a son is given; and the government will be upon his shoulder. (Isaiah 9:6, RSV)

2. Jesus took children in his arms and blessed them.

"Let the little children come to me, do not hinder them."... And he took them in his arms and blessed them, laying his hands upon them. (Mark 10:14–16, RSV)

3. Jesus healed a child of a foreign woman.

"O woman, great is your faith! Be it done for you as you desire." And her daughter was healed instantly. (Matthew 15:28, RSV)

4. Jesus cast a demon out of a child.

And Jesus rebuked him, and the demon came out of him, and the boy was cured instantly. (Matthew 17:18, RSV)

5. Jesus raised a child from the dead.

Taking her by the hand he said to her, "Talitha cumi;" which means, "Little girl, I say to you, arise." And immediately the girl got up. (Mark 5:41–42, RSV)

6. Jesus used a child's loaves and fish to feed five thousand people.

"There is a lad here who has five barley loaves and two fish; but what are they among so many?" Jesus said, "Make the people sit down." (John 6:9–10, RSV)

7. Jesus said you should become like a child.

Truly I say to you, unless you turn and become like children, you will never enter the kingdom of heaven. Whoever humbles himself like this child, he is the greatest in the kingdom of heaven. (Matthew 18:3–4, RSV)

8. When Jesus came, children cried "Hosanna!" to the Son of David.

The chief priests saw...the children crying out in the temple, "Hosanna to the Son of David!" (Matthew 21:15, RSV)

9. Jesus predicted the terrible days when fathers would give their children up to death.

And brother will deliver up brother to death and the father his child. (Mark 13:12, RSV)

10. Jesus said that if you receive a child in his name, you receive him and the one who sent him.

Whoever receives one such child in my name receives me; and whoever receives me, receives not me but him who sent me. (Mark 9:37, RSV)

May the Lord teach us this profound truth—that loving children in the name of Christ is loving God the Son and God the Father. Indeed it is more: It is welcoming and receiving and communing with God. Nursery work "in the name of Christ" is no small wonder.

⌀ﾠﾠﾠ

58

BODIES, BREAKFAST, AND THE MARRIAGE BED

Meditation on Daily Worship

Worship" is the term we use to cover all the acts of the heart and mind and body that intentionally express the infinite worth of God. This is what we were created for, as God says in Isaiah 43:7, "Everyone who is called by My name, and whom I *have created for My glory…*" That means that we were all created to express the infinite worth of God's glory. We were created to worship.

But don't think only about worship *services* when you think about worship. That is a huge limitation which is not in the Bible. All of life is supposed to be worship, as Paul says in Romans 12:1, "Present your bodies a living and holy sacrifice, acceptable to God, which is your spiritual service of worship." All of life is lived in the body. And the body is to be presented to God as our "spiritual service of worship." This is utterly sweeping. Consider a few implications.

Take breakfast, for example, or Pizza Hut, or midmorning snacks. First Corinthians 10:31 says, "Whether you eat or drink or whatever you do, do all to the glory of God." Now eating and drinking are about as basic as you get. What could be more real and human? We eat and drink every day. We do it at home, at work, in the car, anywhere there is a water fountain. Paul says, this all has to do with God. We are to eat and drink in a way that expresses the infinite worth of God. We can do this by preferring God to food in fasting. We can do it by preferring God to food in eating less and sharing more. And we can do it by preferring God to food in feasting, if we "receive [it] with thanksgiving [as] those who believe and know the truth" (1 Timothy 4:3, RSV).

Or take sex, for example. Paul says the alternative to fornication is worship. "Flee immorality [fornication]. Every other sin that a man commits is outside the body, but the immoral man sins against his own body. Or do you not know that your body is a temple of the Holy Spirit who is in you, whom you have from God, and that you are not your own? For you have been bought with a price: therefore *glorify God in your body*" (1 Corinthians 6:18–20, emphasis added).

Don't fornicate with your body. Worship with your body. He even says that the body is a temple, that is, a place of worship. The body is a place for meeting God, not prostitutes. This doesn't mean sex is bad. It means that sex is precious. Too precious to be treated cheaply. God means that we put it in a very secure and sacred place—marriage. There it becomes the expression of the love between Christ and the church. It shows the glory of the intensity of God's love for his people. It becomes worship. "Glorify God in your body."

And *not* doing sex outside marriage also shows the preciousness of what it stands for. So chastity is worship. Continence magnifies Christ above sex. And caring sexuality in marriage magnifies Christ as the great lover of his bride, the church (Ephesians 5:25–30).

Or take death for a final example. This we will do in our body. In fact, it will be the last act of the body on this earth. The body bids farewell. How shall we worship in that last act of the body? We know we can, because Jesus told Peter how he would die and John explained, "Now this He said, signifying *by what kind of death he would glorify God*" (John 21:19, emphasis added). The last deed of the body is to bid farewell to the soul. And our great desire should be that the body bid farewell in a way that expresses the infinite worth of God. The last act should be worship.

How? The answer is explicit in Philippians 1:20–21. Paul said that his hope was that Christ would be exalted in his body by death. Then he added, "For to me...to die is gain." We express the infinite worth of Christ in dying by counting death as gain. Why gain? Because, verse 23 says, death means going to be "with Christ" which is "very much better."

You have a body. But it is not yours. "You have been bought with a price: therefore glorify God in your body" (1 Corinthians 6:20). You are always in a temple. Always worship.

59

THE PISTOL STAR AND THE POWER OF GOD

Meditation on Science, Sight, and Divine Splendor

I thank God for the mind-boggling discoveries of science. It is as though a blind servant should keep bringing gorgeous jewels to the table. Not that all scientists are blind. Or that any of them is totally blind. If they were, I probably would have died of polio or smallpox by now. I would not have electric light, refrigeration, word processing, a combustion engine in my car, instant news on the radio, or flights to Winnipeg (not to mention Mars). Scientists are not dumb and not blind—entirely.

But what word shall I use to describe the eye or the heart that could discover the Pistol Star and not worship God? Or even mention God. Let me catch my breath. There are two breathtaking things in the paper this morning (October 8, 1997). One is the report of the discovery of the largest star ever known. The other is the absence of God. Both of these marvels take my breath away.

The article begins:

> Try to imagine a star so big that it would fill all of the solar system within the orbit of Earth, which is 93 million miles from the sun. A star so turbulent that its eruptions would spread a cloud of gases spanning four light years—the distance from the sun to the nearest star [about 24,000,000,000,000 miles]. A star so powerful that it glows with the energy of 10 million suns, making it the brightest ever observed in our

galaxy, the Milky Way. Actually, a star so big and bright should be unimaginable, according to some theories of star formation. But here it is, near the center of the Milky Way. *(Star-Tribune,* Minneapolis, MN, 8 October 1997, A4)

Jesus loved the Psalms and believed them to be the Word of God. So I do not doubt that he looked into the night sky and worshiped, "I look at your heavens, the work of your fingers, the moon and the stars which you have established" (Psalm 8:3, RSV).

But there is no mention of God in the report of the scientists. There is no worship. Among the "theories of star formation" being exploded by the Pistol Star there is one that will stand unshaken. In fact, it is not a theory but a revealed truth: Stars are "the work of your fingers." Stars are God's fingerwork. This is what Jesus believed. This is true.

Therefore, when I read that scientists have discovered a new star that is ten million times more powerful than the sun that warms my face from ninety-three million miles away and holds the earth in orbit and burns (in its cooler spots) at six thousand degrees centigrade, I see the fingers of God in a new way. I am moved to tremble and to fall on my face in silence before the greatness of God. And as I come back to some degree of composure, the absence of God in this report stuns me. Is there any other word but "blindness" to describe this? Jesus would say, "The heavens are telling the glory of God and the firmament declares the work of his hands" (Psalm 19:1, author's translation). Not to see the glory of God in the Pistol Star is to be blind.

Open your eyes. Pray that God would give you eyes to see. Jesus spoke of those who "hearing do not hear" and "seeing do not see" (Matthew 13:13). Pray that you would not be among that number. The cosmos exists to help you know God, the Maker. And the main message is that he is very *great* and that we are very small. We need to feel this greatness. We need to be able to say, "You are *great,* O Lord GOD; for there is none like You" (2 Samuel 7:22). "You who have done *great* things; O God, who is like You?" (Psalm 71:19). "What god is *great* like our God?" (Psalm 77:13). "For You are *great* and do wondrous deeds; You alone are God" (Psalm 86:10). *"Great* and marvelous are Your works, O Lord

God, the Almighty" (Revelation 15:3). *"Great* is the LORD, and greatly to be praised" (Psalm 48:1). "Bless the LORD, O my soul! O LORD my God, You are very *great;* You are clothed with splendor and majesty" (Psalm 104:1, emphasis added in these texts).

Let us then be doubly stunned as the telescopes bring in the reports of God's greatness—stunned at the power of God and stunned at the absence of worship.

ᏧᏍᏊᎧ

60

IF YOU BELIEVE, YOU WILL SEE THE GLORY OF GOD

Thoughts on Whether Seeing Grounds Faith or Faith Grounds Seeing

In John 11, Jesus speaks of what he is about to do for Lazarus as the ground of faith. He says, "Lazarus is dead, and I am glad for your sakes that I was not there, so that you may believe" (John 11:14–15). But to Mary, the sister of Lazarus, he says what seems to be the opposite: that *if* she would believe, she would see the glory of God. "Did I not say to you, if you believe, you will see the glory of God?" (John 11:40).

Are both true? Does seeing what he did give rise to faith? And does faith enable one to see the glory of God in what he did? Does John 11:45–46 point in this direction? "Many therefore of the Jews, who had come to Mary and beheld what He had done, believed in Him. But some of them went away to the Pharisees, and told them the things which Jesus had done" (John 11:45).

Here, some believe when they see what Jesus did. But then it says, by contrast, others went and told the Pharisees. Evidently John means, by this contrast (some believed, *but* others went and squealed to the Pharisees), that the second group are not truly "believing." But notice what this second group told the Pharisees: They said that Jesus raised a dead man. So they "believed" at least in that sense—the miracle really happened. But they are contrasted with those who believe. So is believing more than consenting to the miracle? Is it, perhaps, seeing *the glory of God* in the miracle? This is what Jesus had said would happen if Mary "believed." "If you believe, you will see the glory of God"—not just a dead man walking out of a grave, but something glorious and wonderful and beautiful and winsome and compelling about God.

But is faith the *means* to seeing the glory of God, or is it the *response* to seeing the glory of God? Maybe they are so close that it is spoken of both ways. "If you believe, you will see the glory of God" may mean, "If your heart is yielded to God, you will recognize God as glorious and beautiful and attractive in this." (You will stay and worship rather than running to the Pharisees to tattle.)

This understanding of preparatory faith is the way Jesus spoke in John 7:17, "If anyone's will is to do [God's] will, he will recognize the teaching whether it is God's" (author's translation). This may be the same as "If you believe, you will see the glory of God." Thus "believe" would mean having a submissive, humble readiness to welcome all of God that you are given to see.

But what about the other part of believing mentioned in John 11:14? Jesus says to his disciples that he is glad he was not there to keep Lazarus from dying, so that now he could do the miracle for the sake of their faith. "I am glad for your sakes that I was not there, so that you may believe." Here faith is a response to seeing the miracle. Yes, and this is not a contradiction but a continuation of what we have seen. "Believe" is used here in a fuller sense not only of being submissive to God and in tune with God in preparation to see what he reveals of himself in the miracle, but also of being properly *responsive* to God's glory after one has seen it. So both aspects of faith are true: seeing to believe, and believing to see.

In sum, faith is a work of God's grace in our hearts that relates essentially to the glory of God seen in the works and words of God in Christ. Faith is awakened by the manifestation of glory in the Word and work of Christ. Its first quickening is a humble willingness to see what is really there for what it really is; and its ongoing life is the glad and submissive response of trust in all that God is for us in Christ.

Lord, grant us to set our eyes steadfastly on the Word and work of your Son. Grant us to fix our attention on what you have revealed. We do not make faith happen. But we know where it happens. It happens in the light of your Word and work. Hold us in that place, O merciful Father, and speak that faith-awakening glory into being in our hearts. For this we watch and wait—in the pages of your book.

61

HOW DOES THE SPIRIT PRODUCE LOVE?

And Why He Does It This Way

The Holy Spirit is God. He has the power to create love in our hearts any way he pleases. Why then does he create that love only through our conscious trust in the promises of Jesus?

That *is* what he does. According to Galatians 5:22, "The fruit of the Spirit is love." So it is clear that the Holy Spirit is the one who produces genuine love in the heart. But Galatians 5:6 says, "In Christ Jesus neither circumcision nor uncircumcision means anything, but faith working through love." This means, at least, that love comes from faith. Faith "works through love."

So which is it? Is love produced by the Holy Spirit (Galatians 5:22)? Or is faith the thing that produces love (Galatians 5:6)?

Galatians 3:5 shows how the two sources of love fit together. Paul asks rhetorically, "Does [God] then, who provides you with the Spirit and works miracles among you, do it by the works of the Law, or by hearing with faith?" In other words, the powerful work of the Spirit in our hearts does not come through works of law but through hearing with faith. So the way that faith and the Spirit combine to bring about love is that the Spirit works his miracles (including love) through faith. When we exercise faith, the Holy Spirit is flowing in the channel of that faith with love-producing power.

But let's be more precise. It says that the Spirit works miracles through *"hearing* with faith." In other words, the faith, through which the Spirit moves, is faith in something heard. It is faith in God's Word, the gospel. Which means it is faith in all that God promises to be for us in Christ. When we read or hear a portion of God's promise to us in Christ, and we trust and rest in it and are satisfied by it, then the Holy Spirit is flowing to our hearts and love is being produced.

So we see that the Holy Spirit does not produce the fruit of love apart from faith in Jesus and his Word. Particular acts of faith in his promises bring empowerments of love. Now the question rises, Why? Why does the Spirit limit himself to bring about love only through conscious faith in the Word of Jesus?

The answer seems to be that the Holy Spirit loves to glorify the all-satisfying dependability of Christ and his Word. This is why the Spirit was sent into the world. Jesus said, "He shall glorify Me" (John 16:14). J. I. Packer put it this way: The Holy Spirit does his work "in order that Christ may be known, loved, trusted, honored and praised, which is the Spirit's aim and purpose throughout, as it is the aim and purpose of God the Father, too" *(Keep in Step with the Spirit* [Old Tappan, N.J.: Fleming H. Revell, Co., 1984], 47).

If the Holy Spirit simply caused acts of love in the human heart without any clear, ongoing causal connection between love on the one hand, and faith in Christ's promises on the other hand, then it would not be plain that Christ's all-satisfying dependability is honored through love. But the Spirit is utterly committed to getting glory for Jesus. Therefore, he keeps himself quietly beneath the surface, as it were, and puts forward "hearing [about Christ and his promises] with faith" as the conscious cause of love. Thus Christ is exalted when love abounds.

You can see this again in John 7:37–38, "Jesus cried out, saying, 'If any one is thirsty, let him come to Me and drink. He who believes in Me, as the Scripture said, "From his innermost being will flow rivers of living water."'" The next verse says that this river of life-giving water flowing out from us is the Holy Spirit. And surely he is flowing out in love. Which means again, then, that the Spirit produces love where Jesus is trusted, that is, where Jesus is found satisfying like a fountain of water.

Conclusion: If you want to become a loving person, by all means pray for the transforming and empowering work of the Holy Spirit. Love is his fruit. But also take down your Bible and look to Jesus in his Word. Meditate longingly on his promises until he satisfies your heart with all that God is for you in him. When that happens, you will be freed from fear and greed and all that hinders love. The Spirit and his fruit of love will flow.

62

CAN THE REGENERATE BE ERASED FROM THE BOOK OF LIFE?

Meditation on Revelation 3:5

> *He who overcomes shall thus be*
> *clothed in white garments;*
> *and I will not erase his name*
> *from the book of life,*
> *and I will confess his name before*
> *My Father, and before His angels.*

The precious biblical truth that the saints will persevere in faith to the end and be saved is relentlessly opposed, generation after generation. Nevertheless the truth endures, resting firmly on the sovereign faithfulness of God to complete the salvation of his elect. He planned it in eternity, purchased it in Christ's death on the cross, and is applying it through the Holy Spirit.

Romans 8:30 says, "[Those] whom He justified, these He also glorified." In other words, between the event of justification by faith at the beginning of our Christian life, and the event of glorification at the resurrection of our bodies (Philippians 3:21), there will be no dropouts, bailouts, or pushouts. "Those whom he justified, he also glorified"—all of them. God will keep and sanctify those whom he has justified and make sure they keep the faith and endure to the end and are saved.

First John 2:19 describes how we should understand the apparent dropouts: "They went out from us, but they were not of us; for *if they had been of us, they would have remained* with us; but they went out, in order that it might be shown that they all are not really of us" (emphasis added). In other words, the failure to persevere is not a sign that you can be truly born again and justified and then be lost. Rather, the failure to persevere is a sign that you were never truly part of the regenerate people of God. That's the explicit point of 1 John 2:19.

Nevertheless, there are texts that have persuaded some to reject this teaching. The one I consider here is Revelation 3:5 where the Lord Jesus says, "He who overcomes shall thus be clothed in white garments; *and I will not erase his name from the book of life,* and I will confess his name before My Father, and before His angels" (emphasis added).

Some say this is a foolproof text against the doctrine of the perseverance of the saints. They assume that when Revelation 3:5 says God will not erase a person's name from the book of life, it implies that he *does* erase some from the book of life, and that these are people who were once justified and then later were condemned. But is that a true assumption?

The promise "I will not erase his name from the book of life," does not necessarily imply that some *do* have their names erased. It simply says to the one who is in the book and who conquers in faith: I will never wipe out your name. In other words, being erased is a fearful prospect which I will not allow to happen. I will keep you safe in the book. That is one of the promises made to those who persevere and conquer. It does *not* say that those who fail to conquer and fall away from Christ were written in the book and got erased.

In fact, there are two other verses in Revelation that seem to teach that to have your name written in the book means that you will most definitely persevere and conquer. Consider Revelation 13:8. "And all who dwell on the earth will worship [the beast], *everyone* whose name has not been written from the foundation of the world in the book of life of the Lamb who has been slain." This verse implies that those whose names are written in the Lamb's book of life "from the foundation of the world" definitely *will not* worship the beast. In other words, having our name in the book of life from the foundation of the world seems to mean that God will keep you from falling and grant you to persevere in allegiance to God. Being in the book means you *will not* apostatize.

Similarly consider Revelation 17:8, "The beast that you saw was, and is not, and is about to come up out of the abyss and go to destruction. And those who dwell on the earth whose names have not been written in the book of life from the foundation of the world, will marvel, when they see the beast, that he was and is not and will come" (author's translation). Again having one's name written in the book of life from the foundation of the world appears to secure one from "marveling" at the beast. Those whose names are *not* written in the book of life from the foundation of the world will marvel. If your name *is* written there, you will *not* marvel at the beast.

The teaching here is that having one's name written in the book is effectual. That is, it has a defining effect on one's responses. To have your name written in the Lamb's book of life from the foundation of the world *guarantees* that you will not worship or marvel at the beast. John does not say, "If you worship the beast, your name is erased." He says, "If your name is written, you *will not* worship the beast."

This fits with Revelation 3:5, "He who overcomes…I will not erase his name from the book of life." The triumph *required* in 3:5 is *guaranteed* in 13:8 and 17:8. This is not a contradiction any more than for Paul to say, "Work out your own salvation…for God is at work in you both to will and to work for his good pleasure" (Philippians 2:12–13, RSV). It is not nonsense to state the condition: If you conquer, God will not erase your name (3:5); *and* to state the assurance: If your name is written, you will conquer (13:8 and 17:8). God's "written-down-ones" really *must* conquer, and really *will* conquer. One side highlights our responsibility; the other highlights God's sovereignty.

The practical impact of this truth is not that we be cavalier about faith and love and holiness. There is necessary vigilance (Hebrews 3:12) and striving (Luke 13:24) and pursuit (Hebrews 12:14) in the Christian life. Rather, the impact is that we rest in the assurance that we are not left to ourselves in this "fight of faith." The God who called you is faithful to "confirm you to the end, blameless in the day of our Lord Jesus Christ" (1 Corinthians 1:8). "Faithful is He who calls you, and He also will bring [your sanctification] to pass" (1 Thessalonians 5:24). He will complete the salvation he began (Philippians 1:6). We are kept by the power of God (1 Peter 1:5). Fight we *must,* for only those who persevere will be saved (Mark 13:13). And fight we *will,* because God is at work in us to will and to do his good pleasure (Phillippians 2:13; Hebrews 13:21).

63

How Dangerous Is Our Faith?

Less and More Dangerous than You Think

One of the ideas that emerged near the end of the twentieth century in American society is that religion is dangerous to public life. And the more religious people are, the more dangerous they are. There is some reason for this. Witness the appearance of "Christ" in Texas with his cache of weapons. And religious mutilations in Pakistan and India and Rwanda and Sudan. And in America, periodic murders by unstable religious people.

But there is another side to the story. George Gallup has developed a way to measure the segment of our population that is "highly spiritually committed." Here is what the Gallup organization has found:

> While representing only 13 percent of the populace, these persons are a "breed apart" from the rest of society. We find that these people, who have what might be described as a "transforming faith," are more tolerant of others, more inclined to perform charitable acts, more concerned about the betterment of society, and far happier. (These findings, in my view [George Gallup's], are among the most exciting and significant that we have recorded in more than a half-century of polling.) *(First Things,* March 1993, 59–60)

In other words, if unstable and sick people are often drawn to religion as a way of expressing their quirky moral delusions, it may not mean that *true* religion is the problem. On the contrary, if one is really interested in showing that religion is bad for public life, one will have to take into account Gallup's study alongside the deranged fanatics.

One would also need to keep in mind that a growing number of violent crimes are committed by utterly irreligious people. Moreover, the reason fraudulent religious leaders are such a sensation is because the religion they profess has taught millions of people not to steal or kill or commit adultery or lie or covet, but to love others as they love themselves. They make news because they don't make sense. Ten thousand honest, self-sacrificing, care-giving pastors are not news, precisely because it is simply expected that they will be that way. Why? Because we take for granted that their faith produces good behavior. The justified media outrage is an indirect testimony to long patterns of uprightness that Christianity has produced.

Our job is not to force secular people to think Christians are not dangerous. Our job is to live according to the truth with hearts of love in reliance on God's grace. This will mean that we declare to be immoral destructive behaviors that many secular people champion (e.g., gambling, extramarital sex, homosexual behavior, abortion). It will also mean that we are engaged in constructive behaviors that bring healing and wholeness and God-exalting eternal joy to as many people as we can.

In the end, the persevering millions of simple saints and ministers will become news. Very big news. Before all the universe their works will follow them and testify to the reality of their faith and the validity of their eternal reward. "Good deeds are conspicuous; and even when they are not, they cannot remain hidden" (1 Timothy 5:25, RSV).

How dangerous is our faith? Far more dangerous than the sword, which we renounce (John 18:36). More dangerous than lying and deceit, which we disown (Ephesians 4:25). More dangerous than greed and theft, which we reject (Ephesians 4:28). More dangerous than hate, which we would rather endure than enact (Matthew 5:43–45). Our faith is as dangerous as the grace and power of God to call what is not into being, to bring untold numbers into conformity to the image of his Son, and to accomplish all his saving purposes for the glory of Christ. "This is the victory that has overcome the world—our faith" (1 John 5:4).

64

FACTS, SEEN AND UNSEEN

What Does It Mean to Walk by Faith and Not by Sight? Meditation on 2 Corinthians 5:7

We walk by faith, not by sight.

Fundamental to Christianity is fact. Once visible, now knowable, historical fact. When Paul said that he walked by faith and not by sight, he had already seen the risen Lord. "Have I not seen Jesus our Lord?" (1 Corinthians 9:1). And when he described the gospel, he described it in factual, visible, historical terms:

> For I delivered to you as of first importance what I also received, that *Christ died* for our sins according to the Scriptures, and that *He was buried,* and that *He was raised on the third day* according to the Scriptures, and that *He appeared* to Cephas, then to the twelve. After that He appeared to more than five hundred brethren at one time, most of whom remain until now. (1 Corinthians 15:3–6, emphasis added).

Therefore, when the Bible says, "We walk by faith, *not by sight,*" (2 Corinthians 5:7, emphasis added), it does *not* mean that there never were any visible evidences. Nor does it mean that there are no visible evidences today.

The heavens are telling of the glory of God *[today!]*; And their expanse is declaring the work of His hands. (Psalm 19:1)

Since the creation of the world *[even to this day!]* His invisible attributes, His eternal power and divine nature, have been clearly seen, being understood through what has been made. (Romans 1:20)

In the first generation of believers, God did not think he was contradicting the grounds of faith by giving visible appearances of the risen Christ, and then later by confirmations of the gospel by visible signs and wonders.

To [the apostles] He also presented Himself alive, after His suffering, by *many convincing proofs, appearing to them over a period of forty days,* and speaking of the things concerning the kingdom of God. (Acts 1:3, emphasis added)

After [our great salvation] was at the first spoken through the Lord, it was confirmed to us by those who heard, *God also testifying with them, both by signs and wonders.* (Hebrews 2:3–4, emphasis added)

What then does Paul mean when he says, "We walk by faith, not by sight"? The context is crucial.

While we are in this tent [that is, the body], we groan…[longing for] what is mortal [to] be swallowed up by life. Now He who prepared us for this very purpose is God, who gave to us the Spirit as a pledge. Therefore, being always of good courage, and knowing that while we are at home in the body we are absent from the Lord—for we walk by faith, not by sight…. (2 Corinthians 5:4–7)

Yes, Christ was seen once, with physical eyes. Yes, he did signs and wonders infallibly with a single word or touch. Yes, he died and rose and appeared to many. But *now* he is gone from sight. We do not see him that way now. As Paul says, "[When we are] at home in the body, [we are] *absent from the Lord!"* That is, we don't see him *now*. Not only that, in this body of ours, we *groan*. We do not even see the full *effect* of his power in our lives now. Rather, Paul says, we have his Spirit as a pledge. The Spirit is an unseen, but experienced, down payment, in advance of the sight of Christ in glory.

So in what sense, then, do we walk by faith and not sight? We walk by faith and not sight because on the basis of the past, visible acts of God in Christ, and because of the compelling testimonies to these acts by the apostles, we now trust in this living Christ and what he promises to be for us, though we do not *now* see him with our physical eyes. Paul says it like this in Romans 8:24–25: "In hope we have been saved, but hope that is seen is not hope; for who hopes for what he already sees? But if we hope for what we do not see, with perseverance we wait eagerly for it."

Peter puts it like this: "Though you have not seen Him, you love Him, and though you do not see Him now, but believe in Him, you greatly rejoice with joy inexpressible and full of glory" (1 Peter 1:8). I have never seen the risen Christ in the flesh. My physical eyes have never beheld Jesus. But there is a kind of seeing that is not the seeing of our physical eyes. Paul prays for us to have it: "I pray also that the eyes of your heart may be enlightened in order that you may know the hope to which he has called you" (Ephesians 1:18, NIV). And Paul speaks of a "light of the gospel of the glory of Christ" (2 Corinthians 4:4) that we "see" when God overcomes the blinding effects of Satan and our own hardness of heart.

So, walking by faith and not by sight means not by the immediate sight of Christ with our physical eyes. It does not mean without historical evidence. And it does not mean without spiritual illumination to the eyes of the heart. The Spirit does grant us the sight of self-authenticating divine glory in the gospel of Christ. The Christ that I see there, has won over my mind and my heart. So I say with Paul in Galatians 2:20, *"I live by faith* [not sight] in the Son of God, who loved me and gave himself for me" (RSV, emphasis added).

If this is not your experience, humbly ask for it. This is not presumption. It is what Paul prayed for in Ephesians 1:18, "I pray that the eyes of your heart may be enlightened, so that you will know what is the hope of His calling, what are the riches of the glory of His inheritance in the saints." It is right to ask for "enlightened hearts." It is right to ask for God to do Psalm 119:18, "Open my eyes, that I may behold wondrous things out of thy law" (RSV). This goes beyond mere reading and mere studying and mere learning. This is a seeing of wonder. And the wonder wakens faith and sustains faith. Fix your eyes on the Son and ask for light.

65

Please, Feed Me More!

The Cry of Dying Faith

Faith feeds on the Word of God. Without a steady diet it gets weaker and weaker. If you are dissatisfied with your Christian courage and joy and purity of heart, check the way you are feeding your faith.

Compare the way you eat. Suppose that you start the day with a glass of orange juice. It's good, and good for you. It takes you maybe five minutes to drink it if you read the newspaper at the same time. Then you go off to work or school. You don't eat anything else until the next morning. And you have another glass of juice. And so you go on drinking one glass of juice a day until you drop.

That's the way a lot of Christians try to survive as believers. They feed their faith with five minutes of food in the morning, or evening, and then don't eat again until twenty-four hours later. Some even skip one or two mornings and don't give their faith anything to eat for days.

Now the effect of starving your faith is that faith starves. Not hard to understand. And when faith is starving, it is getting weaker and not able to do much. It has a hard time trusting God and worshiping and rejoicing and resisting sin. It gasps and stumbles. But someone may say, "How do you know faith needs the food of the Word to thrive and grow?" Well, there are some biblical clues.

First, Romans 10:17 says, "Faith comes from hearing, and hearing by the word of Christ." If faith *comes* from the Word, it *goes* by the absence of the Word.

Second, Psalm 78:5–7 says that God "appointed a law in Israel, which He commanded our fathers, that they should teach them to their children…that they should put their confidence in God." In other words, the aim of teaching the Word of God to our children is to foster confidence (that is, faith) in God. Thus faith feeds on the Word of God.

Third, Proverbs 22:18–19 says, "It will be pleasant if you keep [the words of God] within you, that they may be ready on your lips. So that your trust may be in the LORD, I have taught you today, even you." This shows that the words of God are "so that you may trust in God." Faith feeds on the Word of God.

Fourth, compare Psalm 1:2–3 ("His delight is in the law of the LORD, and in His law he meditates day and night. He will be like a tree firmly planted by streams of water, which yields its fruit in its season") with Jeremiah 17:7–8 ("Blessed is the man who trusts in the LORD, whose trust is the LORD. For he will be like a tree planted by the water, that extends its roots by a stream and will not fear when the heat comes; but its leaves will be green"). One says that *meditating on the Word of God* makes you like a tree that remains strong; and the other says *trusting in the Lord* makes you like a tree that remains strong. Which is it? It's both. Why? Because the person who meditates on the Word of God day and night feeds his faith day and night, so that his trust is strong.

Fifth, it simply stands to reason that faith feeds on the Word because the Word is what faith trusts. And where trustworthy words are not present, faith has nothing to bite into. That's the nature of faith. It exists by what it trusts. It has no life but what it gets from the truth it believes. So if we do not feed it with a substantial diet of life-giving truth, it will shrivel.

All this means that we should memorize Scripture day by day so that we can feed our faith hourly throughout the day. Only a few people have the luxury of being able to open a Bible every hour or so. But all of us can consult our memory every hour. In fact, we need to.

So, with all my heart, I encourage you to do this. When you have devotions in God's Word, find a phrase or a verse—a morsel for your soul—and memorize it. This is like putting faith food in the pantry of your mind. Then throughout the day you reach in and take a bite from that morsel. It may be as simple as, "I will never leave you nor forsake you" (Hebrews 13:5, NKJV). Take that out and chew on it hourly. The nutrition will feed your faith, and your faith will grow strong; you will pray for fruit, and it will come.

66

CHERISHING TRUTH FOR
THE SAKE OF LOVE

Obscuring Truth to Obtain Triumph

Joel Belz, the chief executive officer of *World* magazine, wrote that there is "a perverse assumption now…dominant among evangelicals that feelings, attitudes, and relationships are all more important than truth. Unity is a higher priority than orthodoxy. Division, even for truth's sake, becomes the most offensive of heresies" (12/19 July 1997, 5).

Perhaps the word "perverse" needs qualifying. I don't take Belz to mean that all who prize unity have perverse motives. Nor do I take him to mean that it is always perverse to have unintentional blind spots that keep one from seeing a truth issue behind a relationship issue. What is perverse is intentionally obscuring a truth claim by deflecting attention onto an attitude or style or perceived feeling or motive. This is what seems unusually common today.

For example, you might say, "Nudity, as a part of entertainment, is contrary to God's will for modesty because it fails to treat the body as a sacred trust for God's glory." That's a truth claim. It calls for people to reckon with an objective reality called "God's will." It asks people to think about this claim and form a judgment about its truth. It also carries implications about what kind of entertainment one will approve and how one will spend one's time.

On the level of truth one might respond by saying, "I agree." Or one might say, "I don't agree because I don't think there is a God, and so I don't think you can legitimately talk about his will." Or one might say, "I think God delights in the body he made and does not disapprove of nudity in entertainment." All those responses are on the level of the truth claim being made. Reasons can be given on both sides, and the dialogue can go on. Perhaps some persuasion and change of mind might happen.

But that is not the way it usually goes. More common is a verbal strategy which deflects attention from the truth claim onto an attitude which shrewdly nullifies the truth for unthinking listeners. For example, a response may be, "Too bad you can't handle your own libido and have to project your hang-ups onto others." Or "Long live Victorian prudery!" Or "With eighty thousand refugees unaccounted for in Zaire it is petty to concern ourselves with moral issues on the scale of skirt lengths." Or "Bible-thumping, proof-texting, right-wing moralizers do not understand the nature of art and will never make significant contributions to culture." Or "One senses a repressed youth and a puritan mother behind the priggish anxieties over the human body." Or "It is the height of arrogance to cloak one's private mores in the garment of divine absolutes."

All of these responses ignore the issue of truth. They are evasive. They are the way clever people "win" by tarring a person with labels. This is what Joel Belz calls "perverse."

My prayer for the church is that we put truth and love (orthodoxy and unity, facts and feelings, reality and relationships) in biblical order. For example, Paul said in 1 Timothy 1:5, "The goal of our *instruction* is *love* from a pure heart and a good conscience and a sincere faith" (emphasis added). Notice the order: "Instruction" is the foundation and leads to "love" through purity and faith. Or, again, consider the order in 1 Peter 1:22, "You have in obedience to the *truth* purified your souls for a sincere *love* of the brethren." Again, truth precedes and transforms the soul for the sake of love. Even in the spectacular revelation of 1 John 4:8 that "God is love," "God *is*" provides the foundation for "God is *love.*"

Don't be forced into this false dichotomy. Truth and love are not at odds. Rather, for the sake of love, cherish the truth. Let this love for truth and truth for love govern your use of language the way it did Paul's. "We are not, like so many, peddlers of God's word; but as men of sincerity...in the sight of God we speak in Christ" (2 Corinthians 2:17, RSV). "[We are] not walking in crafti-ness or adulterating the word of God, but by the manifestation of truth commending ourselves to every man's conscience in the sight of God" (2 Corinthians 4:2). Keep in mind the truth that you are speaking "before the face of God," and your language will be the servant of love.

67

AUGUSTINE ON WHAT IT MEANS TO LOVE GOD

Thoughts on Love as Delighting,
Not Just Acting and Willing

What is love to God? Some reduce it to doing things in obedience to God because John 14:15 says, "If you love Me, you will keep My commandments." But that is not what the text says. It says that obedience will *result from* love. It does not say that obedience *is* love. Nor does 1 John 5:3 contradict this when it says, "This is the love of God, that we keep His commandments," because the next phrase is to be taken with it: "and His commandments are not burdensome." In other words, love is not just the doing but the doing from a certain kind of heart that makes the doing "not burdensome."

Others reduce it to acts of willpower or decisions. The reason usually given for this reduction is that love is commanded in the Bible, and people say that if it is commanded, you have to be able to do it no matter how you feel. In other words, since love is commanded (Matthew 22:37), then it must be a decision, not anything deeper and outside our immediate control like an affection or emotion.

But the problem with this reasoning is that it contradicts the Bible. Lots of things are commanded in the Bible that are not mere decisions and are indeed outside our immediate control. For example, joy is commanded (Psalm 100:2; Philippians 4:4); as are hope (Psalm 42:5), fear (Luke 12:5), zeal (Romans 12:11), grief (James 4:9), desire (1 Peter 2:2), tenderheartedness (Ephesians

4:32), brokenness and contrition (Psalm 51:17), brotherly affection (Romans 12:10), and gratitude (Colossians 3:15).

It simply is not true that if something is commanded, it must be a simple act of will lying in our power to do it. This, of course, is offensive to people who deny the deadening effects of original sin. But for those who believe that original sin brought a horrendous hardness and deadness and moral blindness to the human race, then it is not so surprising that the commands of God come to people who cannot simply do them by their own power. Our will is morally and spiritually flawed. Nevertheless we are responsible to do the commandments of God. The moral corruption that cripples us does not relieve us of our responsibility to do what it is right and good to do. "Moses summoned all Israel and said to them, 'You have seen all that the LORD did before your eyes in the land of Egypt.... Yet to this day the LORD has not given you a heart to know, nor eyes to see, nor ears to hear'" (Deuteronomy 29:2, 4). Seeing they did not see. Nevertheless, in spite of this moral blindness and deafness, Israel was responsible to "keep the words of this covenant to do them" (verse 9).

So what then is love to God if not mere action or mere willpower? Here is the way St. Augustine defined it over sixteen hundred years ago: "I call [love to God] the motion of the soul toward the enjoyment of God for his own sake, and the enjoyment of one's self and of one's neighbor for the sake of God" *(On Christian Doctrine,* iii, x, 16). That, I think, is a very good definition. Unlike the other two definitions suggested above, *delight in God* is at the heart of the definition.

This definition accounts for the many texts that summon us not just to obey the Lord or make decisions for the Lord, but to *delight* in the Lord. "Delight yourself in the LORD; and He will give you the desires of your heart" (Psalm 37:4). "Rejoice in the Lord" (Philippians 4:4). "As the deer pants for the water brooks, so my soul pants for You, O God. My soul thirsts for God, for the living God" (Psalm 42:1–2). "O God, you are my God; I shall seek you earnestly; my soul thirsts for you, my flesh yearns for you, in a dry and weary land where there is no water. Thus I have seen you in the sanctuary, to see your power and your glory. Because your lovingkindness is better than life, my lips will praise you" (Psalm 63:1–3). "Then I will go to the altar of God, to God my exceeding joy" (Psalm 43:4). "Yet I will exult in the LORD, I will rejoice in the God of my salvation" (Habakkuk 3:18).

What, then, was this "motion of the soul" which is called love to God, in the life of Augustine? Here is one of his many answers:

> But what do I love when I love my God?... Not the sweet melody of harmony and song; not the fragrance of flowers, perfumes, and spices; not manna or honey; not limbs such as the body delights to embrace. It is not these that I love when I love my God. And yet, when I love him, it is true that I love a light of a certain kind, a voice, a perfume, a food, an embrace; but they are of the kind that I love in my inner self, when my soul is bathed in light that is not bound by space; when it listens to sound that never dies away; when it breathes fragrance that is not borne away on the wind; when it tastes food that is never consumed by the eating; when it clings to an embrace from which it is not severed by fulfillment of desire. This is what I love when I love my God. (*Confessions*, X, 6)

There is no doubt that a love like this will both will and do. But it is oh so much more than mere action and volition. When this inner delight in God is missing, what can the outer casing be but sounding brass or tinkling cymbal?

68

"LORD OF THE DEAD"

*Facing Death When God Is Your God and Jesus Is Your
Lord—Meditation on Romans 14:9*

> *To this end Christ died and lived again,*
> *that He might be Lord of the dead and the living.*

Jesus is Lord of the dead. That's like saying the president of the United States of America is commander-in-chief of all the soldiers in Arlington National Cemetery. Not a very impressive army.

I just looked down at the back of my hand. If I stretch my fingers straight out, the skin on the back of my hand wrinkles, and the creases that connect the pores with diamond shapes are deeper than they were a year ago. This reminds me that I will not always be alive. I will be dead one of these days. Jesus is my Lord now, and he will be my Lord then.

What does this mean?

It was Holy Week when the Sadducees put Jesus to the test. Sadducees don't believe in resurrection. So they try to make the belief look ridiculous: A woman has seven husbands one after the other as each dies. Whose wife will she be in the resurrection? Ha ha ha. But Jesus doesn't laugh. He says: You flunk because you don't know the Bible or the power of God. The Sadducees put much less stock in the prophets than they did in the five books of Moses. Daniel, for example, must have gotten carried away when he wrote that "many of those who sleep in the dust of the earth shall awake, some to everlasting life, and some to shame and everlasting contempt" (Daniel 12:2, RSV). And Isaiah must have let his mind wander when he said, "The dead shall live, their bodies shall rise. O dwellers of the dust awake and sing for joy" (Isaiah 26:19, RSV). The Sadducees preferred the sturdy, down-to-earth Moses. He never said anything about resurrection—or did he?

So Jesus agrees to play on their court. He says, "Have you not read in the book of Moses, in the passage about the bush, how God said to him, 'I am the God of Abraham, and the God of Isaac, and the God of Jacob'? He is not the God of the dead but of the living; you [flunk]" (Mark 12:26–27, RSV). The point is not that God said, "I *am* the God of Abraham" with emphasis on the present tense of "am." The Sadducees would know that's just playing with words. The point is that God said, *"I* am the *God* of Abraham," with the emphasis on the deity of the one speaking about this relationship with Abraham. The assumption is: If *God* is your God, then there is so much power working for you that you can never be robbed of life.

But now back to Jesus, who is Lord of the dead. Isn't it strange that Jesus should say, "God is not the God of the dead," but Paul should say, "Jesus is Lord of the dead"? Think about what each means in its own context. God is not the God of the dead because being God is so great that the one whose God you are can't be dead—or, at least, can't stay dead. So it is with Jesus: If he *is* the Lord of the dead, then the dead can't stay dead. His Lordship is too powerful and too all-encompassing to rule over the dead and leave them dead. Those whom he rules live! If Jesus is Lord of the dead, they are not dead! If God is the God of Abraham, Abraham is not dead!

As my hand gets more and more wrinkled, in this I hope: Jesus is Lord of the dead. And therefore they are not dead. For this he died and lived again: "He who believes in me, though he die, yet shall he live" (John 11:25, RSV). Praise the Lord! The Lord of the dead—who are not dead!

69

HOW DOES ONE SIN MAKE YOU GUILTY OF THE WHOLE LAW?

Degrees of Guilt before God

Meditation on James 2:10–11

> *Whoever keeps the whole law and yet*
> *stumbles in one point, he has become*
> *guilty of all. For He who said, "Do not*
> *commit adultery," also said, "Do not*
> *commit murder." Now if you do not*
> *commit adultery, but do commit murder,*
> *you have become a transgressor of the law.*

You may have heard someone reasoning that no sin is worse than any other sin because every sin makes you guilty of breaking the whole law. Or you may have heard it in another form: No sin is worse than any other because every sin is a crime against an infinitely holy God and therefore worthy of an eternal punishment. We must be careful here. The thinking behind these statements may be well-meant, but biblically skewed.

The first problem with this thinking is that the teachings of Jesus point in another direction. Jesus doesn't seem to support the idea that all guilt is equal because all sins are equally heinous. Rather, there are degrees of guilt and degrees of severity in judgment. For example, he told a parable which ended like this: "That slave who knew his master's will and did not get ready or act in accord with his will, will receive many lashes, but the one who did not know it, and committed deeds worthy of a flogging, will receive but few. From everyone who has been given much, much will be required; and to whom they entrusted much, of him they will ask all the more" (Luke 12:47–48).

Again, Jesus teaches that on the day of judgment there will be greater and lesser degrees of misery. "Woe to you, Chorazin! Woe to you, Bethsaida! For if the miracles had occurred in Tyre and Sidon which occurred in you, they would have repented long ago in sackcloth and ashes. Nevertheless I say to you, it will be *more tolerable* for Tyre and Sidon in the day of judgment than for you" (Matthew 11:21–22, emphasis added). "Whoever does not receive you, nor heed your words, as you go out of that house or that city, shake the dust off your feet. Truly I say to you, it will be *more tolerable* for the land of Sodom and Gomorrah in the day of judgment than for that city" (Matthew 10:14, emphasis added).

Nevertheless, even though Jesus teaches that there will be greater and lesser degrees of guilt and misery in the judgment, yet we must deal with the text that is most commonly brought in to support the case that all sins are equal since they all make us guilty of the whole law. That text is James 2:10–11, "Whoever keeps the whole law and yet stumbles in one point, he has become guilty of all. For He who said, 'Do not commit adultery,' also said, 'Do not commit murder.' Now if you do not commit adultery, but do commit murder, you have become a transgressor of the law."

Notice carefully: James *does* say that to break one commandment of the law makes you "guilty of all." But he does *not* say that this means no sin is worse than another. Well, then, what is the point?

Suppose you avoid five acts of disobedience: theft, murder, lying, swearing, adultery, but, when it comes to coveting or lust, you give way. Then suppose you are caught and brought to account and feel cornered. It may be that you would defend yourself by saying: "Well, I'm really not so bad because there are five other commandments that I obeyed, and I failed only in this one."

James seems to be responding to this kind of thinking. He says that you are not really obeying those other five commandments. Why? Because the same God who tells you not to do those five things also tells you not to covet or lust. So you know God's will in this matter of lust or coveting, but you say no to his will and follow your own desire, contrary to his. What does this say about the "obedience" that you claim to have for the other commandments?

Can you be loving and trusting and submitted to God as a whole Person, and yet distrust his wisdom and goodness in something he says (which is what disobedience is)? If you consistently reject God's counsel in one area, can you really say that your heart is an obedient heart, even if you outwardly comply with other commandments?

True obedience to God (not just to lists of laws) means more than outward performances which can be tallied in percentages (like 80 percent obeyed). Rather, true obedience is to be so transformed that we delight to do God's will at multiple levels. We delight in his will as the excellent expression of his wisdom and justice and love. We delight in personal, close communion with him as our guide, which we would lose, at least for a season, if we acted against his counsel. We delight in his gift of a clean conscience. We delight in the smile of his approval. We delight in God himself whom we see and know more clearly when we walk in unbroken fellowship and obedience. We delight in the prospect of ongoing assurance and hope, which is jeopardized and weakened if we gradually slip away from him in callous disobedience.

The point of James seems to be that willfully doing our own thing in one area while claiming to be doing God's will in several other areas is a misleading and self-justifying way to look at it. As Alfred Plummer says, "To detect ourselves thus balancing a transgression here, against many observances there, ought at once to startle us into the conviction that the whole principle of our lives must be faulty. Our aim is, not to love God, or to obey Him, but to get to heaven, or at least to escape hell, on the cheapest terms" *(The Expositor's Bible,* vol. 6 [New York: George H. Doran Co., n.d.], 588).

Oh, Lord, how devious we can be! Our hearts are deceitful, and we look quickly for reasons to believe that our disobedience is not serious. Humble us before the truth that there is one Judge and one God whose fellowship and fatherly delight is more precious than all the pleasures of sin. Forbid that we would forfeit this fortune—even for a season—while justifying our sin by thinking that it is small and partial and surrounded by other good deeds.

70

ONE DANGER OF DENYING GOD'S FOREKNOWLEDGE OF HUMAN CHOICES

Undermining the New Covenant

One very old false teaching that reemerges periodically in the history of the church is that God can't foreknow responsible human choices. The reasoning goes like this: Choices are free, and "free" means self-created, and "self-created" means outside of knowability before the choices are created. Not even God can know a "nothing." And nothing is what choices are before they are made.

The philosophical presuppositions here abound: 1) that freedom means self-creating; 2) that human choices are free in this sense; 3) that an infinite God cannot know the uncreated, and so on. This old false teaching appears to be philosophically driven. It is not biblically demanded. One recent exponent of the old error spoke of "doctrinal moves that *logic required* and I believed *Scripture permitted* me to make (Clark Pinnock, *The Grace of God, the Will of Man: A Case for Arminianism* [Grand Rapids: Zondervan Publishing House, 1990], 18–19, emphasis added). You see the order: *logic* requires and *Scripture* permits. Something is out of order here, when logic is the requiring king and Scripture gives yielding endorsement.

Denying God's foreknowledge of responsible human choices has never been affirmed by the church as a legitimate part of historic Christian orthodoxy. Both

Calvinists and Arminians historically have affirmed God's exhaustive, definite foreknowledge. John Calvin wrote, "[God] foresees future events only by reason of the fact that he decreed that they take place" *(Institutes of the Christian Religion,* III, 23, 6). Jacobus Arminius wrote, "[God] has known from eternity which person should believe…and which should persevere through subsequent grace" (Carl Bangs, *Arminius* [Nashville: Abingdon Press, 1971], 219, 352). Denying God's foreknowledge of human choices has not been part of Christian orthodoxy.

Among the many reasons to avoid this old error is that it tends to undermine the foundations of the new covenant. The new covenant was predicted by Moses and Jeremiah and Ezekiel. It was inaugurated and purchased by the death of Jesus (Luke 22:20). And Paul was a "minister of the new covenant" (2 Corinthians 3:6).

The essence of the new covenant is that God undertakes to see that the people of the covenant fulfill its conditions of faith and obedience. In the Old Covenant of the Law given at Mt. Sinai, grace was offered (Exodus 34:6–7) and the obedience that comes from faith was demanded. But to most of the people, no transforming grace was given. "To this day the LORD has not given you a heart to know, nor eyes to see, nor ears to hear" (Deuteronomy 29:4).

But in the new covenant the promise is, "The LORD your God will circumcise your heart…to love the LORD your God with all your heart and with all your soul, so that you may live" (Deuteronomy 30:6). "I [the Lord] shall give them one heart, and shall put a new spirit within them. And I shall take the heart of stone out of their flesh and give them a heart of flesh, that they may walk in My statutes and keep My ordinances, and do them…. And I will put My Spirit within you and *cause you to walk in My statutes,* and you will be careful to observe My ordinances" (Ezekiel 11:19–20; 36:27, emphasis added). "I will put My law within them, and on their heart I will write it" (Jeremiah 31:33). "I will put the fear of Me in their hearts so that *they will not turn away from Me"* (Jeremiah 32:40, emphasis added).

In other words, the new covenant is the basis of our hope that—frail and fickle as we are—we will indeed persevere in faith and be saved. It is our ground of assurance that God will "keep [us] from stumbling, and make [us] stand in the presence of His glory, blameless with great joy" (Jude 1:24).

But consider what becomes of this precious hope of the new covenant if God cannot foreknow responsible human choices. The entire fabric of the Covenant unravels. The foundations of it crumble. The new covenant is the promise that God will work to secure the holiness of his people. That means he will work to bring about holy choices in his people. He is at work in us to will and to do his good pleasure; and he is "working in us that which is pleasing in His sight" (Philippians 2:13; Hebrews 13:21). But the old error undermines this very hope by saying God cannot do that, for if he did, he would foreknow our choices, which, it is claimed, he cannot.

Therefore, since our final salvation hangs on the fulfillment of new covenant promises, and since the blood of Jesus purchased the fulfillment of these promises, the undermining of the new covenant promise is an injury to the cross of Christ and a weakening of the work of the Spirit in our lives. May God protect us from the revival of old error and help us cherish the precious, empowering promises of the new covenant.

71

THE GRACE OF BEING BORN TO YOU

*A Tribute to the Supremacy of Grace in
the Life of Ruth Piper*

This is a book about savoring the supremacy of God in all of life. My mother was a massive force of grace in my life. More than I know. And what I know keeps me looking for ways to pay tribute to the grace that gave her to me for twenty-eight years. So here are two Mother's Day poems that I wrote in memory of her. May they stir you up to thank God for someone and find a way to say it.

PICKING UP WHERE MOTHER LEFT OFF

My mother was a workin' Frau:
Teutonic blood flowed in her veins.
The German sweat stood on her brow,
And, like the flawless German trains,
She kept appointments to the dot;
And taught her children it was wrong,
In spite of being sick or not,
To make a person wait for long.
I saw the Munich housewives scrub
The sidewalks with a brush and boots,
And, as I watched them wield the tub,
I learned a lot about my roots.

I heard a German scholar say,
"You must examine every source,"
And smiled, for that was Mama's way,
"The job must be done right, of course!"
I read how Luther stood like stone
gainst the old indulgence tax,
And thought how mother stood alone
Against a church that banished blacks.
I read how Brahms and Schumann said
They craved the Bible every day,
And saw my mother late in bed,
Propped up to read the Book and pray...
For me, no doubt, with all her might.
I never will forget that sight.
God bless you; blue-eyed workin' Frau,
I'll carry on the work for now.

On Grace

Some people tell me I was free,
When I believed in Christ;
And by my power got victory,
When all the world enticed.
I think they did not know my heart,
Nor theirs. Let it be said,
That I for one had sought no part
In rising from the dead.
They wonder at the sovereign rights
That I allow my King,
And puzzle at the worship heights
To which his rule gives wing.

But I will rest God's grace today
On this (I need no other):
He did not give me any say,
But chose for me my mother.

CRINGS

72

How Dispensable Is Gender?

Preserving God's Precious and Satisfying
Patterns of Life

The *Inclusive Language Edition* of the NIV Bible published in Britain in 1995 says in the preface, "It was often appropriate to mute the patriarchalism of the culture of the biblical writers through gender-inclusive language when this could be done without compromising the message of the Spirit" (vii). There are two questionable assumptions in this sentence. One assumption is that the kind of patriarchalism reflected in the Bible is a bad thing and should be muted. The other is that the "message of the Spirit" floats loose from the words inspired by the Spirit. I am not convinced that either of these assumptions is true.

Here are a few questions for you to think about in this regard:

1. Why is God predominantly called our Father rather than our Mother or our Parent? (Matthew 6:9)
2. Why is God revealed as a King not a Queen? (Psalm 95:3)
3. Why did God create man first and then woman? (Genesis 2:7, 22; 1 Timothy 2:13)
4. Why did God create woman as a "helper fit for [man]"? (Genesis 2:18, KJV)
5. Why did Satan address his deceptive scheme to Eve, not to Adam? (Genesis 3:1; 1 Timothy 2:14)
6. Why did God call Adam first to account for the disobedience of the pair? (Genesis 3:9)

7. Why did God give man and woman the name "man" *(adam)*, which in the next verse is the proper name of the husband, Adam? (Genesis 5:2–3)

8. Why were all the priests in the Old Testament men? (Exodus 39:41)

9. Why are the genealogies of the Bible almost entirely patrilineal? (Genesis 5; Matthew 1:1–16)

10. Why was the second Person of the Trinity incarnate as a man? (Luke 2:7)

11. Why does John choose masculine pronouns to refer to the Holy Spirit? (John 16:7–8)

12. Why does Jesus choose all men as apostles? (Matthew 10:2–4)

13. Why did Paul not permit a woman to teach or have authority over men? (1 Timothy 2:12)

14. Why did Paul use the term "brothers" when addressing the church? (Romans 1:13)

15. Why are believers called "sons of God," though in Christ "there is neither male nor female"? (Galatians 3:26, 28)

16. Why is a husband called the head of his wife? (Ephesians 5:23)

17. Why is the wife called to submit to her husband? (Ephesians 5:24)

18. In the comparison of Christ and the church, why is the husband compared to Christ and the wife compared to the church? (Ephesians 5:24–25)

19. Why does Paul say the head of woman is man? (1 Corinthians 11:3)

20. Why does Paul say, "Man was not made from woman, but woman from man"? (1 Corinthians 11:8, RSV)

21. Why does Paul say "man was not created for woman, but woman for man"? (1 Corinthians 11:9, RSV)

22. Why does Paul move from honoring both fathers and mothers to address men in particular, "Fathers, do not provoke your children to anger"? (Ephesians 6:2, 4)

23. Why does the Bible repeatedly refer to our believing ancestors as fathers? (Hebrews 1:1; 3:9; 8:9; 2 Peter 3:4)

24. Why does John say that he writes to the fathers and the young men? (1 John 2:13–14)

25. Why does the Bible often use a generic "he" but never a generic "she"? (Revelation 3:20; John 14:23)

26. Why does Paul urge the entire church to "quit you like men" (KJV) or "act like men"? (Greek: *andrizesthe*, 1 Corinthians 16:13)

The answer to these questions is not bad news for women. God is a God of infinite wisdom and love. His ideas for us as male and female are the best and most satisfying ideas in the universe. His vision of the joyful complementarity of manhood and womanhood is a glorious vision. Sin has distorted it since the Fall, and grace is redeeming it, but not discarding it. The Bible transforms male headship, but does not trash it.

So what is the answer to those twenty-six questions? A rough overall answer might go like this. It's because while man and woman are equally valuable in God's image, and while both of them have essential and satisfying roles to play in the drama of God-exalting human life, nevertheless men bear a primary (not solitary) responsibility for leadership and protection and provision in the human race. Therefore they bear a representative role when it comes to accountability (Genesis 3:9; Romans 5:12–14). This unique calling is a *responsibility* to bear in sacrificial love, not a *right* to seize in dominating power. Where it is embraced with servantlike, Christ-honoring courage, and supported by women with faith-filled, fearless, intelligent joy, the best harmony of man and woman prevails.*

⌒↬↬↬↬⌒

* I have tried to develop this at length with biblical support in John Piper and Wayne Grudem, eds., *Recovering Biblical Manhood and Womanhood: A Response to Evangelical Feminisim* (Wheaton, IL: Crossway Books, 1991).

73

MAKING A DIFFERENCE BY FIRE

"What Are You Doing Here?"

"I Have Been Very Zealous for the LORD of Hosts"

1 KINGS 19:9–10, 13–14

Have you ever prayed a prayer like this? "Lord, let me make a difference for you that is utterly disproportionate to who I am"? That's the prayer I wrote in the margin of a book recently beside a quote from David Brainerd. You recall that Brainerd was a missionary to the New England Indians 250 years ago. He wrote:

> Oh, that I might be a flaming fire in the service of the Lord. Here I am, Lord, send me; send me to the ends of the earth…send me from all that is called earthly comfort; send me even to death itself if it be but in Thy service and to promote Thy Kingdom.

Brainerd has made a difference for God utterly disproportionate to who he was. He was an obscure missionary in New England. He died at the age of twenty-nine. He was not well known. He was extremely vulnerable to depression. But his life has inspired the modern, Protestant missionary movement perhaps more than any other life since the apostles. Why?

One key reason is that he was so utterly *aflame for God.* The great pastor and theologian, Jonathan Edwards, saw this zeal and the knowledge in which it was rooted and the obedience it produced, and was led by God to put Brainerd's brief missionary career of five years into a book. That book and that life have changed the world. It is amazing what God can do through a short life, ablaze for his glory. The impact can be all out of proportion to who a person is.

I hope thousands of you will pray, "O Lord, let me make a difference for you utterly disproportionate to who I am." This is a prayer that the so-called nobodies of the world can pray without fear of presumption. The wording of the prayer contains a disclaimer: "I am not great. But you, Lord, are very great. And in your astonishing sovereignty you can let my little life make a difference far beyond all my little powers."

But what is the key to making a difference for God? Is it not truth-saturated, flaming zeal for God? Twice God asked Elijah in the cave on Mount Horeb, "What are you doing here?" And he answered both times, "I have been very zealous for the LORD of hosts" (l Kings 19:9–10, 13–14). Passion for the glory of the Lord is the key to making a difference all out of proportion to who we are. It is not the prerogative of old or young, intelligent or simple, men or women. This passion can flame up in the heart of any saint. Do we want it enough to seek it?

It comes from prayerful immersion in Scripture. In Luke 24:32 the disciples, who had talked with Jesus on the Emmaus road, said, "Did not our hearts *burn* within us while he talked to us on the road, while he opened to us the *Scriptures?*" (RSV, emphasis added). The fire of zeal for the Lord comes from the opening of the Scriptures in conversation with Jesus (that is, in Scripture-soaked prayer).

Question: If you do not burn with the zeal that you long for, are you willing to make some experiments with high-dosage, extended-time, prayer-driven Bible meditation? Very honestly, there is in my own life a close correspondence between the time and amount of prayerful Bible opening, and the depth and strength and warmth of my zeal for God. Without large and deep doses of God's Word, I am very vulnerable to worldly mindsets. One church in Korea expects its members to read five chapters of the Bible a day and its pastors to read twenty chapters a day. The question is: If you want the flame of the Emmaus road and the flame of Brainerd, are you willing to make serious experiments?

I am praying that thousands who read this book will *burn* for the glory of God. And will pray with me: Oh, Lord, grant me to make a difference for you utterly disproportionate to who I am.

74

WHEN TO SEPARATE AND
WHEN NOT TO

A Letter to an Earnest Inquirer

Dear friend,
Relating to unbelievers who make no profession of faith.

Regarding how to relate to unbelievers, it seems to me that in the New Testament we have two commands that are in tension (not contradiction) with each other. One side is 2 Corinthians 6:14–15, "Do not be bound together with unbelievers; for what partnership have righteousness and lawlessness, or what fellowship has light with darkness? Or what harmony has Christ with Belial, or what has a believer in common with an unbeliever?"

On the other side is 1 Corinthians 5:9–11, "I wrote you in my letter not to associate with immoral people; I did not at all mean with the immoral people of this world, or with the covetous and swindlers, or with idolaters; for then you would have to go out of the world. But actually, I wrote to you not to associate with any so-called brother if he should be an immoral person."

One seems to say that we must be very vigilant lest we be involved with unbelievers in wrong ways, and the other seems to say that you must not take that to an extreme. So we are confronted with the question, what sorts of "being bound together with unbelievers" is wrong? And what sorts are necessary and right? Marriage is clear because of 1 Corinthians 7:39. Marry only in the Lord. What about a business partnership? A bowling team? A neighborhood block club? A working relationship where the boss is an unbeliever?

My principle here would go something like this: *Avoid relations with unbelievers in which your relation endorses the unbelief or consequent sins, and avoid the kinds of relationships that involve the interweaving of deep personal values (like marriage).*

On the other side, don't avoid relationships where you can have clear testimony to the truth and are allowed to stand on Christian principles, even if you are sometimes criticized for getting too close. Jesus was criticized like that, and was called a "glutton and a drunkard" (Luke 7:34).

Relating to those who profess faith in Christ but do not live holy lives or espouse biblical orthodoxy.

With regard to professing believers who live in blatant sin or teach serious false doctrine (you hear some of the ambiguity already in the words "blatant" and "serious") there seems to be a more vigorous ostracism. Thus 1 Corinthians 5:11 says, "But actually, I wrote to you not to associate with any so-called brother if he should be an immoral person, or covetous, or an idolater, or a reviler, or a drunkard, or a swindler—not even to eat with such a one." I take this to mean that if a person has been disciplined or warned in the appropriate way and presses on in his error, we are not to go on hobnobbing with him as if nothing were wrong. We are to say to the professing brother, "You know I love you and would love it if our lives could be woven together more closely, but as long as you live like this (perhaps sleep with your boyfriend or sell drugs or lie on reports at work), I can't act as if things were normal. I don't think we should get together anymore until you change your ways. Otherwise it looks as if nothing is at stake."

What is the principle here that we can apply to various kinds of relations? This person may be my boss at work. Or the person may be the wayward husband who still lives with and is married to a faithful member of our church. It doesn't quite work to say that Matthew 18:17 puts the unrepentant person in the same class as an unbeliever so that the same principle applies as to unbelievers ("If he refuses to listen to them, tell it to the church; and if he refuses to listen even to the church, let him be to you as a Gentile and a tax collector"). If that were true, then 1 Corinthians 5:9–13 would have no meaning when it says, don't separate from those outside, but from those inside. If the "insider" becomes identical to an "outsider" the moment you separate, then he also becomes one that you are not to separate from like that.

The principle seems to be: *If you can, seek for redemptive ways to be separate without writing a person off as an unbeliever.* I say this because of 2 Thessalonians 3:14–15, "And if anyone does not obey our instruction in this letter, take special note of that man and do not associate with him, so that he may be put to shame. And *yet* do not regard him as an enemy, but admonish him as a brother" (emphasis added). In other words, there is a difference between the "ostracism" of this person, and the person in 2 Corinthians 6:14 ("Do not be bound together with unbelievers").

It is not clear to me what form this ostracism should take in each situation. "Do not even eat with such a one" (1 Corinthians 5:11) implies that there are some situations, at least, where the best way to act is to cut off all normal, casual relations. I assume this might still leave room for business contacts or other kinds of togetherness that do not imply that all is well between you.

Second John 9–11 may give a hint as to how to articulate the principle. It says, "Anyone who goes too far and does not abide in the teaching of Christ, does not have God; the one who abides in the teaching, he has both the Father and the Son. If anyone comes to you and does not bring this teaching, do not receive him into your house, and do not give him a greeting; for the one who gives him a greeting participates in his evil deeds."

This would suggest that we should avoid those kinds of gestures or relations that imply our participation in the error or evil of another. Here I think we are going to have to learn to live with differences of opinions about what measures of interaction imply this kind of participation. Strong separatists see participation and endorsement implied earlier than others do. But the principle is there.

I know there is much for me to see. I wish I could give days to every issue that perplexes my mind and presses for decision.

Alas, only one life.

For the supremacy of God in all things,

John Piper

75

SOME QUESTIONS TO ASK WHEN CONSIDERING A JOB

Pondering Vocation as Service to Christ

The freedom to choose your vocation is a historical novelty. Until recent times, if you were a son and your father was a farmer or a blacksmith or shoemaker or a baker, it was almost certain you would be too. If you were a daughter, you would almost certainly be a hardworking homemaker and partner in the home-based family business. Choices were few. And a reading like this one would have been almost unintelligible.

But today, very few sons assume that they will follow in their father's vocation. And daughters have a wide scope of career paths they can follow instead of, or alongside, a more traditional homemaking career. Not only that, midcareer changes are not unusual. Which means that the crisis of choosing a vocation happens not just once, but several times for many people.

One of the things I love to do as a pastor is sow seeds of kingdom restlessness. I picture my preaching as taking trees by the trunk and working them back and forth to loosen the roots. My idea is that this will result in the roots of people's lives going down deeper into God's will where they are, or it will result in the roots being plucked up and planted in a different calling for even greater kingdom fruitfulness. Whatever else, I don't want my people to simply drift into a job or coast along in it with little sense of calling or significance for the supremacy of God in what they do.

So I prepared some questions for them in the hopes that they would be stirred to find jobs and do their jobs, as Paul said, "not in the way of eye-service, as men-pleasers, but as servants of Christ, doing the will of God from the heart" (Ephesians 6:6, RSV).

1. *Can I earnestly do all the parts of this job "to the glory of God," that is, in a way that highlights his superior value over all other things?* "Whether, then, you eat or drink or whatever you do, do all to the glory of God" (1 Corinthians 10:31).

2. *Is taking this job part of a strategy to grow in personal holiness?* "For this is the will of God, your sanctification" (1 Thessalonians 4:3).

3. *Will this job help or hinder my progress in esteeming the value of knowing Christ Jesus my Lord?* "I count all things to be loss in view of the surpassing value of knowing Christ Jesus my Lord" (Philippians 3:8).

4. *Will this job result in inappropriate pressures to think or feel or act against my King, Jesus?* "You were bought with a price; do not become slaves of men" (1 Corinthians 7:23).

5. *Will this job help establish an overall life pattern that will yield a significant involvement in fulfilling God's great purpose of exalting Christ among all the unreached peoples of the world?* "Jesus came up and spoke to them, saying, 'All authority has been given to Me in heaven and on earth. Go therefore and make disciples of all the nations, baptizing them in the name of the Father and the Son and the Holy Spirit, teaching them to observe all that I commanded you; and lo, I am with you always, even to the end of the age'" (Matthew 28:18–20).

6. *Will this job be worthy of my best energies?* "Whatever your hand finds to do, do it with all your might" (Ecclesiastes 9:10).

7. *Will the activities and environment of this job tend to shape me, or will I be able to shape it for the Christ-magnifying purposes of God?* "Do not be conformed to this world, but be transformed by the renewing of your mind" (Romans 12:2).

8. *Will this job provide an occasion for me to be radically Christian so as to let my light shine for my Father's sake, or will my participation in the vision of the firm*

tend to snuff out my wick? "Let your light shine before men in such a way that they may see your good works, and glorify your Father who is in heaven" (Matthew 5:16).

9. *Does the aim of this job cohere with a growing intensity in my life to be radically, publicly, fruitfully devoted to Christ at any cost?* "If anyone wishes to come after Me, let him deny himself, and take up his cross, and follow Me" (Mark 8:34).

10. *Will the job feel like a good investment of my life when this vapor's breath of preparation for eternity is over?* "You are just a vapor that appears for a little while and then vanishes away" (James 4:14).

11. *Does this job fit with why I believe I was created and purchased by Christ?* "Everyone who is called by My name...I have created for My glory" (Isaiah 43:7). "You have been bought with a price: therefore glorify God in your body" (1 Corinthians 6:20).

12. *Does this job fit together with the ultimate truth that all things exist for Christ?* "For by Him all...have been created through [Christ] and for Him" (Colossians 1:16).

76

SWEET SOVEREIGNTY AND THE ASSURANCE OF SALVATION

What Can Be Sweeter Than to Be "Kept by the Power of God"?

When you get the sovereignty of God straight, everything gets straighter. Going wrong here will lead to error in all kinds of unexpected places. Oh, how I pray that God will give us clarity and conviction and joy in our vision of God's absolute sovereignty over our frail and fickle lives!

Take the issue of assurance and eternal security and the possibility of falling away from Christ. One Sunday, I tackled the sobering text of Hebrews 6:4–8. There it says that you can be "enlightened and have tasted of the heavenly gift and have been made partakers of the Holy Spirit, and have tasted the good word of God and the powers of the age to come" and then fall away from it all and be lost. (Sermon, 13 October 1996. Available at http://www.desiringgod.org/library/sermons/96/101396.html)

Instead of saying that you can lose your salvation, I said that the meaning of Hebrews 6:4–8 is something almost as shocking, namely, that you can experience all those things (enlightenment, Holy Spirit, Word of God, and miracles) and *never have been* saved! This is shocking because it means that people may be mistaken in thinking they are Christians when they are not.

So the text and the message raises the question of assurance. How can we be sure we will persevere to the end and not fall away and become like Esau who tried to return but could not repent (Hebrews 12:16–17)? Here is where the sovereignty of God becomes so crucial.

The book of Hebrews exults in the new and better covenant which God has made through the blood of Christ with all who are his people. The old covenant made at Mount Sinai was vulnerable to the people's weakness (Romans 8:3). Hebrews 8:9 says, "'They did not continue in My covenant, and so I paid no heed to them,' says the Lord" (RSV). But the new covenant is radically different in that it is *not* vulnerable to our weakness. Rather, it assures us that God's sovereignty will overcome our weakness and prevent us from breaking the covenant.

Thus Hebrews 8:10 says, "This is the covenant that I will make with the house of Israel after those days, says the Lord: *I will put My laws into their minds, and I will write them upon their hearts.* And I will be their God, and they shall be My people" (emphasis added). In other words, God will not only tell us what we must do, he will see to it that we do it by working in us. This is what Hebrews 13:21 says about the new covenant: "[May God] equip you in every good thing to do His will, *working in us that which is pleasing in His sight,* through Jesus Christ, to whom be the glory forever and ever. Amen" (emphasis added). This is the sanctifying, keeping, saving sovereignty of God. And it is sweeter than honey to the wavering soul.

In the new covenant our assurance rests firmly on the sovereignty of God over our own proneness to wander. We know we will not fall away because this is a promise of the new covenant sealed by the blood of Jesus. For example, in Jeremiah 32:40, God promises, "I will make an everlasting covenant with them that I will not turn away from them, to do them good; and I will put the fear of Me in their hearts so that they will not turn away from Me." If you ask me how I know that tomorrow I will still believe in Christ, my answer is not that I am a disciplined person, or that I finish what I start, or that my will is reliable, or that the benefits outweigh the costs, or even that my church prays for me. My answer is: Christ shed his blood as the price of the new covenant (Luke 22:20), and in this covenant God promises,

"They will not turn away from me." God's sovereign right and grace over my fickle will is my only hope for persevering to the end.

This is the sweet reality of the sovereignty of God. I pray that you will understand it and believe it and revel in the security and joy of it. What can be sweeter than to be "kept by the power of God"? (1 Peter 1:5).

77

MORE, MORE, MORE

Seventeen Aspects of Holy Dissatisfaction

One mark of Christian authenticity is discontentment with anything less than "all the fullness of God" (Ephesians 3:19). Coasting is not discipleship. Drifting in self-contentment is not like basking in the pool of security, but like floating, fast asleep, toward the falls. "We must pay much closer attention to what we have heard, so that we do not *drift* away" (Hebrews 2:1, emphasis added).

There is a holy discontentment. It is not a nail-biting uncertainty about our standing with God. It is the increased appetite of those who have tasted and seen that the Lord is good (1 Peter 2:2–3). It is the pursuit of those who have been pursued and captured by the strong arms of love. "Not that I have already obtained it, or have already become perfect, but *I press on* so that I may lay hold of that for which also I was laid hold of by Christ Jesus" (Philippians 3:12, emphasis added).

Therefore the biblical passages that follow are a way of waking our drowsy souls to feel a pure and holy dissatisfaction and stirring us up to pursue "all the fullness of God" (emphasis added in the following verses).

- "Grow in *grace.*" "But he gives more *grace.*" (2 Peter 3:18; James 4:6)
- "We...pray for you...that you may be...increasing in the *knowledge of God.*" "Grow in the...*knowledge of our Lord* and Savior Jesus Christ." (Colossians 1:9–10; 2 Peter 3:18)

- "Increase our *faith!*" "We...give thanks...because your *faith* is growing abundantly." (Luke 17:5; 2 Thessalonians 1:3, RSV; see also 2 Corinthians 10:15)

- "May the God of hope fill you with all joy and peace in believing, so that by the power of the Holy Spirit you may abound in *hope.*" (Romans 15:13, RSV)

- "May the Lord cause you to increase and abound in *love* for one another and for all men." (1 Thessalonians 3:12; 4:10; 2 Thessalonians 1:3; Philippians 1:9)

- "As you learned from us how you ought to...*please God*...do so more and more." (1 Thessalonians 4:1, RSV)

- "And we all, with unveiled face, beholding the glory of the Lord, are being changed into *his likeness* from one degree of *glory* to another." (2 Corinthians 3:18, RSV)

- "Let us cleanse ourselves from every defilement of body and spirit and make *holiness* perfect in the fear of God." (2 Corinthians 7:1, RSV)

- "[God] will cause the fruits of your *righteousness* to grow." "Unless your *righteousness* exceeds that of the scribes and Pharisees, you will never enter the kingdom of heaven." (2 Corinthians 9:10; Matthew 5:20, RSV)

- "Be steadfast, immovable, always abounding in *the work of the Lord.*" (1 Corinthians 15:58; 2 Corinthians 9:8)

- "Be filled with the *Spirit.*" (Ephesians 5:18)

- "The *word of God* grew and multiplied." (Acts 12:24; 6:7)

- "The *number of the disciples* multiplied greatly in Jerusalem." "I have made myself a slave to all, that I might win the more *[people].*" (Acts 6:7, RSV; 1 Corinthians 9:19; see also Acts 16:5)

- "Since you are eager for manifestations of the Spirit, strive to excel in *building up the church.*" (1 Corinthians 14:12, RSV)

- "As you received Christ Jesus the Lord so live in him...abounding in *thanksgiving.*" "Always and for everything [give] thanks." (Colossians 2:6–7; Ephesians 5:20; 2 Corinthians 4:15)

- "Speaking the truth in love, we are to grow up *in every way* into him, who is the head." (Ephesians 4:15)

- "You shall be *perfect*, as your heavenly Father is perfect." (Matthew 5:48; Philippians 3:12)

Father, we fear our deadly fondness for floating toward the falls when we ought to be swimming against the current. Oh, God, have mercy to waken us again and again to the perils of drifting in the Christian life. Help us heed Hebrews 2:1, "We must pay much closer attention to what we have heard, so that we do not drift away from it." Woe to the drifters in a world where all the current is toward destruction! Grant us to see and to feel that not only life, but also joy, is in the "good fight" that does not end until the final rest.

78

ON LENDING TO GOD

Meditation on Proverbs 19:17

> *He who is kind to the poor lends to the Lord,*
> *and he will repay him for his deed. (RSV)*

Ihave a great deal of trouble picturing myself as the creditor of God. How can I possibly presume to say that I have loaned to God from my storehouse and now he is my debtor? Didn't God say, "If I were hungry, I would not tell you, for the world and all that is in it is mine" (Psalm 50:12, RSV)? Surely that means we insult God if we presume to barter with him. We forget that everything we have to barter is already God's. We are merely stewards or trustees of God's possessions. He is the rightful owner of all that is. It is impossible, isn't it, to give to God such that he then becomes our debtor? "Who has given a gift to him that he might be repaid?" (Romans 11:35, RSV). So how can a steward lend to his master what already belongs to him?

To understand Proverbs 19:17, I think we should start with a more fundamental teaching of this book: "Trust in the Lord with all your heart and do not rely on your own insight" (Proverbs 3:5, RSV). The only way to have a fulfilling life is to stop relying on our own savvy and to start relying on God to provide the necessary turns of affairs. Now, a person who knows that God aims to bless him because of his faith rather than because of his wealth-accumulating "insight" will look upon the needy from a new perspective. He will say, "Well now, here is a person a lot like myself. He has no power or means for bartering with God.

All he can do is trust him. Which is all I can do. So I better not boast over this person. And not only that, here is an opportunity for me to express my trust in God. If I give this poor man some of my money or some of my time or some of my energy to help him find a job, then I won't have as much money or time or energy left over to do the things I was planning to do to make me happy. So that means I will have to trust God and not rely on my own insight. But that's really no big risk because I know how much God loves to be trusted. In fact, God loves to be trusted so much that he always blesses those who trust him with a life more fulfilling than if they hadn't trusted him. So, of course, I will give this poor man my help."

If being kind to the poor is an act of trusting God to take care of us, there is a sense in which God becomes a debtor. He is a debtor to his own glory. If I trust him and reckon his Word and wisdom and love worthy to be counted on, then God is honor-bound, glory-bound, to uphold the worth of his Word and wisdom and love. Trust is the one thing that can put God in debt. The reason trust can do this is that it is the one human attitude that looks away from our sufficiency to God's sufficiency. When God's sufficiency is at stake, he will prevail.

Which means that the focus of Proverbs 19:17 is not on the Lord's need, but on the certainty of our receiving back from the Lord something corresponding to what we gave to the poor. God treats our gifts to the poor as obligating his own divine generosity back to us with the same certainty as if we lent the money to him and made his integrity the guarantee of our return. When our investment in the poor is an expression of faith in God's provision, then God himself is committed to bringing that investment back to us with the same certainty as though he were in our financial debt. Jesus taught something similar when he said to his disciples, "Sell your possessions and give alms; make yourselves money belts which do not wear out, an unfailing treasure in heaven, where no thief comes near nor moth destroys" (Luke 12:33, author's translation). If we will give alms to the poor, it is a way of putting our money in heaven ("lending to the Lord"), as it were, so that the investment will never be lost but bear eternal dividends ("he will repay him for his deed"). Similarly, Jesus said to the rich man, "Sell what you possess and give to the poor, and you will have treasure in heaven; and come, follow me" (Matthew 19:21, RSV). Giving to the poor means having treasure in heaven.

So, whether we think of giving to the poor as "lending to the Lord," who will surely pay us back in due season, or "putting our treasure in heaven," where it will be safe for us in the age to come, the point is the same: God will bless those who bless the poor with the same commitment that he has to his own integrity as the guarantor of our investments with him.

You do not have to look far to find a need greater than your own in this world. When you find it, let your first act be to trust in God's provision; and let your second act be the demonstration of that trust by investing your earthly resources in that need. God so values being trusted that he will not let this investment be in vain.

79

"The Terror That Is Named the Flight of Time"

"In the Lord Your Labor Is Not in Vain"

The clock never stops ticking. Nothing but God is more persistent than the passing of time. You can't stop it or slow it. It is sovereign over all human resistance. It will not be hindered or altered or made to cease. It is utterly oblivious to young and old, pain and pleasure, crying and laughing. Nothing, absolutely nothing, makes a difference to the unstoppable, unchangeable tick, tick, ticking of time. Anna Akhmatova, a Russian poet, said that war and plague pass, but no one can cope with "the terror that is named the flight of time" (quoted in D. M. Thomas, *Alexander Solzhenitsyn* [New York: St. Martin's Press, 1998], 270).

I have an unusual habit when I go to bed. After Noël and I pray, I crawl into bed and situate myself on my left side, facing the red glow of the radio-alarm-clock numbers on the bedside table. I pull my hands up in front of me at about face level and wait for a few minutes in stillness, usually praying silently with gratitude for the wife who lies behind me, and for my children, and for the ministry God has given me. Then I take my right hand and curl my fingers around my left wrist and find my pulse. I watch the red minute number until it changes, and then I begin counting. One…two…three… When the number changes and one minute has passed, I stop.

I began this peculiar habit out of the vain notion that if my heart rate is very slow, from good exercise (or genes), it may mean that my heart is healthy and I will live long. Such is the silliness of human thought. The effect has been otherwise.

Now, as I count the beats, it is not the *rate* that fixes my attention, but the *succession.* One beat, then another, then another, on through the night, about twenty-one thousand times while I sleep. The effect of this little exercise is that I fall asleep most nights, lulled by the steady rhythm of my heart and with a sober sense of my very fragile existence. Any one of those beats could be my last. I cannot will my heart to beat one more time. If it stops, it stops. I and my time on earth are over. "If I should die before I wake, I pray the Lord my soul to take."

Time is precious. We are fragile. Life is short. Eternity is long. Shall we not then enter on every venture with a vigilance like that of the young Jonathan Edwards when he wrote his fifth resolution: "Resolved, Never to lose one moment of time, but to improve it in the most profitable way I possibly can;" which is really a subpoint of his sixth resolution: "Resolved, To live with all my might, while I do live" *(The Works of Jonathan Edwards,* vol. 1, ed. Edward Hickman [Edinburgh: The Banner of Truth Trust, 1974], xx). Yes, this can become compulsive and unhealthy. But for those of us who need to hear it as an antidote to squandering the preciousness of irretrievable time, let us hear it.

The church I serve is generous to me beyond all my deserving. As I write these words I am on a one-month leave to complete this book. I enter the month with a sense that every minute counts. Oh, to be a faithful steward of the breath God has given me. Three texts resound in my ears. 1) "Redeem the time" (Ephesians 5:16, KJV). 2) "It is required of stewards that one be found trustworthy" (1 Corinthians 4:2). 3) "His grace toward me was not in vain; but I labored even more than all of them, yet not I, but the grace of God with me" (1 Corinthians 15:10, author's translation).

Surely God means for our minutes on earth to count for something significant. Paul said, "In the day of Christ I will have reason to glory because I did not run in vain nor toil in vain" (Philippians 2:16). In the same way, I have good hope from the Lord that my "labor is not in vain in the Lord" (1 Corinthians 15:58, KJV). And I commend this promise to you. No minute need be lived in vain. Eternity will render it significant if lived in faith for the glory of God. In the end we rest in this: "My times are in Your hand" (Psalm 31:15).

80

FOUNDATIONS FOR THINKING ABOUT RACE AND INTERRACIAL MARRIAGE

Pondering the Primacy of Being Created in the Image of God

If we think that issues of race and racism in America were settled with the civil rights movement in the sixties, we are not awake to the real world. Take just one angle, transracial adoption. As controversial as they are, Richard Neuhaus's words at least show that the issue is alive, well, and in need of biblical treatment:

> In recent years all kinds of policies and procedures have been put into place making interracial adoption impossible or extremely difficult. Such policies must be called what they are. They are racist. Hundreds of thousands of children have their lives blighted by being shuffled from place to place in foster care while millions of American couples yearn to adopt them. Couples pay many thousands of dollars to have people search out children in Asia and Latin America, while ideologically driven social workers and psychologists here at home tell us it is better for a child to die in a drive-by shooting than to have his "black identity" confused because he is adopted by white people. This is madness and cruelty of a high order. ("Counting by Race," *First Things,* No. 60, February 1996, 78)

For starters, then, let us ponder these eight biblical truths:

1. God designed all ethnic groups from one human ancestor.

> [God] made from one, every nation [*pan ethnos* means "every ethnic group"] of mankind to live on all the face of the earth. (Acts 17:26)

2. Members of every ethnic group are made in the image of God.

> God created man in His own image, in the image of God He created him; male and female He created them. (Genesis 1:27)

3. In determining the significance of who you are, being a person in the image of God compares to ethnic distinctives the way the noonday sun compares to a birthday candle.

Being a person is infinitely more significant than being a white person or black person. In the real world on this earth, race is significant; but in the more real world of heaven redeemed personhood is ten thousand times more significant than race.

4. The prediction of a curse that Noah spoke over some of the descendants of Ham is irrelevant in deciding how the black race is to be viewed and treated.

> When Noah awoke from his wine, he knew what his youngest son had done to him. So he said, "Cursed be Canaan; a servant of servants he shall be to his brothers." (Genesis 9:24–25)

The prediction is that the Canaanites will eventually be overpowered by the descendants of Shem and Japheth, which they were when the Israelites took possession of the Promised Land. Canaan is the one son of Ham who is *not* the ancestor of African peoples (Genesis 10:15–18). So the curse doesn't fall on the African peoples but on the Canaanites.

5. *It is God's purpose and command that we make disciples for Jesus Christ from every ethnic group in the world, without distinction.*

> All authority has been given to Me in heaven and on earth. Go therefore and make disciples of all the nations, baptizing them in the name of the Father and the Son and the Holy Spirit, teaching them to observe all that I commanded you; and lo, I am with you always, even to the end of the age. (Matthew 28:18–20)

6. *All believers in Jesus Christ, of every ethnic group, are united to each other not only in a common humanity in the image of God, but even more, as brothers and sisters in Christ and members of the same body.*

> Just as we have many members in one body and all the members do not have the same function, so we, who are many, are one body in Christ, and individually members one of another. (Romans 12:4–5)

> See how great a love the Father has bestowed upon us, that we should be called children of God; and such we are. (1 John 3:1)

7. *The Bible forbids intermarriage between believer and unbeliever, but not between members of different ethnic groups.*

> A wife is bound as long as her husband lives; but if her husband is dead, she is free to be married to whom she wishes, *only in the Lord.* (1 Corinthians 7:39, emphasis added)

This is the new covenant application of the Old Testament warnings about intermarrying with the pagan nations. For example, Deuteronomy 7:3–4:

> You shall not intermarry with [the nations]; you shall not give your daughters to their sons, nor shall you take their daughters for your sons. For they will turn your sons away from following Me to serve other gods; then the anger of the LORD will be kindled against you.

The issue in intermarriage is fundamentally religious and not racial. Will you unite your heart and life to a person who does not love your Savior? That is the question.

8. Therefore, against the spirit of indifference, alienation, and hostility in our land, let us embrace the supremacy of God's love to take new steps personally and corporately toward racial harmony, expressed visibly in our communities and in our churches.

⁂

81

CONTROVERSY: ESSENTIAL AND DEADLY

Communing with God in the Doctrines for Which We Contend

Doctrinal controversy is both essential and deadly. The attitude toward controversy in various groups of Christians depends largely on which of these two they feel most strongly. Is it essential? Or is it deadly? My plea is that we believe and feel *both* of these. Controversy is essential where precious truth is rejected or distorted. And controversy is deadly where disputation *about* truth destroys exultation *in* truth.

The reason controversy is essential, even in the face of rejection and distortion, is that God has ordained that the truth be maintained in the world partly by human defense. For example, Paul says in Philippians 1:7 that he is in prison for the *"defense and confirmation* of the gospel" (emphasis added). And Jude 1:3 says that we should *"contend earnestly* for the faith which was once for all delivered to the saints" (emphasis added). And Acts 17:2–3 says that Paul's custom in the synagogue was to "reason" from the Scriptures and "explain and give evidence" that Jesus was the Christ. So the preservation and transmission of precious truth from person to person and generation to generation may require controversy where truth is rejected or distorted.

And controversy is deadly because it feels threatening, so it tends to stir up defensiveness and anger. It's deadly also because it tends to focus on the *reasons* for truth rather than the *reality* behind truth and so replaces exultation *in* the truth with disputation *about* the truth. This is deadly because thinking rightly about truth is not an end in itself; it's a means toward the goal of love and worship. Paul said in 1 Timothy 1:5 that "the goal of our instruction is *love.*" And he prayed in Philippians 1:9–11 that our "love…abound in knowledge…unto the glory and *praise* of God." Controversy tends to threaten both love and praise. It's hard to revel in a love poem while arguing with someone about whether your sweetheart wrote it.

So controversy is *essential* in this fallen world, and controversy is *deadly* in a fallen world. We must do it, and we must fear doing it. A good counselor for us in this is John Owen, the Puritan pastor from three centuries ago. He was involved in many controversies in his day—theological and denominational and political. But he never ceased to be a deep lover of God and a faithful pastor of a flock. He counsels us like this concerning doctrinal controversy:

> When the heart is cast indeed into the mould of the doctrine that the mind embraceth—when the evidence and necessity of the truth abides in us—when not the sense of the words only is in our heads, but the sense of the thing abides in our hearts—when we have communion with God in the doctrine we contend for—then shall we be garrisoned by the grace of God against all the assaults of men. *(The Mystery of the Gospel Vindicated* [1655], *Works* I, lxiii–lxiv)

I think that was the key to Owen's life and ministry: He didn't merely contend for doctrine; he loved and fellowshipped with the God behind the doctrine. The key phrase is this one: "When we have *communion with God* in the doctrine we contend for—then shall we be garrisoned by the grace of God against all the assaults of men." In other words, we must not let disputation replace contemplation and exultation.

As a pastor, I am eager that my ministry of preaching avoid two great errors: losing truth in the quest for exultation and losing worship in the noise of disputation. May God grant us the grace to walk the biblical tightrope, balanced by the necessity of controversy on the one side, and the dangers of it on the other.

⁕

82

"FINALLY, BRETHREN, PRAY FOR US"

A Plea for Pastors

The apostle Paul gave a clear, straightforward plea to the church at Thessalonica: "Brothers, pray for us" (2 Thessalonians 3:1). I love its simplicity. It is emotionally understated. Can you hear the depth of need this apostle feels for God's help? "…on frequent journeys, in dangers from rivers, dangers from robbers, dangers from my countrymen, dangers from the Gentiles, dangers in the city, dangers in the wilderness, dangers on the sea, dangers among false brethren…in labor and hardship, through many sleepless nights, in hunger and thirst, often without food, in cold and exposure" (2 Corinthians 11:26–27).

We hear it again with more vehemence in Romans 15:30: "Strive together with me in your prayers to God for me." Here is a great man. He has great gifts and great experiences with God. He is a brilliant intellect. He is a valiant spiritual warrior. He is a chosen instrument of God. And he pleads for prayer. "Pray for me." "Strive with me in your prayers to God for me."

Why? Two reasons:

1. Because what counts most in the Christian ministry cannot be accomplished by man left to himself.

   • I will not presume to speak of anything except *what Christ has accomplished through me,* resulting in the obedience of the Gentiles. (Romans 15:18, emphasis added)

- By the grace of God I am what I am, and His grace toward me did not prove vain; but I labored even more than all of them, yet not I, but the grace of God with me. (1 Corinthians 15:10)
- Whoever renders service, [do it] as one who renders it *by the strength which God supplies;* in order that in everything God may be glorified through Jesus Christ. (1 Peter 4:11, RSV, emphasis added)
- Now the God of peace…equip you in every good thing to do His will, *working in us that which is pleasing in His sight,* through Jesus Christ, to whom be the glory forever and ever. (Hebrews 13:20–21, emphasis added)

2. Because God has set up the world so that a) moral transformation and b) ministry triumphs, come by prayer.

a) Moral transformation:
- And this I pray, *that your love may abound* still more and more in real knowledge and all discernment. (Philippians 1:9, emphasis added)
- We have not ceased to pray for you…*so that you will walk in a manner worthy of the Lord…bearing fruit in every good work.* (Colossians 1:9–10, emphasis added)
- Pray that you may *not enter into temptation.* (Luke 22:40, emphasis added)

b) Ministry triumphs:
- [Pray] that *I may be rescued* from those who are disobedient in Judea, and *that my service for Jerusalem may prove acceptable to the saints.* (Romans 15:30–31, emphasis added)
- Pray for us *that the word of the Lord will spread rapidly and be glorified.* (2 Thessalonians 3:1, emphasis added)
- Pray on my behalf, that utterance may be given to me in the opening of my mouth, *to make known with boldness the mystery of the gospel.* (Ephesians 6:19, emphasis added)

- [Pray]...for *us...that God will open up to us a door for the word,* so that we may speak forth the mystery of Christ, for which I have also been imprisoned; *that I may make it clear in the way I ought to speak.* (Colossians 4:3–4, emphasis added)

I speak on behalf of thousands of pastors. We humbly plead: Pray for us. Let these texts be your guide. Imagine what God might do! Dream of the ripple effect across the nation—and across the decades. "Finally, brethren, pray for us."

ᏪᎳᎧ

83

BEING LOVED AND BEING HATED
Thinking About the Dark Side of Missions

I will try to be sensitive in the way I give the details of this story—a few name and detail changes to protect the innocent. It comes from an e-mail that I received after speaking outside my own state.

I had finished my second talk to this group, stressing the sovereignty of God in suffering and even martyrdom. One of the women at the conference (call her Mary) discovered that evening that a friend she had not seen for ten years (call her Rachel) was staying in adjacent conference housing. They reconnected. Rachel told Mary that ten years ago when they went their separate ways she moved to France (we'll say), met and married a former Muslim, now turned Christian (call him Ahmed). They had come back from France three years ago.

This year, the week before the conference where I was speaking, Ahmed went back to his homeland in Northern Africa for a family matter and also with some Bibles he wanted to smuggle in for believers. To make a complicated story short, he was discovered, arrested, jailed, and tortured. Mary e-mailed me and said, "His trial is today, and if guilty, he will be executed." As I write this, the outlook is more positive. But that's not the point.

The point is what she said about Rachel during this crisis. She said that Rachel was a living example of faith in God's sovereign care as she waited to hear the outcome of her husband's trial from three thousand miles away. Her words were, "She is screaming God's sovereignty just with her demeanor. I am so very humbled to watch her walk through it, contemplating that I would most likely be *un*like her. However, by God's grace, He is changing me so that I can glorify Him through the trials He has for me and my family to go through."

Why tell this story here? Because I am praying for God to raise up "Rachel's" and "Ahmeds" through the readings in this book. Oh, God, give us men and women who count everything as loss for the surpassing value of spreading a passion for your supremacy for the joy of unreached peoples. Lord, raise up radical disciples who know the "dark side of missions" and count it all joy.

What do you mean "dark side"? Well, take the phrase "all the nations" (Greek: *panta ta ethne*). We usually think of this phrase in connection with the great commission in Matthew 28:19, "Go and make disciples of *all the nations*" (emphasis added). But there is another use of the phrase in Matthew 24:9, "You will be hated by *all the nations* because of My name" (emphasis added). That's the dark side of missions. The hatred will be as widespread as the harvest.

In the face of that reality, may the Lord raise up real, radical Christians who are willing not only to love the nations, but also to be hated by the nations. That's how Jesus accomplished his mission. That is the only way ours will be accomplished. "If the world hates you," Jesus said, "you know that it has hated Me before it hated you. If you were of the world, the world would love its own; but because you are not of the world, but I chose you out of the world, because of this the world hates you" (John 15:18–19).

Pray with me that thousands would embrace the call to be hated for the sake of loving others. If your driving motive in life is to be liked and loved, you will find it almost impossible to be a Christian, especially a Christian missionary. Missionaries are people who have decided that being loved by God is enough to enable love. We don't need to be loved by others. Yes, it feels good. But it is not essential. Loving, not being loved, is essential.

Oh, Lord, put your Spirit of love in the hearts of thousands for the sake of the nations.

84

EMBRACING A GOD-CENTERED GOD
WITH GOD-CENTERED LOVE

A Letter to One Longing to Love
the God of Romans 9

I wrote the following letter to a woman who told me that she was intellectually persuaded that God is sovereign in salvation. She no longer resists the force of Romans 9:16–20, RSV:

> So [God's election of who will be saved] depends not upon man's will or exertion, but upon God's mercy.... He has mercy upon whomever he wills, and he hardens the heart of whomever he wills. You will say to me then, "Why does he still find fault? For who can resist his will?" But who are you, a man, to answer back to God? Will what is molded say to its molder, "Why have you made me thus?"

Now, she said, the battle lines have shifted. They are in her heart and not her head. In a word, "Now that I understand intellectually that God elects, how can I love a God who reprobates?" In other words, she agrees that if God chooses unconditionally who will be rescued from the corruption and condemnation of sin (in which he sees all humanity even before the creation, 2 Timothy 1:9), then he also passes over many and leaves them in sin and truly-deserved condemnation (which is called reprobation). "How shall I love him," she asks, "in his electing and reprobating freedom?" Let's call her Priscilla.

Dear Priscilla,

My basic response, though I am sure inadequate in itself, is that what you are experiencing needs to be experienced by thousands of evangelicals. How I wish one could pass by this step more easily, and some in fact do. But in the long run I am afraid that if we are ever to make the move from a man-centered God to a God-centered God there will be no other way. I think the problem is that not only must our vision of God change, but our very understanding of the nature of loving him must also change.

It isn't surprising, is it, that if our mind undergoes a kind of Copernican revolution in regard to the place of God in our intellectual universe, another kind of Copernican revolution in our very experience of the love of God might be required? I don't think this can be put neatly into words, but my guess is that a supernatural and spiritual God-centered love for God is going to be of such a different kind than the love for God that we experienced before he took his rightful place, that the two will seem almost like opposites.

I don't think that they are necessarily opposites in those who are truly born of God. A little seedling looks almost opposite to an oak tree, but they are of one piece. The oak tree has some hard bark and some stiff wood and some very thick and heavy branches. Only taken as a whole is it a beautiful thing. Up close it looks like a place for ants to crawl and woodpeckers to drill. But taken as a whole from a distance it is a grand and glorious thing.

There's a great deal of trust in the love of God, and a great deal of love in the trust of God. He is of such a kind that what he reveals will always be in part awesome, in part threatening, in part winsome, in part tender, in part severe, and we will find ourselves pulled in many directions as we try to get our heart around him. And then we cannot begin to stretch that far without breaking, yet trusting still. He has revealed enough of himself in Christ, and especially in the glorious Pauline sentence, "I live by faith in the Son of God, who loved me and gave himself for me" (Galatians 2:20, RSV), that we can cast ourselves on him. We can do this even when the awesome realities of election and definite atonement scratch at our finite and limited sense of what infinite wisdom and infinite goodness and infinite justice must really look like.

The last thing I would heartily recommend: Every time you think of God's reprobation, you also think of the infinite, true sinfulness that those who perish are guilty of and the judgment that is really deserved. If our minds cry out that we do not understand in what measure they can be so guilty, let us rest our minds in the teaching of Scripture. This one thing stands for certain in Scripture, "that every mouth will be closed, and all the world will become accountable to God" (Romans 3:19).

Let us tremble that we, for absolutely no cause in ourselves, have been plucked from this horrid condition and have been made to trust him and have been covered by his infinitely valuable blood so that we will render to him praise for his mercy forever and ever.

I know that in one sense what I have spoken here are words, words, words. But I am closing with the prayer that the Holy Spirit will come and set them on fire with light and passion and love.

For the supremacy of God in all things,

Pastor John

85

BETWEEN RESIGNATION AND TRIUMPHALISM

Finding the Way Between Presumption and Paralysis

Monday morning I was savoring my minutes in a great book—*Holiness* by J. C. Ryle. I read these words:

> All things are growing older: the world is growing old; we ourselves are growing older. A few more summers, a few more winters, a few more sicknesses, a few more sorrows, a few more weddings, and a few more partings, and then—what? Why the grass will be growing over our graves!

Sometimes this is great comfort and sometimes it is a great threat. It depends much on whether we are overwhelmed with the burdens of life or invigorated with the challenges of life.

We oscillate between two errors: resignation and triumphalism. Resignation has a truth in it, but it is not God's way. The shortness of life, the obscurity of our labors, the smallness of our influence, the weakness of our powers, the shortfall of our efforts, the disappointments of unfulfilled dreams, the relentless debauching of our culture—all these can make us wistful for heaven and for the end of our warfare. And so we fall into resignation and lose energy for the work at hand.

Triumphalism also has a truth in it, but it is not God's way either. Some good success of our labor or a timely encouragement from a respected person or the birth of a righteous movement somewhere in the world or the vindication of a famous Christian leader or a doctor's clean bill of health or a bright spring morning or a new friendship—all these can so fill us with a sense of life's possibilities and challenges and energy that we fall into a triumphalistic forgetfulness that we are dust. Our perspective is profoundly limited; our importance in the world is relatively minute; our time is short; and the church and the mission and the kingdom are all able, under God, to survive when we are gone and forgotten.

Neither resignation nor triumphalism is a safe place to live and minister. My prayer for my own church and for Christians around the world is that God will make plain to us where we are in this oscillation, and that he would move us to the place where we ought to be. And where is that? A place of deep faith in two complementary biblical truths:

Truth # 1: "You do not know about tomorrow. What is your life? For you are a mist that appears for a little while and then vanishes. Instead [when your heart presumes with great plans upon the future of God], you ought to [humbly] say, 'If the Lord wills we shall live and we shall do this or that.'" (James 4:14–15, RSV)

Truth #2: "All authority has been given to Me in heaven and on earth. Go therefore and make disciples…and lo, I am with you always, even to the end of the age." (Matthew 28:18–20) "Let us not grow weary in well-doing, for in due season we shall reap, if we do not lose heart." (Galatians 6:9, RSV)

Between presumption and paralysis—that is where we must learn to live. We all tend toward one or the other. And in different times of our lives we tend to different extremes. The young have one bent and the old have another. One culture leans to one side and another culture leans to another. Know your natural excesses and press to the other side. God will help you. He gives strength and he gives rest. He gives passion and he gives quietness of soul. "Commit your way to the LORD; trust in him, and he will act" (Psalm 37:5, RSV).

86

How to Be Strong in the Lord

Pondering the Power of Joy in the Lord

The Bible commands us to "be strong in the Lord and in the strength of His might" (Ephesians 6:10). What does this mean? How can we be strong in the strength of another? The pathway to power in Christ is a hard and happy road. Ponder with me these four biblical markers on the way called *strength in the Lord.*

1. The joy *of the Lord is your* strength! *(Nehemiah 8:10, emphasis added)*
Is it not good to belong to a God that makes gladness the pathway to power? Satan is a very gloomy god. But Jesus said, "Rejoice in that day, and leap for joy, for behold, your reward is great in heaven" (Luke 6:23). Satan cannot abide the songs of the saints. (Knowing this, he fabricates "musical" substitutes which are not the heart-songs of happy people, but the grunts and gasps and screams of people without peace.) I have seen Satan driven out with the songs of hope-filled Christians. And I know that, in my own life, finding the pace to finish the race means recovering the joy of the Lord again and again. Joy is a great power.

2. [We] rejoice *in hope of the glory of God. (Romans 5:2, KJV, emphasis added)*
Some joy comes from what we have now—forgiveness of sin, fellowship with God, purposeful lives, worship, fellowship, sunrise, sunset, precious friends and family. But the simple and painful fact is "our outer nature is wasting away" (2 Corinthians 4:16, RSV). "We are afflicted in every way…perplexed…persecuted…struck down"

(2 Corinthians 4:8–9); and we who have the Spirit "groan inwardly as we wait for adoption...the redemption of our bodies" (Romans 8:23, RSV). Therefore if we're going to have an unwavering joy in this life, it will have to be "in hope." "For in this hope we were saved. Now hope that is seen is not hope. For who hopes for what he sees? But if we hope for what we do not see, we wait for it with patience"—and with *joy* (Romans 8:24–25, RSV). Therefore "rejoice in hope!" (Romans 12:12). This will prove to be your *strength* in the Lord.

3. He will wipe away every tear from their eyes, and death shall be no more, neither shall there be mourning nor crying...any more, for the former things have passed away....The city has no need of sun or moon to shine upon it, for the glory of God *is its light, and its lamp is* the Lamb. *(Revelation 21:4, 23, RSV, emphasis added)*

This is our hope. The glory of God will one day stand forth in a new creation and wipe away all evil and all pain and all sorrow and all fear and all guilt. All obedience and faithfulness will be vindicated and rewarded. All self-denial and suffering in faith will be recompensed a hundredfold. He who did not spare his only Son, but gave him up for us all, will freely give us all things with him (Romans 8:32). All that God owns will be the inheritance of his children for their everlasting enjoyment. Therefore put your hope in the glory of God, and rejoice in that hope, and let that joy be your strength for the warfare of this life.

4. I...do not cease to...pray for the eyes of your hearts to be enlightened, that you may know what is the hope of your calling and what is the wealth of the glory of God's inheritance in the saints. (Ephesians 1:15–18, author's translation)

The great challenge for us now is to know the glory of our hope. To see it with the eyes of the heart and not think about it with the mind alone. This is the great spiritual battle. And this is fought with the television off, on our knees, in the Word. God forbid that seeing we would not see and hearing we would not hear (Matthew 13:13). Let us pray with all our heart that the God who said, "Let there be light," will shine in our hearts "to give the light of the knowledge of the glory of God in the face of Christ" (2 Corinthians 4:6). This is what Paul is asking for in Ephesians 1:16–18, that something supernatural would happen in our hearts—a kind of seeing that is different from the seeing of physical eyes. This is a spiritual apprehension. This is the miracle of what Jonathan Edwards called "a divine and supernatural light immediately imparted to the soul, by the Spirit of God" *(The Works of Jonathan Edwards,* vol. 2, ed. Edward Hickman [Edinburgh: The Banner of Truth Trust, 1974], 12).

How then shall we be strong in the Lord? We must first pray for the divine enabling of spiritual sight and spiritual knowledge. Without this we are blind. Seeing we do not see. Second, we must see with the eyes of the heart the greatness and glory of our future with God. He will wipe away every tear, and he will be our light, and the Lamb will be our lamp. Third, we must rejoice in that firm and certain glory. This must be our daily delight and our abiding treasure. Finally, this joy will be our strength. It will mightily free us from all the competing pleasures of the world that weaken us and make us listless soldiers instead of mighty for God.

87

"For Your Sake He Became Poor"

Taking the Poverty of Jesus to Heart

If Christ had evangelized only his own kind, no one would be saved. There is only one of his kind—and God did not need evangelizing. Therefore, "though He was rich, yet for your sake He became poor, so that you through His poverty might become rich" (2 Corinthians 8:9). Similarly, if the well-fed church evangelizes only "its own kind," massive stretches of lost humanity will go untouched because they are absolutely poor. Not only that, there are millions of Christians among the poor who are our brothers and sisters.

> We share our planet with one billion people that live in a condition called absolute poverty. Absolute poverty isn't quite starvation, but it isn't quite subsistence either. Absolute poverty means earning less than $370 per year. Half of all children in this population will not survive to their fifth birthday....
>
> Of the one billion people living in absolute poverty, David Barrett estimates that fully 200 million of these people are fellow believers in Jesus Christ. Something is desperately wrong in the international body of Christ when some of us live palatially, and others can't keep their kids fed. (Tom Sine, "The Demographic Revolution and Whole-Life Stewardship," *Faces of Poverty and Population* [Monrovia, CA: World Vision, 1992], 18)

But even more important and more powerful in our lives than such statistics is the life and teaching of Jesus Christ, our Lord. We need to keep our eyes fixed on him—the real Jesus of history, not just some vague idea of God floating in the air. What he did and how he lived and what he said will change us, if we really listen to him and ponder the purpose of our predestination: "Those whom [God] foreknew he also predestined to be conformed to the image of his Son" (Romans 8:29, RSV).

1. He became poor.

For you know the grace of our Lord Jesus Christ, that though He was rich, yet for your sake He became poor, so that you through His poverty might become rich. (2 Corinthians 8:9)

2. His mother was poor.

For [God] has had regard for the lowly state of His bondslave; for behold, from this time on all generations will count me blessed. (Luke 1:48)

3. He was born in a cow stall.

She gave birth to her firstborn son; and she wrapped Him in cloths, and laid Him in a manger, because there was no room for them in the inn. (Luke 2:7)

4. He was dedicated with the poor offering.

When the days for their purification according to the law of Moses were completed, they brought Him up to Jerusalem to present Him to the Lord…and to offer a sacrifice according to what was said in the Law of the Lord, "a pair of turtledoves, or two young pigeons." (Luke 2:22–24; see also Leviticus 12:6–8)

5. He was anointed to preach to the poor.

> The spirit of the Lord is upon me, because he anointed me to preach the gospel to the poor. He has sent me to proclaim release to the captives, and recovery of sight to the blind, to set free those who are downtrodden. (Luke 4:18)

6. He called the poor blessed and the rich woeful.

> And turning His gaze on His disciples, He began to say, "Blessed are you who are poor, for yours is the kingdom of God.... But woe to you who are rich, for you are receiving your comfort in full." (Luke 6:20, 24)

7. He said it was hard for the wealthy to be saved.

> Jesus looked at him and said, "How hard it is for those who are wealthy to enter the kingdom of God! For it is easier for a camel to go through the eye of a needle, than for a rich man to enter the kingdom of God." (Luke 18:24–25)

8. He called for anxiety-free sell-offs to get to a wartime lifestyle.

> Do not be anxious for your life, as to what you shall eat; nor for your body, as to what you shall put on.... But seek for His kingdom, and these things shall be added to you. Do not be afraid, little flock, for your Father has chosen gladly to give you the kingdom. Sell your possessions and give to charity.... For where your treasure is, there will your heart be also. (Luke 12:22, 31–34)

9. He called for a passionate search for the poor.

> Go out at once into the streets and lanes of the city and bring in here the poor and crippled and blind and lame. (Luke 14:21)

When you give a reception, invite the poor, the crippled, the lame, the blind, and you will be blessed, since they do not have the means to repay you; for you will be repaid at the resurrection of the righteous. (Luke 14:13–14)

10. He lived without accumulating even a home.

The foxes have holes, and the birds of the air have nests; but the Son of Man has nowhere to lay His head. (Matthew 8:20)

There is in the life and teachings of Jesus a relentless tendency toward simplicity. There is a steady impulse toward living at risk, and with a kind of abandon to the Father's care that looks foolish to the well-off world. There is an unsettling otherworldliness that made Jesus and his first followers radically useful in this dead-end world. There is a freedom *from* things and *for* the kingdom that thrills the heart of his disciples.

Lord, give us this freedom. At any cost, free us from the bondage to this world, and its images of success and power. Open our eyes to see that "what is exalted among men is an abomination in the sight of God" (Luke 16:15, RSV). Grant us to live as aliens and exiles. And fix our eyes on the all-satisfying, everlasting joy of arriving in heaven on the Calvary road of love and service.

88

From Shadow to Substance for the Sake of Christ

Pondering the Shift from Old Testament to New

One of the main points of the book of Hebrews is that the Old Testament system of worship is a shadow replaced by the reality of Christ himself. So the coming of Christ is a massive change in the history of redemption. Many things change substantially. Christ replaces shadows with reality. You can see this in Hebrews 8:5 where it says that the priests offer gifts that "serve a *copy and shadow* of the heavenly things" (emphasis added).

To understand how Christianity and Old Testament Judaism relate to each other, we need to know which shadows have been replaced by something more substantial since Christ has come. Consider six shadows that the coming of Christ replaces with reality.

The shadow of the Old Testament priesthood

The former priests, on the one hand, existed in greater numbers, because they were prevented by death from continuing, but [Christ], on the other hand, because He abides forever, holds *His priesthood permanently.* (Hebrews 7:23–24, emphasis added)

The Old Testament priesthood comes to an end with the perfect priestly ministry of Christ. He is the one Mediator with God (Hebrews 8:6; 9:15; 12:24). He enters into the heavenly Holy of Holies as our one High Priest (Hebrews 4:14; 9:24; 10:21). He puts the priesthood to an end because he does not die and need to be replaced, but holds his priesthood "by the power of an indestructible life" (Hebrews 7:16).

The shadow of the Passover sacrifice

> Clean out the old leaven, that you may be a new lump, just as you are in fact unleavened. For *Christ our Passover* also has been sacrificed. (1 Corinthians 5:7, emphasis added)

Christ is, in fact, the end of all animal sacrifices, not just the Passover. Hebrews makes this plain with that wonderful phrase "once for all." "[Christ] does not need daily, like those high priests, to offer up sacrifices, first for His own sins, and then for the sins of the people, because this He did *once for all* when He offered up Himself" (Hebrews 7:27; see also 9:12, 26).

The shadow of the tabernacle and temple

> Now the main point in what has been said is this: we have such a high priest, who has taken His seat at the right hand of the throne of the Majesty in the heavens, a minister in the sanctuary, and in *the true tabernacle,* which the Lord pitched, not man. (Hebrews 8:1–2, emphasis added)

In one sense, the risen Christ himself is our tabernacle, in that we have access to God in him and not by the holiness of any building (John 2:19–21). But in another sense heaven itself is the "true tabernacle" that Christ himself enters into, where God dwells and where Christ intercedes for us the way the priests once did in the old tabernacle on earth.

The shadow of circumcision

> *Circumcision is nothing,* and uncircumcision is nothing, but what matters is the keeping of the commandments of God. (1 Corinthians 7:19, emphasis added)

> In Christ Jesus neither circumcision nor uncircumcision means anything, but faith working through love. (Galatians 5:6)

> Neither is circumcision anything, nor uncircumcision, but a new creation. (Galatians 6:15)

The shadow of dietary laws

> And He said to them, "Are you so lacking in understanding also? Do you not understand that whatever goes into the man from outside cannot defile him; because it does not go into his heart, but into his stomach, and is eliminated?" (Thus *He declared all foods clean.)* (Mark 7:18–19, emphasis added)

The shadow of feast days

> Therefore let no one act as your judge in regard to food or drink or in respect to a festival or a new moon or a Sabbath day—things which are a mere shadow of what is to come; but the *substance belongs to Christ.* (Colossians 2:16–17, emphasis added).

Circumcision, dietary laws, and feast days were part of the old constitution of Israel that set them apart from the nations and represented their separation for God. With Christ, a decisive shift from separation ("come see") to declaration ("go tell") occurred in redemptive history. This made many of the marks of cultural and ceremonial separation less fitting because now Christianity is to be rooted in many cultures, not just one.

This is why the matter of shadow and substance is so important. What a tragedy to get hung up on ritual and form, when the New Testament is oriented on spiritual substance, namely, Christ. So, flee from the shadow to the Substance and from pattern to the Person. Look to the Person of Christ, as it says in 2 Corinthians 3:18, "We all, with unveiled face, beholding the glory of the Lord, are being changed into his likeness from one degree of glory to another" (RSV). Where will you find him to look at? In the gospel, which Paul calls "the light of the knowledge of the glory of God in the face of Christ" (2 Corinthians 4:6).

89

THE SOVEREIGNTY OF GOD: A PRECIOUS AND PRACTICAL DOCTRINE

Savoring the Sovereignty of God in the Life of George Mueller

One of the great joys of ministering in one church for twenty years is that you get to see people pass through the darkest seasons of life, leaning on the sovereign goodness of God, and come out on the other side with unshakable faith and joy. The sovereignty of God is a most precious doctrine. It is the strong wood of the tree that keeps our lives from being blown over by the winds of adversity. It is the rock that rises for us out of the flood of uncertainty and confusion. It is the eye of the hurricane where we stand with God and look up into the blue sky of his mastery when everything is being destroyed. "When all around my soul gives way," this is all my hope and stay.

The word "sovereignty" (like the word "trinity") does not occur in the Bible. I use it to refer to this truth: God is in ultimate control of the world, from the largest international intrigue to the smallest bird-fall in the forest. Here is how the Bible puts it: "I am God and there is no other…my counsel shall stand and I will accomplish all my purpose" (Isaiah 46:9–10, author's translation). "[God] does according to his will in the host of heaven and among the inhabitants of the earth; and none can stay his hand or say to him, 'What doest thou?'" (Daniel 4:35, RSV). "Are not two sparrows sold for a cent? And yet not one of them will fall to the ground apart from your Father" (Matthew 10:29). "He is unchangeable and who can turn him? What he desires, that he does. For he will complete what he appoints for me" (Job 23:13–14, RSV). "Our God is in the heavens; he does whatever he pleases" (Psalm 115:3). "[He] works all things after the counsel of His will" (Ephesians 1:11). "I will have mercy on whom I have mercy, and I will have compassion on whom I have compassion" (Romans 9:15). "You ought to say, 'If the Lord wills, we shall live and we shall do this or that'" (James 4:15).

One reason this doctrine is so precious to believers is that we know that God's great desire is to show mercy and kindness to those who trust him. "I will make with them an everlasting covenant, that I will not turn away from doing good to them; and I will put the fear of me in their hearts, that they may not turn from me. I will rejoice in doing them good...with all my heart and all my soul" (Jeremiah 32:40–41, RSV). God's sovereignty means that this design for us cannot be frustrated. Nothing, absolutely nothing, befalls those who love God and are called according to his purpose, except what is for our deepest and highest good (Romans 8:28; Psalm 84:11).

Therefore, the mercy and the sovereignty of God are the twin pillars of my life. They are the hope of my future, the energy of my service, the center of my theology, the bond of my marriage, the best medicine in all my sickness, the remedy of all my discouragements. And when I come to die (whether soon or late) these two truths will stand by my bed and, with infinitely strong and infinitely tender hands, lift me up to God.

George Mueller has been admired for 150 years as a great man of faith because of the work he did, especially with orphans in London. Not as many know that he lived his wonderful life in utter reliance on the cherished truth of God's sovereignty. When Mueller's wife of thirty-nine years died, he preached her funeral sermon from the text "Thou art good and doest good" (Psalm 119:68). He recounts how he prayed when he discovered she had rheumatic fever:

Yes, my Father, the times of my darling wife are in Thy hands. Thou wilt do the very best thing for her, and for me, whether life or death. If it may be, raise up yet again my precious wife—Thou are able to do it, though she is so ill; but howsoever Thou dealest with me, only help me to continue to be perfectly satisfied with Thy holy will. *(Autobiography of George Müller* [London: J. Nisbet and Co., 1906], 442)

The Lord's will was to take her. Therefore, with great confidence in the sovereign mercy of God, Mueller said:

I bow, I am satisfied with the will of my Heavenly Father, I seek by perfect submission to his holy will to glorify him, I kiss continually the hand that has afflicted me.... Without an effort my inmost soul habitually joys in the joy of that loved departed one. Her happiness gives joy to me. My dear daughter and I would not have her back, were it possible to produce it by the turn of a hand. God himself has done it; we are satisfied with him. *(Autobiography,* 444, 440)

This is the preciousness of the doctrine of the sovereignty of God.

90

How Is the Wrath of God Being Revealed Now?

Meditation on Romans 1:18

> *The wrath of God is being revealed from heaven against all ungodliness and unrighteousness of men who suppress the truth in unrighteousness. (author's translation)*

Are you the object of God's wrath? There are few questions more important than this one. To answer it we need to know where and how the wrath of God is being revealed now, and whether we are under it. Romans 1:18 says that "the wrath of God is being revealed from heaven against all ungodliness and unrighteousness of men who suppress the truth in unrighteousness." Where and how is this happening in the world? The book of Romans answers in three ways.

First, from Romans 5, we see that universal human *death* is a manifestation of the wrath of God. In the middle of verse 15, we read, "By the transgression of the one [namely, Adam] the many *died.*" Then in the middle of verse 16, death is called a judgment and a condemnation: "For on the one hand the *judgment* arose from one transgression resulting in *condemnation.*" Then in the middle of verse 18 you see it again: "Through one transgression there resulted *condemnation* to all men" (emphasis added). So the first answer is that the wrath of God is being revealed against human sin in universal human death.

Second, from Romans 8, we see that universal futility and misery are evidence of God's wrath against human sin. Consider verses 18–20: "I consider that the sufferings of this present time are not worthy to be compared with the glory that is to be revealed to us. For the anxious longing of the creation waits eagerly for the revealing of the sons of God. For *the creation was subjected to futility*" (emphasis added). What does that mean?

It means that the "sufferings" of verse 18 are inevitable in this fallen world. You may plan well for retirement, but the year before you begin to enjoy it, you have a stroke. You work with your own hands for years to build a simple home, but the week before you're ready to move in, lightning strikes and it burns to the ground. You labor all during the spring to plant your crops but when the grain is just ready to sprout, a flood or a drought takes it all away. The creation was subjected to futility. In verse 21 it's called "slavery to corruption."

Now let's read on in Romans 8:20 to see where this subjection to futility came from: "The creation was subjected to futility, not willingly, but because of Him who subjected it, in hope." This means that God subjected the creation to futility. Satan and Adam could not be the ones who did this because Paul said it was done "in hope." Neither Satan nor Adam in the garden of Eden was planning for the hope of the human race. They simply sinned. But God showed his wrath against sin and subjected creation to futility, not as the last word. But *in hope.* There would come a day when the seed of the woman would crush the serpent's head (Genesis 3:15). But the misery and futility of the world we live in is owing to God's subjecting creation to futility and is a testimony to his wrath against sin.

The third way that God's wrath is revealed against human sin is the one most immediately in Paul's mind in Romans 1, namely, the sinking degradation of human thinking and behavior. You see this three times in verses 24–28.

After describing the ungodliness and unrighteousness of man in verses 19–23, Paul says in verse 24, "Therefore God gave them over in the lusts of their hearts to impurity, so that their bodies would be dishonored among them." In other words, God reveals his wrath against sin by giving people up to be more sinful. Again in verse 26: "For this reason God gave them over to degrading passions." And again in verse 28: "And just as they did not see fit to acknowledge God any longer, God gave them over to a depraved mind, to do those things which are not proper."

So these are three of the ways that the wrath of God is being revealed now in this age against the ungodliness and unrighteousness of man. He has consigned all to death, he has subjected all to futility, and he has given many over to the degradation of their own minds and hearts. Now what about the question we started with: Are you the object of God's wrath? Is wrath the only thing that unbelievers receive from God in this age? The next reading deals with these questions.

91

THE WRATH OF GOD ON BELIEVERS AND UNBELIEVERS NOW

What Wrath Becomes in the Life of Believers

In the previous reading we saw that "the wrath of God is being revealed against all ungodliness and unrighteousness of men" (Romans 1:18). That wrath is seen in universal death, the suffering of futility, and the degradation of human morality. We were left with the burning question: Is that God's only response to the ungodliness and unrighteousness of men? The answer to that question is no—neither in the case of unbelievers or believers.

Take the case of *unbelievers* first. Wrath is always mingled with mercy in this age of hope. In Romans 2:4–5 Paul speaks to those who are missing this great truth: "Or do you think lightly of the riches of His kindness and tolerance and patience, not knowing that the kindness of God leads you to repentance? But because of your stubbornness and unrepentant heart you are storing up wrath for yourself in the day of wrath and revelation of the righteous judgment of God."

Yes, there is kindness in the midst of wrath. God is always doing more than one thing. Jesus said, "He causes His sun to rise on the evil and the good, and sends rain on the righteous and the unrighteous" (Matthew 5:45). Paul said to the pagans of Lystra, "[God] did not leave Himself without a witness, in that He did good and gave you rains from heaven and fruitful seasons, satisfying your hearts with food and gladness" (Acts 14:17).

God warns with his wrath and he woos with his kindness. He speaks both languages: severity and tenderness. Do you recall how Jesus interpreted the coming of John the Baptist as a severe, leather-girded, locust-eating, desert-living, adultery-condemning prophet and his own coming as a party-going, wine-making, child-healing, sin-forgiving Savior? He said, "We played the flute for you, and you did not dance; we sang a dirge, and you did not mourn." Instead you said: John has a demon and Jesus is a glutton (Matthew 11:17–19).

Oh, unbeliever, God is speaking to you in your pain to warn you, and God is speaking to you in your pleasure to woo you. Don't misread the voice of God.

And, second, consider the case of *believers*. What is our situation? According to Romans 1:17 we have the gift of God's righteousness by faith. God's punishment of us was poured out on Jesus who died in our place. Romans 8:1 says, "There is therefore now no condemnation for those who are in Christ Jesus." First Thessalonians 5:9 says, "God has not destined us for wrath." What then of our death and our suffering and our sin? Are they still the wrath of God against us? If not, why do they still happen to us?

The answer is that death and suffering and sin are not the wrath of condemnation from our heavenly Father. Each one is fundamentally altered by the gospel of Christ crucified in our place.

For believers, the sting and victory of *death* has been removed. "'O death, where is your victory? O death, where is your sting?' The sting of death is sin, and the power of sin is the law; but thanks be to God, who gives us the victory through Lord Jesus Christ" (1 Corinthians 15:55–57). For believers, death is not the condemning wrath of God toward them, it is the last gasp of a defeated enemy who opens a door to paradise.

For believers, *futility* is removed from suffering. For those who love God and are called according to his purpose "all things work together for good" (Romans 8:28). Punishment is transformed into purification. Destructive forces become disciplinary. And the seeming chaos and futility of life's calamities become the severe but loving hand of our Father in heaven (Hebrews 12:3–11).

Finally, not only is the sting of death replaced with hope and the futility of suffering replaced with meaning; but the dominion of *sin* is replaced with a love of righteousness (the point of Romans 6). God does not give us over to a depraved mind; he gives us the gift of the Holy Spirit.

Therefore let us awaken to the truth of Romans 1:18 that the wrath of God is being revealed now in this age against the ungodliness and unrighteousness of man. But let us also awaken to the truth that God is revealing something else at the same time. He reveals the gift of righteousness for all who will believe on Christ. And with that righteousness there is no wrath or condemnation on us anymore. For us who believe, death becomes a gateway to paradise; suffering becomes a pathway to holiness; and sin becomes a dethroned enemy that we fight by the power of God's Spirit.

So let us flee the wrath of God and take refuge in the precious power of the gospel of God.

92

WHAT DOES THE SLAUGHTER OF THE AMORITES MEAN?

When to Leave Judgment to God

To understand what was happening when the people of Israel stormed the cities of Canaan and slaughtered their inhabitants, we need to go back about five hundred years before the Israelite invasion. In Genesis 15:13, 16, God says to Abraham, "Your descendants will be strangers in a land that is not theirs [Egypt], where they will be enslaved and oppressed four hundred years…. Then in the fourth generation they shall return here, *for the iniquity of the Amorite is not yet complete"* (emphasis added).

The return of Israel to the Promised Land from Egypt would correspond with the "completion" of the iniquity of the Amorites. This is the meaning of the slaughter of the peoples of Canaan. God timed the arrival of his judgment with the fullness of the sin to be judged. Not before. God did not jump the gun. He was, in fact, long-suffering and endured the idolatry and sins of the nations for centuries, giving them "rains from heaven and fruitful seasons, satisfying [their] hearts with food and gladness" (Acts 14:17). As Derek Kidner says, "Until it was *right* to invade, God's people must wait, if it cost them centuries of hardship. [Genesis 15:16] is one of the pivotal sayings of the Old Testament" *(Genesis* [Downers Grove: InterVarsity Press, 1967], 125).

But there comes a time when the sins of a people are "complete." That is the time for decisive judgment. The appointed instrument of God's judgment was the army of Israel. But God sees *himself* as the effective warrior and judge behind the defeat of the Amorites. He says to Joshua, "I brought you into the land of the Amorites…and they fought with you; and I gave them into your hand, and you took possession of their land when *I destroyed them* before you" (Joshua 24:8, emphasis added). *God* did the destroying. It was by the hand of Israel, but it was the judgment of God. This does not mean that Israel's motive was always holy. At times it was not. But the just purposes of God were being carried out, even if Israel at times had wrong motives.

In fact, God warned the people against pitiless pride in Deuteronomy 9:4–5, "Do not say in your heart when the LORD your God has driven them out before you, 'Because of my righteousness the LORD has brought me in to possess this land,' but it is because of the wickedness of these nations that the LORD is dispossessing them before you…in order to confirm the oath which the LORD swore to your fathers, to Abraham, Isaac and Jacob." In other words, this carnage is not about human justice, but divine judgment. The Amorites provoked God to anger for centuries by their idolatry—so much so that centuries later the wicked king Ahab was compared to the Amorites: "He acted very abominably in following idols, according to all that the Amorites had done, whom the LORD cast out before the sons of Israel" (1 Kings 21:26).

One implication of this for us is that we, as the church of Jesus Christ, may *not* imitate Israel. The church is not God's instrument of judgment in the world, it is his instrument of evangelization and reformation. We have no ethnic or geographic or political identity. We are "aliens and exiles" (1 Peter 2:11). God's dealing with Israel was unique in redemptive history. He chose them and ruled them as a demonstration of his holiness and justice and electing grace among the nations. But to the church he says, "My kingdom is not of this world, if it were, my servants would fight, that I might not be handed over to the Jews; but my kingship is not from the world" (John 18:36, author's translation).

Therefore let us tremble at the prerogatives of God to judge and to destroy. And let us love our enemy and pray for those who persecute us. And let us testify, if necessary with the loss of our lives, that "here we have no lasting city, but we seek the city which is to come" (Hebrews 13:14, RSV).

93

A Life Well-Lived Is like Writing a Good Poem

Meditation on 1 Corinthians 15:10
and the Process of Writing and Living

By the grace of God I am what I am, and
his grace toward me was not in vain.
On the contrary, I worked harder than any
of them, though it was not I, but the grace
of God which is with me. (RSV)

It is more plain to me than ever that living the Christian life the way Paul lived it is like writing an Advent poem. Paul said, "By the grace of God I am what I am, and his grace toward me was not in vain. On the contrary, I worked harder than any of them, though it was not I, but the grace of God which is with me" (1 Corinthians 15:10). Very great grace brings about very hard work.

What is an Advent poem? It is a tradition at our church. Since Christmas of 1982, I have written four poems, one for each Sunday of each Advent, which I read to the church as a kind of Christmas gift. They are usually an imaginative retelling of some biblical story with a view to helping our people savor the sweetness of God's sovereignty.

It is sheer hard work. The reading of them on Sunday morning is often a spiritually moving moment (at least for me), but the making of the poems is toil and cannot be elevated to a mystical moment of revelation. I hit brick walls again and again in writing, unable to make the rhyme work so that it is not hackneyed or unnatural. Or I can't find a way to say a complex thought in understandable language for people who must get it on the first hearing. And then there is the sheer exhaustion factor: how to keep awake and thinking and creating at 2 a.m. two nights in a row. Not always, but sometimes. So at those moments I cry out, "Oh, Lord, I need a breakthrough. Please help me!"

And here is what I have learned. At that moment, after that prayer, I should not and must not sit there with an empty mind waiting for something to pop into an idling mind. It does not happen. God simply does not work that way. Neither in writing, nor in living. I have proved it for decades now, and with almost twenty years of Advent poems in particular. Nor is there biblical warrant to think it will happen. The biblical rule is "I worked harder than any of them."

Instead of leaving the mind idle, I pray, and then I bend every fiber of effort in my mind and body to think and create. And the breakthroughs come. They do not feel miraculous. They feel agonizingly natural. But they come. And because I asked God for them, I give him thanks. "It was not I, but the grace of God which was with me."

Each poem takes fifteen to eighteen hours to write. I have tried repeatedly to shorten the time. But this appears to be an irreducible minimum. God has appointed, I believe, that good things be hard work. I see this in Philippians 2:12–13 ("Work out your salvation with fear and trembling") and 1 Corinthians 15:10 ("I labored even more than all of them") and 2 Timothy 2:15 ("Be diligent…a workman who does not need to be ashamed") and many other places. Work is appointed for us. Prayer is not a replacement for work. It is the atmosphere of work. It is what gives to work its supernatural effectiveness.

It is the same with my other pastoral ministry. And the same in your life and work. "Lord, I need a breakthrough. I want my life, my ministry, to be true and beautiful and life-changing for people." And the breakthroughs come. Not immediately. Not without hard thought and tossed-away drafts.

Life, well lived, is like writing a poem. And therefore it is hard, very hard. A sloppy prose life or an unintelligible, free verse life would not be as hard. And the effect would not be as great. God is beautiful, and the life that expresses his glory should be beautiful. And, if I have learned anything in these twenty years of Advent effort, it is that beauty and truth do not come by mystical revelations and inspirations in a moment of motionless mental waiting. Beauty and truth and compelling depth come by painstaking thinking and trial and praying and self-correcting.

So, Lord, I go back to my work now and pray that you will write a poem in all the messages and ministries of my life. "Unless the Lord builds the house [or poem or sermon], those who build it labor in vain" (Psalm 127:1, RSV). "I worked harder than any of them, nevertheless, it was not I but the grace of God which was with me."

94

MARTIN LUTHER'S RULES FOR HOW TO BECOME A THEOLOGIAN

Prayer, Meditation, and Suffering—

the Path to Understanding

Martin Luther was born on November 10, 1483, in Eisleben, Germany. He died February 18, 1546. In those years he preached over three thousand sermons and wrote fifty thousand pages. From his Bible professorship at the University of Wittenberg, he played the decisive human role in creating the Reformation.

He gives profound counsel to us about getting the most from the Bible. Don't be put off by the word "theology." What he has in mind is good solid reading and thinking about what God says. It is for everybody: "I want you to know how to study theology in the right way. I have practiced this method myself…. The method of which I am speaking is the one which the holy king David teaches in Psalm 119…. Here you will find three rules. They are frequently proposed throughout the psalm and run thus: *Oratio, meditatio, tentatio* [prayer, meditation, trial]." (All quotes from Ewald M. Plass, compiler, *What Luther Says: An Anthology* [St. Louis: Concordia Publishing House, 1959], vol. 3, 1359f.)

1. Prayer

"You should completely despair of your own sense and reason, for by these you will not attain the goal…. Rather kneel down in your private little room and with sincere humility and earnestness pray God through His dear Son, graciously to grant you His Holy Spirit to enlighten and guide you and give you understanding. As you see, David constantly prays in the psalm...."

PSALM 119
Verse 18: "Open my eyes, that I may behold wonderful things from Your law."

Verses 27, 33: "Make me understand the way of Your precepts.... Teach me, O LORD, the way of Your statutes."

Verses 34–37: "Give me understanding, that I may observe Your law.... Make me walk in the path of Your commandments, for I delight in it. Incline my heart to Your testimonies, and not to dishonest gain.... Revive me in Your ways."

"He uses many more words of this nature, although he knew the text of Moses well and that of other books besides, and heard and read them daily. Yet he desires to have the real Master of Scripture in order by all means to make sure that he does not plunge into it with his reason and become his own master."

2. Meditation
"Second, you should meditate. This means that not only in your heart but also externally you should constantly handle and compare, read and reread the Word as preached and the very words as written in Scripture, diligently noting and meditating on what the Holy Spirit means.... Therefore, you observe how in this psalm David always says that he will speak, think, talk, hear, read, day and night and constantly—but about nothing else than God's Word and Commandments. For God wants to give you His Spirit only through the external Word."

PSALM 119
Verse 11: "Your word I have treasured in my heart, that I may not sin against You."

Verse 15: "I will meditate on Your precepts, and regard Your ways."

Verse 48: "I shall lift up my hands to Your commandments, which I love; and I will meditate on Your statutes."

Verse 24: "Your testimonies also are my delight; they are my counselors."

Verse 47: "I shall delight in Your commandments, which I love."

Verse 93: "I will never forget Your precepts."

Verse 97: "O how I love Your law! It is my meditation all the day."

3. Trials

"Third, there is the *tentatio,* the trial *[Anfechtung].* This is the touchstone. It teaches you not only to know and understand, but also to experience how right, how true, how sweet, how lovely, how mighty, how comforting God's Word is: it is wisdom supreme. This is why you observe that, in the psalm indicated, David so often complains of all sorts of enemies…. For as soon as God's Word becomes known through you, the devil will afflict you, will make a real [theologian] of you."

PSALM 119
Verses 67–68: "Before I was afflicted I went astray, but now I keep Your word. You are good and do good; teach me Your statutes."

Verse 71: "It is good for me that I was afflicted, that I may learn Your statutes."

Perhaps you say you do not want to be a theologian. Don't stumble over the word. Luther means: a true knower of God. Do you want to know God? Do you want to know his ways in the world and in your life? Do you want to be able to understand and apply the Bible to your situation? Do you want to be a good soul doctor for the hurts of others? Then this is good counsel. Ponder the Word of God day and night. Pour out your heart in prayer for illumination and love. Be patient in suffering. Do not let its lessons fall to the ground while you grumble over God's hard gifts. Trust him and learn the deepest things of all.

⁗

95

Is the Holy Spirit Phase Three of God's Word?

Preserving the Finality of Phase Two

Meditation on Hebrews 2:3–4, RSV

> *How shall we escape if we neglect such a*
> *great salvation? After it was at the first*
> *spoken through the Lord, it was confirmed*
> *to us by those who heard. God also*
> *bearing witness with them, both by signs*
> *and wonders and by various miracles and*
> *by distributions of the Holy Spirit*
> *according to His own will.*

The point of Hebrews 1 is to make us realize the enormous value of God's speaking to us through the Son of God and revealing to us a way of salvation. We know this because the chapter begins with the trumpeting of the superior value of God's speaking "in these last days by a Son," and because chapter 2 begins by saying, "For this reason we must pay much closer attention to what we have heard." In other words, the whole first chapter is to help us pay attention to the Word of God spoken through the Son.

Then again in Hebrews 2:2–3 this great Word of salvation is contrasted with the word of angels: "For if the word spoken through angels proved unalterable, and every transgression and disobedience received a just recompense, how shall we escape if we neglect so great a salvation?" So again the point is the superiority of the Word that God has spoken through Jesus concerning our salvation. Listen! Listen! Take heed! Don't take it for granted! That is the message.

Then, in Hebrews 2:3, the writer tells us how this Word comes to the generations who were not there to hear it from Jesus himself or to see it with their own eyes when he died and rose again. There are three stages. Look for them in this text: "After it was at the first spoken through the Lord, it was confirmed to us by those who heard."

The three stages in this verse are: 1) the Lord spoke, once for all, by his life and teaching and death and resurrection, 2) those who heard and saw him (the apostles) testify and confirm the truth of the Lord's Word, and finally, 3) others hear or read the confirming testimony of the apostles.

But what is the role of the Holy Spirit in this connection? The answer is given in verse 4: "God also bearing witness with them, both by signs and wonders and by various miracles and by distributions of the Holy Spirit according to His own will." This verse says that God himself testified to the Word in three ways: 1) by signs and wonders, 2) by various miracles, and 3) by distributions of the Holy Spirit.

The function of the "distributions of the Holy Spirit" was to testify to the Word, that is, the "great salvation" which was "at the first spoken through the Lord" (verse 3). In other words, the role of the Holy Spirit is to direct attention and conviction toward the Word of the Son of God which has been spoken "in these last days." Which means that the work of the Holy Spirit is not a "third phase" of divine communication after phase one (the Old Testament) and phase two (the incarnation of the Son of God). The work of the Holy Spirit is a clarification and application and certification of phase two.

Thus one test of the Spirit's voice is whether it orients us more and more on the Word of God spoken once for all "in these last days" through the Son of God, Jesus Christ, in his decisive work of redemption. If a claim to spiritual revelation leads us to depend less on the once-for-allness of the historical Word that comes to us by Jesus Christ through the apostles (2:3), then that claim is dubious.

"In these last days God has spoken *to us* in His Son" (1:2, emphasis added). The "us" in this verse is a third generation of Christians—the ones to whom the apostles delivered the message in 2:3. This means that, in principle, any of us after the apostles, whether third generation or fiftieth generation, can hear God in the Son. He has spoken *to us*. This is where we hear God. He is not silent. Nor has any of us exhausted this Word. Oh, let us read and ponder and meditate and memorize and saturate our minds in this great, final Word—which the Holy Spirit serves by all his gifts.

96

WHO GOVERNS THOUGHT AND TONGUE?

Meditation on Proverbs 16:1

> *The plans of the heart belong to man,*
> *but the answer of the tongue is from the LORD.*

A s I ponder this remarkable statement, the question that presses upon me is not whether God rules over what people say. That seems plain from the second half of the verse: "The answer of the tongue is from the LORD." The work of the tongue is not outside God's governance. The tongue, no less than the foot, is finally governed by the sovereign God, though without removing human accountability: "I know, O LORD, that a man's way is not in himself, nor is it in a man who walks to direct his steps" (Jeremiah 10:23). The step of the foot and the answer of the tongue are finally "from the Lord."

Rather, the question that presses on me is this: Does the first half of this verse mean that God does not govern the plans of the heart? "The plans of the heart belong *to man.*" Does God govern only the final formations of the tongue or also the plans of the heart? If God governed the tongue's answer but not the heart's planning, this would be strange from the standpoint of our experience. For the one thing that we feel we have most control over is not the ebb and flow of how our minds cast about for truth, but rather the final choice to give expression to our conclusion. But this verse seems to put in God's hands the choice we feel is ours and put in our hands the process that seems so uncontrolled.

I think the answer to this perplexity is that both the plans of the heart and the answer of the tongue involve God's governance and our responsible choices. To illustrate this, let us ask: Does the second half of the verse ("The answer of the tongue is from the LORD") mean that the answer of the tongue is in no sense man's doing, but only God's?

Well, experience as well as other Scriptures teach us that in some sense the answer of the tongue is also ours, and we are responsible for the errors we make and the ill-chosen words we speak. We are commanded, "Let no unwholesome word proceed from your mouth" (Ephesians 4:29). Jesus says, "By your words you will be justified, and by your words you will be condemned" (Matthew 12:37). And Proverbs 21:23 says, "He who guards his mouth and his tongue, guards his soul from troubles." Clearly we are responsible for "the answer of the tongue" even though it is finally "from the LORD."

So if this was assumed and left unsaid in regard to the second half of the verse, may it not also be that the same was assumed and left unsaid in regard to the first half of the verse? In other words, when it says, "The plans of the heart belong to man," does it mean that the Lord does not have a decisive hand in shaping those human plans? Or is it not likely that, as the writer did not mean to rule out human accountability in regard to the answer of the tongue, he probably does not mean to rule out divine sovereignty in regard to the plans of the heart?

This is the more likely in view of Proverbs 21:1, "The king's heart is a stream of water in the hand of the LORD; He turns it wherever he will." Here it is not simply the king's tongue that is "from the LORD," but also the king's heart. This is illustrated with the ten kings of Revelation 17:16–17, "These will hate the harlot and will make her desolate…. For God has put it in their hearts to execute His purpose by having a common purpose, and by giving their kingdom to the beast, until the words of God will be fulfilled." So it is not just answers of the tongue that God governs, but also purposes of the heart—yet not (as mysterious as it may seem) undermining human accountability.

So what would be the point of saying that the answer of the tongue is from the Lord while the thoughts of the mind are man's? First, it means that the reasonings of our minds are indeed ours, and we are responsible for them and should take heed how we think. But, second, it means that when man has done all he should and can do in his thinking, the upshot will be God's sovereign design and outcome.

The point can perhaps best be brought out by understanding "although" to be in front of the verse: "[Although] the plans of the heart belong to man, [nevertheless] the answer of the tongue is from the LORD." In other words, the fact that your thoughts and plans are your responsibility does not imply that God is not in control of the outcome. Do all that you can with what is yours, and God will bring his sovereign plan to pass.

It is the same with our steps as with our words: "The mind of man plans his way, but the LORD directs his steps" (Proverbs 16:9). "Man's steps are from the LORD, how then can man understand his way?" (Proverbs 20:24). He may just as truly have said, "The promises of the tongue belong to man, but the steps he takes are from the Lord." The point is not to deny human accountability for thinking or speaking or acting; the point is to say that when you have used your God-given powers to plan, do not think that the outcome of the tongue is your sovereign creation: It is "from the LORD." And when your tongue has spoken all your plans and promises, do not think that the outcome of your steps is your sovereign creation: It is "from the LORD." All this is for our humility and for our courage (James 4:13–16; 2 Samuel 10:12).

97

ANSWERS TO PRAYER IN THE MIDST OF NONANSWERS

Meditation on the Detours of God

On the way to South Carolina in the heat of June, our water pump locked up sixteen miles east of Knoxville on the interstate. The car immediately overheated and we had to stop. The nearest station was fifteen miles away, and it was Sunday morning. Pretty bleak. The sun was blazing down, pushing the temperature into the nineties, and I had no idea what to do. We were hurrying to get to Myrtle Beach for a once-in-a-lifetime five days with my father. He and his only grandsons (my sons) were planning to do some deep-sea fishing which was all scheduled.

After piddling around with the motor for twenty minutes or so, I knew there was nothing I could do. No cars were stopping to help. But we needed help. Can you imagine how hard it was for me to try to stop a car on that freeway? It took me ten minutes of walking in circles to get up the courage (or to get down the pride) to try to flag down a car.

Finally, I got a rag from under the front seat and went out behind the U-Haul trailer we were pulling, and held it up in the air to signal our distress. I stood there for two or three or four minutes, and the cars just whizzed on by. I couldn't believe it. Here I was on my knees, as it were, with a flag in my hand, standing like the Statue of Liberty, and they didn't stop. It was humiliating. (It's not hard to see why the white-flag-waving truce of repentance and saving faith is so hard for people.)

Abraham (who was nine at the time) came up to me and said, "I think we need to pray." I said, "You're right." So I put down my flag for a moment. Abraham and I prayed right there by the trailer. When we opened our eyes, two vehicles had pulled over. One of them was a mechanic. He looked at the car, diagnosed the problem, and said, "You know everything is closed today. If you go into town, you'll have to wait till Monday. I could go get the part and fix it here on the road for you." Well, that is what happened, and we were on our way again in about four hours.

Now here's the puzzling thing. I believe with all my heart that God answered Abraham's prayer, and that he answered it with a one-in-a-thousand possibility—a mechanic, Sunday morning, sixteen miles from home, working for a trucking firm that was open for trucks on Sunday, and willing to go all the way to town and back to help us. Incredible! I believe that was God. *But,* the skeptic says, "If your God is so powerful and so wonderful, why didn't he just keep the water pump working?" In fact, we had asked the Lord for his help earlier that morning. We asked for a good-working car all day.

But God did not give us a trouble-free day. Instead he let us come into trouble (which, of course, he could have kept from happening) and then helped us in some amazing ways in the midst of our fear and frustration and sweat and disappointment. So here, as in a thousand other times of my life, I was thanking the Lord for his grace, not to keep me from trouble and sickness and frustration and disappointment, but to give me amazing help in the midst of it.

Why does he work this way? Four answers (for starters):

1. God knows better how to run the universe than I do, including the timing of my arrival in Myrtle Beach (or not!); "I am God, and there is no one like Me...saying, 'My purpose will be established, and I will accomplish all My good pleasure'" (Isaiah 46:9–10).
2. God loves to teach nine-year-olds (and forty-three-year-olds!) lessons in faith and prayer. "Our affliction...came to us...so that we would not trust in ourselves, but in God who raises the dead" (2 Corinthians 1:8–9). "It is good for me that I was afflicted, that I may learn Your statutes" (Psalm 119:71).

3. God prizes the discipline of humility more than trouble-free days. "God has chosen the foolish things...and...the weak things of the world...so that no man may boast before God" (1 Corinthians 1:27–29).

4. God had a gospel word for that mechanic. I gave him the tract *Quest for Joy*, and on the way with him to Knoxville to get a new water pump, I spoke to him of faith in Christ.

Only eternity will show the full wisdom and mercy of God in the curious derailing of our plans and "reinterpretation" of our prayers for a "good" day. Such are the good purposes of God in the detours of our lives. With such a God, surely we should be the most trusting and grumble-free people in the world.

98

WHO WAS JESUS' GRANDFATHER?

How to Think About Apparent Contradictions in the Bible

Doubts about God's Word can arise when we find apparent contradictions and don't see immediate solutions. For example, who was Jesus' grandfather? We know that, although Jesus was supernaturally conceived by the Holy Spirit (Luke 1:34–35), his earthly, legal father was Joseph. But Luke says that Joseph is the son of *Eli* (3:23), while Matthew says that he was the son of *Jacob* (1:16).

One of the best treatments of this problem is *The Virgin Birth of Christ* by J. Gresham Machen (New York: Harper Brothers, 1930). The solution Machen argues for is that "while Matthew's genealogy traces the successive heirs to the throne of David from David to Joseph, Luke's genealogy traces the ancestors of Joseph [without respect to royal inheritance] back to David" (206).

He explains, "The Lucan genealogy, in other words, starts with the question, 'Who was Joseph's "father"?' the answer to that question is, 'Heli' [Eli].... In the Matthean genealogy, on the other hand, we start with the question, 'Who was the heir to David's throne?' The answer is, 'Solomon,' and so on down to Joseph." (207).

You can see the signal that something like this is happening by comparing how the two genealogies are the same from Abraham to King David, and then they diverge. For example, in Luke 3:31 it says that *Nathan* is David's son, while in Matthew 1:6 it says that David was the father of *Solomon*. Now we know from

2 Samuel 5:14 that Nathan *and* Solomon were both sons of David. But only Solomon was the heir of the throne (1 Kings 1:13).

So the possible solution to why the genealogies are different from David down to Joseph is that Luke is giving the physical ancestors (or in one or two cases, a very close adoptive relation), while Matthew is most interested in showing that the father of Jesus is the legal heir to the throne of David.

The correctness of this view of the purpose and the meaning of each genealogy is confirmed by the fact that the genealogy in Luke begins at the end and works backward, whereas the genealogy in Matthew begins at the beginning. Where the point was merely to trace the descent of Joseph back to David, that could be done by recording the tradition of the family as to his actual father, Eli, and then recording Eli's father, and so on, back to Nathan whose father was David. But where the point was to mention the successive heirs of the Davidic throne, it was natural to begin with David and work forward (207).

What then actually happened in the generations just before Jesus? Here is one possible scenario. And all we can do is offer plausible solutions since some of the facts are hidden from us.

MATTHEW'S GENEALOGY	LUKE'S GENEALOGY
Eleazar>Matthan>Jacob>Joseph	Levi>Matthat>Eli>Joseph

Suppose that Eleazar, the legal heir of David's throne, died without widow or son. Customarily a more or less close relative would be counted as his legal descendent and be said to have been "begotten" by him. Suppose also that Matthan is that relative and is the same person as Matthat (in Luke) with an alternative spelling. That would mean that Jacob and Heli are brothers. Then suppose that Jacob dies before he has sons. According to the custom of Levirate marriage (see Matthew 22:25), the brother of the deceased man is to marry and raise up descendants for the sake of the name of the dead brother. Thus Heli marries Jacob's wife and they give birth to Joseph, Jesus' father. In this way, Joseph is the legal heir through Jacob's line, but the actual physical son of Eli.

Perhaps the best lesson from this complicated hypothetical case is simply that apparent contradictions in the Bible do have plausible and possible solutions, and we should be slow to throw out a book that has proved itself for thousands of years as the mighty, saving, transforming Word of God.

CINIS

99

"THEY LOVE ALL MEN"

Thoughts on How to Make a Name for Christ

The best way to begin this reading would be to take five seconds right now and pray, "Heavenly Father, let your love be done in my life the way it's done in heaven." With all his *teaching* on love, the apostle Paul also *prayed* that God would make love grow in the hearts of Christians. "I pray that your love may abound still more and more in real knowledge and all discernment" (Philippians 1:9). "May the Lord cause you to increase and abound in love for one another, and for all men, just as we also do for you" (1 Thessalonians 3:12). "[I pray] that you [would be] rooted and grounded in love" (Ephesians 3:17).

It was an urgent plea when Paul prayed this way. Why? Because what is at stake in "increasing and abounding in love to one another and to all men" is immense. At stake is a compelling demonstration of God's reality in the world. Jesus described the impact of the unity of love like this: "[I pray, Father] that they may all be one; even as You, Father, are in Me and I in You, that they also may be in Us; that the world may believe that You sent Me. The glory which You have given Me I have given to them; that they may be one, just as We are one; I in them, and You in Me, that they may be perfected in unity, so that the world may know that You sent Me, and loved them, even as You have loved Me" (John 17:21–23). We may not fully understand this. But it is clear that something tremendous is at stake in the practical unity of love in the body of Christ.

Or consider John 13:34–35, where Jesus says, "A new commandment I give to you, that you love one another, even as I have loved you, that you also love one another. By this all men will know that you are My disciples, if you have love for one another." One indispensable public mark of a Christian is love for other Christians. Jesus assumes that the world is watching this and that judgments are being made. He means it to be this way.

Or consider Matthew 5:16: "Let your light shine before men in such a way that they may see your good works, and glorify your Father who is in heaven." The glory of our heavenly Father is at stake in the pattern of good deeds that flow out from our lives.

On the basis of all these texts, I infer that growing in love is also growing in evangelism and missions and pastoral care and marriage and how to get along with people you disagree with—and virtually everything else. Small wonder that Paul calls love "the greatest of these" (1 Corinthians 13:13).

In the early centuries of the Christian church, Christians lived a kind of love that did not always win approval, but, in truth, testified to Christ. *The Epistle to Diognetus,* from the second century, says, "They love all men, and are persecuted by all…. They are poor and make many rich; they lack everything and in everything they abound…. They are abused, and they bless; they are insulted, and repay insult with honor. They do good, and are punished as evildoers; and in their punishment they rejoice as gaining a new life therein" (quoted in J. Stevenson, ed., *A New Eusebius* [London: SPCK, 1968], 59).

Justin Martyr, writing at about the same time, described the Christians of his day: "We who hated and destroyed one another, and on account of their different manners would not live with men of a different tribe, now, since the coming of Christ, live familiarly with them, and pray for our enemies, and endeavor to persuade those who hate us unjustly to live conformably to the good precepts of Christ, to the end that they may become partakers of the same joyful hope of a reward from God, the ruler of all" *(First Apology,* chapter 13).

Do not these testimonies of the early church fill you with a longing to love the way they loved? Oh, to make a name for Christ by the radical difference of our love—for enemy and friend. To that end I pray in the words of Paul, "May the Lord cause you [and me] to increase and abound in love for one another, and for all people" (1 Thessalonians 3:12). This is the great work of God. The great and first fruit of the Holy Spirit (Galatians 5:22). "Now faith, hope, love, abide these three; but the greatest of these is love" (1 Corinthians 13:13).

100

PLURALISM: WE HAVE BEEN HERE BEFORE

Meditation on Why We Are Here

> *"You are My witnesses," declares the LORD,*
> *"And My servant whom I have chosen....*
> *I, even I, am the LORD; and there is no*
> *savior besides Me.... So you are My*
> *witnesses," declares the LORD,*
> *"And I am God."*
>
> ISAIAH 43:10–12

Year by year, our neighborhoods are culturally less uniform and more diverse. For example, in the neighborhood of our church, the arrival of Somali people in recent years has changed the face of the street. Many of them are Muslim. Indians with Hindu backgrounds wait with African-Americans and Anglo moms to put their kids on the bus in the morning. No problem. The local, secular "natives" espouse relativism with ease: What's true for you is your god, and what's true for me is my god—whatever works is fine.

It would be a mistake to reel back on our heels as if good old white Protestant America has taken a blow on the chin. Rather, Christians should think that God is designing a situation like the first three centuries in the Roman Empire where Christianity took root and spread so dramatically. There was no

Christian consensus. There was no reigning Judeo-Christian ethic. There was no most-favored religion status. There were, in fact, no guaranteed rights for Christians nor any constitutional freedoms. There were no common categories of monotheism or sin or eternity that Christian witnesses could assume. There was no TV and no radio and no *Time* magazine giving cultural uniformity to the empire. There were no bestselling books linking Spain with Egypt in a common way of thought.

Instead there was pervasive pluralism. There were many gods and many philosophies. There were stoical and sensual lifestyles. There were trade routes from the East and West with religious and philosophical worldviews from far and near spreading their beliefs. There were popular, New Age–like religious practices that cared nothing for objective truth, but only subjective experience and claims to inner light. The similarities to our own day could be multiplied.

In this pervasive pluralism, Christians came not primarily with a new idea to think about, but with *news* of something that had *happened*. It was relentlessly objective and historical and particular—and therefore absolute and offensive in its claim on people's lives. God had sent his Son into the world to die for sins. He had lived in Palestine and had taught for a few years, and had been killed like a criminal, though innocent, and had risen from the dead to show that his death was a ransom for sin, and had ascended into heaven where he rules the world until the time when he will come and establish his kingdom for all those who have put their life in his hands. It was a shocking message. Nothing like it had ever been spoken or heard before.

In this process they had a lot of explaining to do. There is a God. There is truth. There is sin. There is wrath and judgment. There is love and redemption. There is Jesus and the Holy Spirit. There is faith. There is heaven and hell. Is it any wonder that when Paul evangelized the great pagan center of Ephesus, he spent two years *teaching* for (possibly) five hours a day (Acts 19:9–10)? There was so much to explain.

Today God has a great work for us to do. We are his witnesses. Don't be daunted by the developments of pluralism. Ask for the wisdom and the boldness and the love that drove the early believers and gave them such amazing triumphs. Don't bemoan the disappearance of a lightly Christianized America. Rejoice that the Word of God has run and triumphed before (2 Thessalonians 3:1) in the very situation we find ourselves today. "'You are my witnesses,' declares the LORD." And he does not send his witnesses in vain.

101

"God Has Allotted to Each a Measure of Faith"

Meditation on Romans 12:3

> *For through the grace given to me I say to*
> *everyone among you not to think more*
> *highly of himself then he ought to think;*
> *but to think so as to have sound*
> *judgment, as God has allotted to each*
> *a measure of faith.*

According to Romans 12:3, God gives varying measures of faith to his people. Paul says that we ought "to think so as to have sound judgment, *as God has allotted to each a measure of faith*" (emphasis added). In the context, this is not a limited reference to the unique spiritual gift of faith which only some believers have (1 Corinthians 12:9). For Paul says, "I say to *everyone among you* not to think more highly of himself than he ought to think; but to think so as to have sound judgment, as God has allotted *to each* a measure of faith" (emphasis added). *"To each"* refers back to *"everyone among you."* God has given *all* Christians varying measures of faith. This is the faith with which we receive and use our varying gifts. It is the ordinary daily trust in the Son of God (Galatians 2:20) by which we live and minister.

In the context, Paul is concerned that people were "thinking of themselves more highly than they ought to think." His final remedy for this pride is to say that, not only are spiritual gifts a work of God's free grace in our lives, but so also is the very faith with which we use those gifts. This means that every possible ground of boasting is taken away. How can we boast if even the qualification for receiving gifts is also a gift?

That's how important humility is in God's eyes. This is exactly the same aim of God mentioned in Ephesians 2:8–9 where Paul stresses that saving faith is a gift: "By grace you have been saved through faith; and *that not of yourselves, it is the gift of God;* not of works, *so that no one may boast"* (emphasis added). Faith is a gift from God, *so that no one may boast.* Or, as Romans 12:3 says, so that we will not think too highly of ourselves. The last bastion of pride is the belief that we are the originators of our faith.

Paul knew that the abundant grace of God was the source of his own faith. He said in 1 Timothy 1:13–14, "I was formerly a blasphemer and a persecutor and a violent aggressor. Yet I was shown mercy because I acted ignorantly in *unbelief;* but the grace of our Lord overflowed [for me] with the *faith* and love which are in Christ Jesus" (author's translation, emphasis added). He was an unbeliever. But then grace overflowed to him with faith.

So he knew this was the case with every other believer too. He said to the Philippians, "To you *it has been given* for Christ's sake, not only *to believe in Him,* but also to suffer for His sake" (Philippians 1:29, emphasis added). This is why he thanked *God* and not human resourcefulness for the faith he saw in his churches: "We ought always to give *thanks to God* for you, brethren, as is fitting, because *your faith* is greatly enlarged" (2 Thessalonians 1:3, emphasis added). We thank God for the enlargement of faith because *"God has allotted to each [his own] measure of faith"* (Romans 12:3, emphasis added).

This truth has a profound impact on how we pray. Jesus gives us the example in Luke 22:31–32. Before Peter denies him three times, Jesus says to him, "Simon, Simon, behold, Satan has demanded to sift you like wheat; but *I have prayed for you, that your faith may not fail;* and you, when once you have turned again, strengthen your brothers" (emphasis added). Jesus *prays* for Peter's faith to be sustained even through sin, because he knows that God is the one who sustains faith.

So we should pray for ourselves and for others this way. Thus the man with the epileptic boy cried out, "I do believe; *help my unbelief*" (Mark 9:24, emphasis added). This is a good prayer. It acknowledges that without God we cannot believe as we ought to believe. Similarly the apostles pray to Jesus, "Increase our faith!" (Luke 17:5). They pray this way because Jesus is the one who can do that.

This teaching about faith being a gift of God raises many questions. God has answers for them all, even if we don't. Let us seek to put the teaching to its practical biblical use, namely the humbling of our pride and the stimulation of our prayers. In other words, let us pray daily: "Oh, Lord, thank you for my faith. Sustain it. Strengthen it. Deepen it. Don't let it fail. Make it the power of my life, so that in everything I do you get the glory as the great Giver. Amen."

102

SHALL WE GOOF OFF THAT GRACE MAY ABOUND?

Why Does the Gift of Faith Not Produce Passivity?

In the previous reading we saw from Romans 12:3 that God gives faith to his people in varying measures. Believing this should have the good effects of humility in ministry and prayer for sustaining grace. But viewing faith as a gift is easily perverted into passivity. The danger is that we will become passive and say, "Well, if I am to do my ministry by faith, and faith is a work of God's grace, then there is nothing for me to do. I will just stay at home and watch TV." Now that is an unbiblical and irrational response to the teaching of Romans 12:3.

We know it is unbiblical because right there in the text the whole point of Romans 12:6–8 is to exhort the Christians in just the opposite way, namely, to *do* something. "Since we have gifts that differ according to the grace given to us, *each of us is to exercise them accordingly:* if prophecy, according to the proportion of his faith; if service, in his serving; or he who teaches, in his teaching; or he who exhorts, in his exhortation; he who gives, with liberality; he who leads, with diligence; he who shows mercy, with cheerfulness" (emphasis added). In other words, *exercise* your gift. Don't let it lie dormant. Take hold of it by faith and use it.

Resist passivity and look to God and say: "Lord, I know that you have given me a gift for some kind of ministry. I am tired, and I am anxious that I will not do a good job. But, Lord, I trust *you,* not me and not my gift. I trust your enabling grace. In fact, I trust you even to help me trust you because you said that faith is your gift. And I go to my ministry (say my small group leadership) tonight in the strength that *you* supply so that in everything you might get the glory." That's the point of 1 Peter 4:11, RSV (emphasis added), "Whoever renders service, [let him do so] as one who renders it *by the strength which God supplies;* in order that in everything God may be glorified through Jesus Christ." The gift of faith doesn't replace service; it trusts in power to do service.

We also know that passivity is unbiblical because of Paul's own testimony in 1 Corinthians 15:10, "By the grace of God I am what I am, and His grace toward me did not prove vain; but I labored even more than all of them, yet not I, but the grace of God with me." He *labored* more than all of them! That is not passivity! But look at the conviction beneath it: "Nevertheless it was not I, but the grace of God with me."

The great words "Not I, but grace" are not energy-destroying words, but energy-producing words. Listen to Paul again from Colossians 1:28–29, "We proclaim [Christ], admonishing every man and teaching every man with all wisdom, so that we may present every man complete in Christ. For this purpose also I *labor, striving* according to His power, which mightily works within me" (emphasis added). Paul labors. Paul strives. But it is by the mighty power of Christ that works in him, enabling him.

The point is this: God does not will *instead of* our willing; he wills in and *through* our willing. God does not work instead of our working, but through our working. God does not energize instead of our having energy; he energizes our energy. Therefore it is unbiblical and irrational to say that because the grace of God produces an active trust in God, we don't need to exert an active trust in God.

At the end of your life, after decades of loving ministry, however God uses you to stir up the obedience of faith in others, what are you going to say about the grace of God and your lifelong labors? Are you going to boast? No. You are going to use the words of Paul in Romans 15:18, "For I will not presume to speak of anything except what Christ has accomplished through me, resulting in the obedience of the Gentiles." You will say something like a paraphrase of 1 Corinthians 4:7, "What did I have that I did not receive? If then I received it, why should I boast as if it were not a gift?"

The Lord gives spiritual gifts to every Christian, including the faith to use them. Let us pray that he will measure out to us mighty measures of faith. Find your gift. Embrace it by faith. Use it in the strength that God supplies so that God will get the glory and you (and those you love) will get the joy.

103

ANOTHER PARADOX OF PRAYER: "VAIN REPETITIONS" VERSUS "CONTINUAL COMING"

Pondering Matthew 6:7, Luke 11:8, and Luke 18:5

What's the difference between the "vain repetitions" of the Gentiles who want their prayers to be "heard for their many words" (in Matthew 6:7), and the "continual coming" of the widow to wear down the judge and get her legal protection (in Luke 18:5), or the "persistence" of the man at midnight who prevails on his friend to get up and give him bread (in Luke 11:8)?

- In Matthew 6:7–8, Jesus introduces the Lord's Prayer by saying, "And when you are praying, do not use *vain repetitions* as the Gentiles do, for they suppose that they will be heard for their many words" (emphasis added).
- In Luke 11:5–8, Jesus follows the Lord's Prayer with a parable about a persistent friend at midnight: "I tell you, even though he will not get up and give him anything because he is his friend, yet because of his *persistence* he will get up and give him as much as he needs" (verse 8, emphasis added).
- In Luke 18:1–5, Jesus tells a parable about a widow pleading with an unjust judge. He says that the point of the parable is "to show that at all times [we] ought to pray and not to lose heart" (verse 1). The breakthrough comes with these words: "Because this widow bothers me, I will

give her legal protection, otherwise by *continually coming* she will wear me out" (verse 5, emphasis added).

Even though Matthew 6:7 warns against "vain repetitions," all these texts have at least one thing in common: They all encourage praying to God over and over and over again. In Matthew, after the warning about "vain repetitions," Jesus says, "Pray, then, in this way:... Give us *this day* our daily bread" (6:9, 11, emphasis added). Notice the phrase "this day." It means that Jesus expects us to pray like this at least *daily.* He does not want us to pray on January 1, "Give us this year sufficient bread every day," and then not pray about bread anymore that year. No, he says ask for daily bread "this day." So, even though "vain repetitions" are bad, asking for daily bread at least 365 times a year is not bad.

And if the petition about bread is supposed to be repeated daily, then probably the same applies to the other petitions in the Lord's Prayer. Every day we should pray for the hallowing of God's name, the coming of his kingdom, the heaven-like doing of his will, and the forgiveness of sins. So the teaching in Matthew 6 agrees with the teaching in Luke 11 and 18, to the effect that "continual" or "persistent" praying is a good thing.

The key question, then, is this: What danger does Matthew 6:7–8 warn us against in this continual, persistent kind of praying that does not give up but keeps on asking and seeking and knocking (Matthew 7:7; Luke 11:9)? There are two clauses that give us the clues in Matthew 6:7–8, "When you are praying, do not use vain repetitions as the Gentiles do, for *they suppose that they will be heard for their many words.* So do not be like them; *for your Father knows what you need before you ask Him"* (emphasis added).

1. *"They suppose that they will be heard for their many words."*
The warning here seems to be against thinking of our praying as impressive or coercive to God. It is as if Jesus wants to say, "Yes, you could take the parables about the persistent friend or tenacious widow to mean that God is impressed with many words or other human resources. But in fact, that is not what I mean to call attention to. I mean to call attention to the absence of human resources anywhere but in God." Right praying feels destitute, not resourceful. If we find

ourselves reaching inside of us for more and better phrases to tell God what we mean, we are in danger of "vain repetitions." If we grasp for more words with a view to showing God we are more worthy than if we had one simple cry, we are in danger of "vain repetitions."

2. *"For your Father knows what you need before you ask Him."*
The warning here is that there is a kind of praying that makes God look unaware and uncaring. Jesus says, "He knows what you need," and so he is not unaware, and "He is your Father," so he is not uncaring. Therefore, don't pray in a way that makes him look ignorant or apathetic.

Yes, but why does the persistence and tenacity of continual prayer not make God look this way? It might. And we are being called by Jesus to find the balance. There is a reason why Jesus not only calls us to simplicity and brevity, but also to persistence and tenacity. The demand for prevailing prayer exposes those who pray in a passing way, as if they are just trying to cover all their bases. They are not looking to God as their only hope. They are trying God out alongside other resources. Such praying does not prevail.

In other words, there are dangers on both sides; one danger needs the admonition to "always pray and not lose heart" (Luke 18:1), and the other danger needs the admonition to avoid "vain repetitions" (Matthew 6:7). Let us not be more fearful of persistence than Jesus was, when he prayed all night (Luke 6:12), nor more fearful of repetition than Jesus was, when he prayed three times the same thing: "Father, if it is possible, let this cup pass from me" (Matthew 26:39, 42, 44). If we pray in the Spirit and feel that God is our only hope, we will find our way.

104

DOES UNCONDITIONALITY CONCEAL THE REAL REMEDY?

Wisdom from Another Century

J C. Ryle's nineteenth-century book *Holiness* (Grand Rapids: Baker Book House, 1979) is full of remedies for twentieth-century problems. For example, I find these words to be a very needed antidote to much careless talk today about the "unconditionality" of God's love, in the context of healing our sense of distance and disharmony with him.

> Above all, grieve not the Spirit. Quench not the Spirit. Vex not the Spirit. Drive Him not to a distance, by tampering with small bad habits and little sins. Little jarrings between husbands and wives make unhappy homes; and petty inconsistencies, known and allowed, will bring in a strangeness between you and the Spirit.... The man who walks with God in Christ most closely, will generally be kept in the greatest peace. The believer who follows the Lord most fully and aims at the highest degree of holiness will ordinarily enjoy the most assured hope, and have the clearest persuasion of his own salvation. (181)

Can you really "drive [God] to a distance, by tampering with small bad habits"? Do "petty inconsistencies bring strangeness between you and the

Spirit"? Is the greatest peace really enjoyed by those who "walk with God most closely"? Is the greatest assurance known by those who "aim at the greatest degree of holiness"?

Yes. This is clearly taught in Scripture. "Draw near to God and he will draw near to you" (James 4:8).

This means that there is a precious experience of peace and assurance and harmony and intimacy that is not *un*conditional. It depends on our not grieving the Spirit. It depends on our putting away bad habits. It depends on forsaking the petty inconsistencies of our Christian lives. It depends on our walking closely with God and aiming at the greatest degree of holiness.

If this is true, I fear that the unguarded reassurances today that God's love is unconditional may stop people from doing the very things the Bible says they need to do in order to have the full experience of peace that they so desperately crave. In trying to give peace through "unconditionality" we may be cutting people off from the very remedy the Bible prescribes.

Let us declare untiringly the good news that our justification is based on the worth of Christ's obedience and sacrifice, not ours (Romans 5:19, "For as through the one man's disobedience the many were made sinners, even so through the obedience of the One the many will be made righteous"). Let us declare that our election and our calling are totally unconditional (Romans 9:11; 11:5–6; Ephesians 2:5). But let us also declare the biblical truth that the enjoyment of that justification, in its effect on our joy and confidence and power to grow in likeness to Jesus, is conditioned on our actively forsaking sins and renouncing bad habits and mortifying lusts and pursuing intimacy with Christ and not grieving the Spirit.

It is true that God is the initiator and enabler of our meeting these conditions. "Work out your salvation with fear and trembling; for it is God who is at work in you, both to will and to work for His good pleasure" (Philippians 2:12–13). "I labored even more than all of them, yet not I, but the grace of God with me" (1 Corinthians 15:10). Yes, that is true. But the conditions are still there and still real and still mine to fulfill—with God's enabling.

Not to tell people the truth that Ryle is teaching is to mislead people into shallow and weak Christianity. In fact, I ask: Is the healing technique today (which stresses unqualified "unconditionality") producing deep, strong, durable, wise people? Or is it helping produce a generation of fragile people whose hold on reality is tenuous because it is based on an oversimplified understanding of how we relate joyfully and sturdily to God?

105

WHERE DOES CHRISTIAN LIVING COME FROM?

Reflections on the Power of Right Knowing

I t is remarkable that again and again the apostle Paul confronts failure to *do* what's right with failure to *know* what's right. For example:

Right knowing prevents continuing in sin.

> Are we to continue in sin that grace might increase? May it never be!…
> *Or do you not know* that all of us who have been baptized into Christ Jesus
> have been baptized into His death?" (Romans 6:1–3, emphasis added)

Right knowing prevents the prostituting of grace.

> Shall we sin because we are not under Law but under grace? May it
> never be! *Do you not know* that when you present yourselves to some-
> one as slaves for obedience, you are slaves of the one whom you obey,
> either of sin resulting in death, or of obedience resulting in righteous-
> ness? (Romans 6:15–16, emphasis added)

Right knowing prevents boasting.

> Your boasting is not good. *Do you not know* that a little leaven leavens
> the whole lump of dough? (1 Corinthians 5:6, emphasis added)

Right knowing empowers good dispute settling.

> Or *do you not know* that the saints will judge the world? And if the world is judged by you, are you not competent to constitute the smallest law courts? *Do you not know* that we shall judge angels? How much more, matters of this life? (1 Corinthians 6:2–3, emphasis added)

Right knowing prevents fornication.

> *Do you not know* that your bodies are members of Christ? Shall I then take away the members of Christ and make them members of a harlot? May it never be! *Or do you not know* that the one who joins himself to a harlot is one body with her? For He says, "The two will become one flesh."... *Do you not know* that your body is a temple of the Holy Spirit who is in you, whom you have from God, and that you are not your own? (1 Corinthians 6:15–19, emphasis added)

Paul is simply continuing the emphasis of Jesus who said, "You will know the truth, and *the truth will set you free"* (John 8:32, emphasis added). *"Sanctify them in the truth;* your word is truth" (John 17:17, emphasis added).

Therefore don't coast in your thinking. Don't be passive with your mind. Instead...

> *Make your ear attentive to wisdom,*
> *Incline your heart to understanding...*
> *Cry for discernment,*
> *Lift your voice for understanding...*
> *Seek her as silver,*
> *And search for her as for hidden treasure.*
>
> PROVERBS 2:2–4

106

CAN YOU BE WORTHY OF GOD?

Finding What Fits with the Faithfulness of God

The Greek adverb *aksios* is translated "worthy of" in all six of its New Testament uses in the *New American Standard Bible*. Five of those uses refer to our acting "worthy of God" or the gospel or our heavenly calling. What does this mean? Does it mean that we are to become "worth" God's favor? That is, does "worthy of" mean deserving or meriting or earning God's favor? Does it call attention to our worth which God is obliged to acknowledge because it enriches his worth, the way a great computer programmer might be worth a huge salary to a leading software company?

Consider these five uses of the word *aksios:*

3 John 6, "You will do well to send them on their way in a manner *worthy* of God."

1 Thessalonians 2:12, "Walk in a manner *worthy* of the God who calls you into His own kingdom and glory."

Colossians 1:10, "Walk in a manner *worthy* of the Lord, to please Him in all respects, bearing fruit in every good work and increasing in the knowledge of God."

Philippians 1:27, "Conduct yourselves in a manner *worthy* of the gospel of Christ."

Ephesians 4:1, "Walk in a manner *worthy* of the calling with which you have been called." (Emphasis added in above verses.)

I don't think these texts mean that we merit God or the gospel or our call, but that they merit from us. That is, to "walk worthy of the Lord" means to walk in a way that the Lord is worthy of. Walk so as to show what the Lord deserves from us, not to show what we deserve from the Lord. A clue is found in Colossians 1:10 which says, "Walk worthy of the Lord, *to please him*" (emphasis added). But Hebrews 11:6 says, "Without faith it is impossible to please him." So the call to walk "worthy of the Lord" is at least a call to walk by faith.

But *faith* looks away from itself to the worth and ability and grace and strength of another. So walking "worthy of the Lord" would mean acting in a way that shows how worthy and able and gracious and strong the Lord is. Faith calls attention to the worth and ability of the one trusted. Therefore living by faith is evidence that the trusted Lord is worthy of our trust and obedience. "Walk worthy of the Lord"—as strange as it may sound (which is often the case when dealing with the absolute uniqueness of God's grace)—means that the Lord deserves or is worthy of being trusted.

Another clue to this interpretation would be Matthew 3:8, NKJV, where John the Baptist says, "Bear fruit worthy of *(aksios)* repentance." This surely does not mean: Act in a way that deserves repentance or merits repentance. That doesn't even make sense—I am worth repentance. Rather, "bear fruit worthy of repentance" assumes that repentance is there as something extremely valuable, and calls us to act in a way that *fits the value and nature of repentance.* Thus the NASB translates it, "Bear fruit *in keeping with* repentance," and the RSV translates it, "Bear fruit *that befits* repentance."

So it is with the phrases "worthy of God" and "worthy of the Lord" and "worthy of the gospel" and "worthy of the calling." They mean: Act in a way that fits the great value and glorious nature of God and the gospel and your calling. And what is it that fits with that great value? Faith. Above all things, faith and its fruit of love fit the worth and trustworthiness of God and the gospel.

So think this way. *Not:* I must have faith and love so as to be worth God's favor; *But rather:* God's favor is free and it is infinitely worth trusting. Walking *worthy* of that favor means walking by faith because faith is the one thing that agrees with (and fits) our bankruptcy and God's infinite "worth." Looking to God's infinite worth for our help and satisfaction is "walking worthy of God."

Set your minds on this greatness. Savor the incomparable trustworthiness of God's promises. Ponder what acts will fit with this. And then rise up and be doing—"worthily of the Lord."

107

IF I HAVE FOUND FAVOR, LET ME, O GOD, FIND FAVOR

Meditation on Knowing God in Exodus 33:13

> *Now therefore, I pray You, if I have found favor in Your sight, let me know Your ways that I may know You, so that I may find favor in Your sight. Consider too that this nation is Your people.*

The remarkable thing about this text is that it makes clear what is only implicit in many other places in the Bible, namely, that the conditions placed on receiving blessings from the Lord are themselves fulfilled as blessings from the Lord. Fulfilling the conditions for receiving grace is itself a gift of grace.

First, Moses finds grace in the eyes of the Lord. This was spoken by the Lord in verse 12 with no reference to any prior condition being met. The Lord had said to him, "I have known you by name, and you have also found favor in my sight." We see in verse 19 that God is utterly free in the giving of favor (grace): "I will be gracious to whom I will be gracious, and will show compassion on whom I will show compassion." So Moses knows himself a recipient of free and unconditional grace in that God has "known him by name" and that he has found favor in God's eyes.

On the basis of this wonderful grace, Moses cries out to God for the privilege of knowing God's ways: "If I have found favor in Your sight, let me know Your ways" (Exodus 33:13). Or, as one old commentator paraphrases Moses, "Show me thy views and purposes, thine *intended ways* of acting and thy requirements of me in reference to this great object" (George Bush, *Notes on Exodus,* vol. 2, 234, emphasis added).

More importantly, Moses' aim in knowing God's ways is so that he may know God himself. "Let me know Your ways *that I may know You.*" Seeing the aims and purposes of God are a means of seeing and knowing God personally. This is why there is a redemptive history: We see and know God in his ways. We are to read God from his path in the history of his people and from his ways in the world. This is not mere academic knowledge. There is a knowing of God in the working of God. This is real personal knowledge, if God will by his grace grant that we have a spiritual apprehension of his glory and his person in his ways. That is what Moses is asking for. "Let me know Your ways that I may know You."

But then he says that the reason for wanting to know God is that he "may find favor in [God's] sight." "Let me know Your ways that I may know You, *so that I may find favor in Your sight.*" So we see that the blessing of knowing God is the condition which Moses says has to be fulfilled so that some additional blessing might come. So when you take the whole verse into account, knowing God is, first, the *result* of God's being gracious to Moses, and then, second, it is also the *cause* of God's being more gracious to Moses. "If I have *found favor in Your sight,* let me know Your ways that I may know You, s*o that I may find favor in Your sight.*" Knowing God is the result of grace and the cause of grace. Or we may say, grace is the cause of Moses' knowing God and the result of Moses' knowing God.

free grace > knowing God > more grace

So if we read somewhere in Scripture that grace is conditional upon human knowing or some other human act, we must not assume that human willing is the bottom line in whether the grace is given. There may be a grace behind the act of willing or doing that is simply not mentioned. Here it is mentioned and we are taught that when grace is the *response* of God to human knowing, it has also been the prior *cause* of that knowing, so that the *ultimate* condition of grace is grace.

And what would this added grace be that Moses wants? The simplest answer is more of the same. If the first grace shown to Moses fills Moses with a desire for knowing God's ways and knowing God himself, then the new grace that he longs for would be to know God more, and this time, perhaps, not *mediately* through God's ways, but *immediately* by a more direct revelation. Which is, in fact, exactly what Moses asks for in verse 18, "I pray You, show me Your glory!"

But before he asks for that, he asks that God would go up to Canaan with the people, so that they might be distinguished from all the other peoples, by virtue of God's presence among them (verse 16). So the larger grace that Moses wants, after he has known the ways of the Lord and the Lord himself, is that the people would be marked by the Lord's presence among them—that the knowledge of the Lord and the manifestation of his ways would be plain in the midst of his people.

In other words, Moses is concerned not only for his private experience of God's ways and God's glory. He also wants it to be a public experience, a shared experience. The greater grace is both more revelation of God's glory to Moses himself (verse 18) and a manifestation of that glorious presence among the people, both for their good and the praise of God's name among the nations.

This is the great passion of our lives: to know God himself by grace, and to make him known by grace. To see him in his ways among his people, and to see him as immediately as he will allow in this fallen world and the other glorious world. To so pray and so minister that we spread to others a passion for the glory of this great God for the joy of all peoples.

⟨ΤΤΤΛΘ⟩

108

ARE CHRISTIANS FULLY SATISFIED?

Pondering (Again) the Path Between Paralysis and Triumphalism

Flase expectations can turn a good relationship into a bad one. Jesus did say, "Whoever drinks of the water that I shall give him will never thirst" (John 4:14). One might then enthusiastically jump to the conclusion that once you come to Jesus, all your longings are satisfied then and there. No more dissatisfaction.

But consider the following biblical indications that some dissatisfaction not only is, but *ought* to be, part of our Christian experience.

- "Not that I have already obtained [the resurrection] or am already perfect; but I press on to make it my own, because Christ has made me his own." (Philippians 3:12, RSV)
- "Weep with those who weep." (Romans 12:15)
- "Will not God vindicate his elect who cry to him day and night?" (Luke 18:7, RSV)
- "Wretched man that I am! Who will deliver me from this body of death?" (Romans 7:24, RSV)
- "If we say we have no sin, we deceive ourselves, and the truth is not in us…. If we say we have not sinned, we make him a liar, and his word is not in us." (1 John 1:8, 10, RSV)

- "We ourselves, who have the first fruits of the Spirit, groan inwardly as we wait for adoption as sons, the redemption of our bodies." (Romans 8:23, RSV)

When we invite a person to Christ—to come to the fountain of living water—we *do* offer satisfaction. Christ is the source of all deep and lasting satisfaction. We are even told to pray that our experience of God be full of satisfaction: "Oh *satisfy us* in the morning with Your lovingkindness, that we may sing for joy and be glad all our days" (Psalm 90:14, emphasis added). But the depth of this satisfaction is not drunk all at once.

For example, in this life our bodies will decay and give us pain and eventually die. As Paul says, "our outer nature is wasting away" (2 Corinthians 4:16, RSV). It is true that this decaying experience is transformed by hope and by God's use of it for our good (Romans 8:24, 28). But still we are not satisfied with this painful condition. We know God promises something better, and Romans 8:23 is painfully realistic: "We ourselves, having the first fruits of the Spirit, even we ourselves *groan within ourselves,* waiting eagerly for…the redemption of our body" (emphasis added).

Another example of our partial satisfaction now is the remaining corruption in our hearts. We still sin and need forgiveness. "If we say we have no sin, we deceive ourselves, and the truth is not in us" (1 John 1:8, RSV). Indeed we sin every day, which is why the Lord taught us to pray daily not only, "Give us this day our *daily* bread," but in the same way, "Forgive us our debts" (Matthew 6:12). Yes, this imperfection too is transformed by hope, and by the daily cleansing we can have from Jesus! But still we are not satisfied with this sinfulness, and cry out to be more pure and holy and loving. "I pray that your love may abound still more and more" (Philippians 1:9).

Another example is the sheer weakness of the flesh. Jesus said to the sleeping disciples, "The spirit is willing, but the flesh is weak" (Matthew 26:41). We want to worship and pray and serve, but we find that weakness makes us sluggish. We have to be urged out of this: "[Do] not be *sluggish*…. Strengthen the hands that are weak and the knees that are feeble" (Hebrews 6:12; 12:12). We languish when we would like to experience only white-hot zeal. So we are dissatisfied even with our best efforts at worship and obedience. This, too, is changed by Christ because he is willing to accept less than perfect sacrifices of praise and obedience that come from hearts of faith. "The sacrifices of God are a broken spirit; a broken and a contrite heart, O God, You will not despise" (Psalm 51:17).

So, yes, Christ does offer *total* satisfaction, much of it right now in hope and forgiveness and growing power to love, but *all* of it only in the age to come when we will be made perfect in a perfect world. Then there will be no sense in which we will be disappointed in ourselves or in our circumstances at all.

We must learn to walk the narrow way between despair and presumption. On the one side lies the pitfall of hopeless paralysis, and on the other side lies the pitfall of premature triumphalism. "Let not him who girds on his armor boast like him who takes it off" (1 Kings 20:11). Between is humble, energetic, joyful, ever repentant confidence in the power and promise of grace.

109

Going Beyond the Limits of Unlimited Atonement

Christ Died for All, but Especially for His Bride

Arminians take all the passages which say the death of Christ is "for us" (Romans 5:8; 1 Thessalonians 5:10) or for "his own sheep" (John 10:11, 15) or for "the church" (Ephesians 5:25; Acts 20:28) or for "the children of God" (John 11:52) or for "those who are being sanctified" (Hebrews 10:14) and say that the meaning is this: God designs and intends the atonement for all people, but he applies it as effective and saving only for those who believe and become part of "us" and "the sheep" and "the church" and "the children of God."

In this view, then, the sentence, "Christ died for you," means: Christ died for all sinners, so that *if* you will repent and believe in Christ, then the death of Jesus will become effective in your case and will take away your sins. "Died for you" means if you believe, the death of Jesus will cover your sins.

Now, as far as it goes, this is biblical teaching. But then Arminians *deny* something that I think the Bible teaches. They deny that the texts about Christ's dying for "us" or his "sheep" or his "church" or "the children of God" were intended by God to obtain something *more* for his people than the benefits they get *after they believe.* They deny, specifically, that the death of Christ was intended by God not only to obtain benefits for people *after* they believe (which is true), but even more, Christ's death was intended by God to obtain *the very willingness to believe.* In other words, the divine grace that it takes to overcome our hardness of heart so that we become believers was *also* obtained by the blood of Jesus. This they deny.

There is no dispute that Christ died to obtain great saving benefits for all who believe. Moreover there is no dispute that Christ died so that we might say to all persons everywhere without exception: God gave his only begotten Son to die for sin so that if you believe on him you may have eternal life. John 3:16 stands affirmed. Amen.

The dispute is whether God intended for the death of Christ to obtain *more* than these two things: 1) saving benefits after faith, and 2) a *bona fide* invitation that can be made to any person to believe on Christ for salvation. Specifically, did God intend for the death of Christ to obtain the free gift of faith (Ephesians 2:8) and repentance (2 Timothy 2:25)? Did the blood of Jesus obtain *both* the benefits after faith, *and* the benefit of faith itself?

Does the historic Arminian interpretation of any of the "universal" texts on the atonement necessarily contradict this "more" that I am affirming about God's intention for the death of Christ? Texts like 1 Timothy 2:6; 1 John 2:1–2; Hebrews 2:9; 2 Corinthians 5:19; John 1:29.

I don't think so—at least it doesn't have to. Arminians historically are just as eager as Calvinists to avoid saying that these texts teach "universal salvation." So they do not teach that the death of Christ "for all" in fact saves all. Rather they say, in the words of Millard Erickson, "God intended the atonement to make salvation *possible* for all persons. Christ died for all persons, but this atoning death becomes *effective* only when accepted by the individual." Erickson then says, "This is the view of all Arminians" *(Systematic Theology* [Grand Rapids: Baker Book House, 1985], 829, emphasis added).

It is crucial to see what Arminians do *not* say. They do *not* say that in the death of Christ, God intends to *effectively* save all for whom Christ died. They say only that God intends to *make possible* the salvation of all for whom Christ died. But this interpretation of these "universal" texts does *not* contradict the Calvinist assertion that God *does* intend to obtain the grace of faith and repentance for a definite group by the death of Christ.

Arminians may deny this assertion, but they cannot deny it on the basis of *their* interpretation of the "universal" texts of the atonement. That interpretation simply affirms that all may have salvation *if* they believe. I do not dispute that. I only go beyond it.

Here's the rub: If God did this "more" in the death of Christ, he didn't do it for everyone; and so, at this level, the atonement becomes "limited." And this is what Arminians stumble over: Is there anything that God would do to get some unbelievers saved that he would not do for all? Such a "limitation" of "more grace" to some implies a choice on God's part to intervene decisively, and effectively save some and not all. This is the real stumbling block for those who give man and not God the final determination of who is saved.

What difference practically does all this make? A great deal. In affirming not only the essence of what Arminians believe (see the Erickson quote above), but also the "more" that Calvinists believe (that the blood of Christ obtains the faith and perseverance of the elect), Christians are able to cherish the death of Christ as an act of omnipotent love by which Christ, our husband, pays for us, pursues us, overpowers us with love, and preserves us as his uniquely loved bride forever. The Lover of our souls paid his own blood, not just to make his marriage possible, but to break down doors of the prison and take his beloved to himself. Strength and stability and joy and courage flow from knowing ourselves loved like this.

110

WHEN ADULTERESSES ARE MEN

Spillover of a Sermon on Abortion

Meditation on James 4:2–4

In James 4:4, "adulteresses" refers to men (and women). It refers to nominal or very immature Christians who make a cuckold out of God. "Cuckold" is an old-fashioned word that means "a man whose wife is unfaithful." This is a terrible thing to do—to make a cuckold out of God. We should be aware of how it is done. The key verses are James 4:2–4:

> You lust and do not have; so you commit murder. You are envious and cannot obtain; so you fight and quarrel. You do not have because you do not ask. You ask and do not receive, because you ask with wrong motives, so that you may spend it on your pleasures. *You adulteresses,* do you not know that friendship with the world is hostility toward God? Therefore whoever wishes to be a friend of the world makes himself an enemy of God. (emphasis added)

James has in his mind a picture of people who use prayer to try to get from God something they desire more than God. He calls these people—men and women—"adulteresses." Why? Because in his mind God is like our husband who is jealous to be our highest delight. If we then try to make prayer a means of getting from him something we want more than we want him, we are like a wife who asks her husband for money to visit another lover.

As if it were not clear enough, James explains (in verse 5) why this is offensive to God: "He jealously desires the Spirit which He has made to dwell in us." In other words, God is jealous to be the object of our spirit's greatest delight. And verse 4 says, if we become "friends" with the world, we become "enemies" of God. That means if we find our most satisfying relationships with others besides God, we make him our enemy. God is either our first and greatest delight, or he is our enemy.

Now this, James says, is the explanation of where killing comes from: You desire and do not have; so you commit murder. If God were your desire, you *would* have what you desired, namely God, and so you wouldn't murder. Murder, as in abortion. Dads would not pressure daughters to have abortions— if they delighted in God. Boyfriends would not pressure girlfriends to abort their own children—if they delighted in God. Men would not be the doctors who do abortions—if they delighted in God. Men, not just women, are "adulteresses." They use the very life and gifts their God has given them to pursue another lover. It may be money or freedom or good standing in the community. These are their paramours.

Men are adulteresses when they exploit God's grace to get God's rival. Therefore one great work needed in the cause of life—and every other form of abuse of women and children—is for men to repent and seek their full and final joy in God. When this happens, it will be impossible for men to assault the image of God in the womb of their daughters, their wives, and their girlfriends. In fact, the very drive for wanton sexual satisfaction that begets so many babies outside marriage will be swallowed up in the flames of a higher passion, and either consumed in noble labors or sanctified in the covenant of married love.

I call on men to cease being adulteresses and to pursue the pleasure you were made for: knowing and loving and being conformed to God. Fight for this against all obstacles. Yield to nothing till you find it. Don't be weakly fatalistic and say, "That's for mystics." It is for men created in the image of God. And when enough of us find it, abortion will virtually vanish.

111

A Joyful Meeting with
Josef Tson

The Camaraderie of a Common Vision of Suffering

I relished two hours with Josef Tson in my office on Wednesday, January 31, 1996. At that time Dr. Tson, who lived in his native land of Romania, was the president of the Romanian Missionary Society and president of Emmanuel Bible Institute in Oradea, Romania. When I heard he was in town, I was very eager to have time with him because his writing on the "Theology of Martyrdom" had deeply moved me several years before.

In the spring of 1972, when he was completing his undergraduate studies in theology at Oxford, England, he was warned that if he returned to communist Romania, he would probably be arrested, imprisoned, and possibly killed. Should he go home?

> One of the most popular professors of Bible in Oxford at that time was G. B. Caird. I loved to sit in his classes and to absorb his commentaries on different books of the New Testament.... I picked up his commentary on the book of Revelation. It was this book that introduced me to the biblical teaching on martyrdom. It was there that I saw how God always conquers by a love that is self-giving and self-sacrificing. It was here that I understood God's method of sending His Lamb into the world, followed by many thousands of other

lambs, to overcome the world by proclaiming the love of God and by dying for the sake of their proclamation.

This astonishing biblical principle that God always conquers through people who will preach the gospel and then die for it helped me immeasurably to be able to go back to Romania. It gave me the solid rationale I needed for the dangerous return home. Buttressed by this teaching, I preached, lectured and wrote for nearly a decade, ready to be martyred for what I was doing, yet knowing that death would be my supreme weapon of conquest and my road to the highest glory in heaven. [Preface to Josef Ton [variant spelling], *Suffering, Martyrdom, and Rewards in Heaven* [Lanham: University Press of America, 1997], xi–xii.)

What an amazing time we had together on that January winter afternoon. I had not experienced anything quite like it before. There was almost no small talk. Immediately we were catapulted into the weightiest matters of suffering and biblical theology. On the surface he vehemently disapproved of my term "Christian hedonism" which I describe and defend in *Desiring God: Meditations of a Christian Hedonist* (Sisters, Ore.: Multnomah Publishers, 1996). One does not suffer at the hands of communism and easily embrace anything called "hedonism."

But beneath the surface (where we went very quickly) there was an almost instantaneous camaraderie. At one point, well into our conversation, he startled me by standing up from his chair and taking two steps toward me with a big smile on his face and shaking my hand because of the delight he felt in our agreement theologically with regard to the role of suffering and self-denial in the plan of salvation and in the completion of the great commission. In recent years I have come more and more to the conclusion that suffering is at the heart of what it means to be a Christian and what it means to do missions. (See the chapters on suffering in *Let the Nations Be Glad* [Grand Rapids: Baker Book House, 1993] and *Future Grace* [Sisters, Ore.: Multnomah Publishers, 1995] and *Desiring God* [Sisters, Ore.: Multnomah Publishers, 1996]).

Dr. Tson told me of his personal relationship with Martyn Lloyd-Jones, the great London pastor who died in 1981. He described how he was the only foreigner in the Monday pastors' meetings while he was studying at Oxford. He knew the doctor personally and was told by Martyn Lloyd-Jones how he and his wife prayed regularly for Josef.

On *joy*, he said that at one point in the days of oppression in Romania, his house was searched by Communist officials because he was a leading pastor. Almost all his books were confiscated. He said that the soldiers needed proof that they were getting his books from him. So they told him to sit at a table and write in each book that it was found in his house. Then he had to sign the book while they took pictures of him. At one point in the tense process, he took down a book whose title was "Joy Unspeakable and Full of Glory" with the subtitle "Is This Your Experience NOW?"

As he read the title, he asked himself that question and was filled—at that very moment—by the Holy Spirit with amazing joy. The change was so profound that he told his wife to get these soldiers some coffee, and he was freed from his anger and fear. Later that week he had to preach. All in his congregation knew that he had been stripped of his books and was daily questioned by the authorities so that he had no time to minister or prepare. When he preached, he spoke on "The joy of the LORD is your strength" (Nehemiah 8:10). He said that one man was so overwhelmed with the sheer force of his joy in that setting of suffering that he could not hear anything after the text and was broken in his own heart and deeply changed.

Lord, I thank you for this meeting and this man. I pray that I will be faithful to your call, and that the *joy* of the Lord will be the strength that frees me to love soldiers and preach truth (whether anyone calls it *Christian hedonism* or not). Amen.

112

WHEN JESUS WILL NOT ANSWER A QUESTION

How Not to Be a Pig or a Dog

Meditation on Mark 11:27–33

The scribes and elders asked Jesus, "By what authority are You doing these things, or who gave You this authority to do these things?" Instead of answering immediately, Jesus said, "I will ask you one question, and you answer Me, and I will tell you by what authority I do these things" (Mark 11:28–29).

This just might be an illustration of Jesus' command, "Do not give what is holy to dogs, and do not throw your pearls before swine" (Matthew 7:6). In other words, what Jesus is doing is testing the scribes and elders with his question. He wants them to show if they are "swine." If they are, he will not answer their question. He will not give what is holy to dogs or cast his pearls before swine.

So Jesus asked, "Was the baptism of John from heaven, or from men?" (Mark 11:30).

The scribes and the elders were cornered by this question. They reasoned (if you can call it that): "If we say, 'From heaven,' He will say, 'Then why did you not believe him?' But shall we say, 'From men'?—they were afraid of the people, for everyone considered John to have been a real prophet" (Mark 11:31–32). What is this so-called reasoning? This is posturing, not truth-seeking. This is evasion and the prelude of deception. It is living by the book of expediency, not integrity.

So they answer Jesus, "We do not know." This is a politically driven answer with no allegiance to the truth. This is the very opposite of what Paul modeled for the believers in Corinth: "As from sincerity...as from God, we speak in Christ in the sight of God" (2 Corinthians 2:17). For Paul, communication among men had to do primarily with God. The scribes and elders huddled and calculated in the dark as if there were no God listening—as if the main Person in the universe did not matter in their dealing with truth.

Therefore, Jesus said to them, "Nor will I tell you by what authority I do these things" (Mark 11:33). In other words, I will not answer people like you. I will not cast the pearl of truth before those who trample truth with the whisperings of expediency. I will not answer questions that come from hearts that elevate self-preservation above honesty. Dogs and pigs don't care about truth. They care only about not getting stoned by the crowds.

When Paul said to the Philippians, "Beware of the dogs" (3:2), he explained what they were like: people "whose god is their belly, and whose glory is in their shame—who set their minds on earthly things" (Philippians 3:19, NKJV). That is what pigs and dogs do: They set their minds on the immediate payback of slop and roadkill. This is their god.

Honesty and truth, that might cost them some comfort, is not what dogs and pigs care about. When the elders and the scribes (or you and I) act like that, we earn the names "swine" and "cur."

If you want to walk with Jesus, you can't be a pig or a dog. He will not speak to you if you play games with words and conceal your meaning with politically correct evasions. So let us come near to Christ and speak "from sincerity...as from God...in Christ in the sight of God" (2 Corinthians 2:17).

113

IN QUEST OF REST

Pondering the God-Centered Purpose of Sleep

This time of year at 5:00 a.m., Sunday morning, the world is not dark, but there is still no color. Everything is black and white and gray, except for the orange light on the garage across the street that shines through my bedroom window. There is no breeze, and the poplar leaves are caught like a snapshot in stillness. The stars are gone, but the sun is not up yet; so you can't tell if the gray sky is overcast or clear. Very soon we will know.

I sit on the edge of my bed trying to develop a theology of sleep. Why did God design us to need sleep? We sleep a third of our lives. Just think of it: a third of our lives spent like dead men. Think of everything being left undone that could be done had God not designed us to need sleep. There is surely no doubt that he could have created us with no need for sleep. And what an amazing thing that would be: Everyone could devote himself to two careers and not feel tired. Everyone could be a "full-time Christian worker" and still keep his job. There is so much of our Father's business we could be about.

Why did God imagine sleep? *He* never sleeps! He thought the idea up out of nothing. He thought it up for his earthly creatures. Why? Psalm 127:2 says, "It is in vain that you rise up early and go late to rest, eating the bread of anxious toil; for he gives to his beloved in his sleep" (author's translation). According to this text, sleep is a gift of love, but the gift is often spurned by anxious toil. Peaceful sleep is the opposite of anxiety. God does not want his children to be anxious, but to trust him. Therefore I conclude that God made sleep as a continual reminder that we should not be anxious but should rest in him.

Sleep is a daily reminder from God that we are not God. "He who keeps Israel will neither slumber nor sleep" (Psalm 121:4). But we will. For we are not God. Once a day God sends us to bed like patients with a sickness. The sickness is a chronic tendency to think we are in control and that our work is indispensable. To cure us of this disease, God turns us into helpless sacks of sand once a day. How humiliating to the self-made corporate executive that he has to give up all control and become as limp as a suckling infant every day.

Sleep is a parable that God is God and we are mere men. God handles the world quite nicely while a hemisphere sleeps. Sleep is like a broken record that comes around with the same message every day: Man is not sovereign…. Man is not sovereign…. Man is not sovereign. Don't let the lesson be lost on you. God wants to be trusted as the Great Worker who never tires and never sleeps. He is not nearly so impressed with our late nights and early mornings as he is with the peaceful trust that casts all anxieties on him and sleeps. "His delight is not in the strength of the horse, nor his pleasure in the legs of a man; but the LORD takes pleasure in those who fear him, in those who hope in his steadfast love" (Psalm 147:10–11, RSV).

114

WILL WE LOVE CHRIST AT THE END OF THE YEAR?

Meditation on 1 Corinthians 16:22

If anyone does not love the Lord,
he is to be accursed.

Will we love Christ at the end of the year? It is an absolutely crucial question because Paul says, in 1 Corinthians 16:22, "If anyone does not love the Lord, he is to be accursed." If we do not love Christ we will be cursed and not saved. The same urgency of love is expressed in Matthew 24:12–13. "Because lawlessness is increased, most people's love will grow cold. But the one who endures to the end, he will be saved." Some kinds of love can grow cold and die. That is not a love that "endures to the end" and is "saved." So again we must love Christ in order to be saved. It is serious and essential. It is not a matter of options or icing on the cake of Christianity. Eternity is at stake. But how do you know you will love Christ to the end of this year, let alone to the end of your life? What is your hope and plan to sustain love to Christ?

I found help with this in a 350-year-old book by Thomas Shepard, the founder of Harvard University and pastor in Cambridge, Massachusetts, who had been exiled from England as a Puritan. *The Parable of the Ten Virgins* (Morgan, Pa.: Soli Deo Gloria Publications, 1997) is 635 pages of rich biblical meditations on the difference between two kinds of Christians—the real and the false: the virgins with oil, who go in to the Bridegroom, and the virgins without oil, who are shut out of the marriage feast of eternity.

One section is titled "True Saving Grace in the Hearts of Believers Can Never Fail." The great thing about this book and this section is that it is so permeated with Scripture. Reading a book like this is like reading the Bible through the eyes of a great saint who has learned to fight unbelief with the weapon of the Bible and win a thousand battles.

Here is a glimpse into how he answers our question. He addresses one fear after another that might take away our confidence in the perseverance of our love for Christ. Do you fear Satan? he asks. Then consider Matthew 16:18 ("I also say to you that you are Peter, and upon this rock I will build My church; and *the gates of Hades will not overpower it*" [emphasis added]). He shall not prevail against thee, but thou shalt give the last blow and wound (357).

Do you fear the world, the deceits of it? He counsels, consider Matthew 24:24 ("For false Christs and false prophets will arise and will show great signs and wonders, so as to mislead, *if possible, even the elect*" [emphasis added]). It is not possible, take heart. Do you fear the evil or the good things of the world? Then consider John 17:15 ("I do not ask You to take them out of the world, but to keep them from the evil one"). Jesus has prayed for you that the Father will guard you from the evil in the world. How much more the dangerous good!

Do you fear that your sin will separate you from God? Consider Romans 6:2 ("How shall we who died to sin still live in it?"). "It is a strong, but a wounded, but a dying enemy" (358). Do you fear the Lord, that you have walked unworthily of him? Consider Matthew 12:20 ("A bruised reed shall he not break, and smoking flax shall he not quench, till he send forth judgment unto victory" [KJV]). "Oh, therefore, be comforted against this in these times, which are declining evil days, and bless the Lord" (358).

This is very serious business. "If anyone does not love the Lord, he is to be accursed." Do you love the Lord? Not just believe things about him. But love him. Does your family love the Lord? Do your Christian friends love Christ? And just as crucial is the question: Will you keep on loving him? What Thomas Shepard teaches us is that knowing the Word of God is essential to fighting the fight to stay in love with Jesus. I beg of you all: Don't assume that love for Christ is self-perpetuating. It isn't. It must be nurtured by the Word again and again. Its enemies are countless in this world. But "he who is in you is greater than he who is in the world" (1 John 4:4, RSV). And the Word of God is greater than all the love-killing promises of sin. Let us read it often, study it deeply, memorize it wisely, and wield it decisively against every foe of love to Christ. Stir yourself up to this with warnings like 1 Corinthians 16:22, and with promises like 1 Corinthians 2:9, "What no eye has seen, nor ear heard, nor the heart of man conceived…God has prepared for those who love him" (RSV). Love him. Love him.

"Take Heed How You Hear!"

Ten Practical Preparations for Hearing the
Word of God on Sunday Morning
A Meditation on Luke 8:18, RSV

> *Take heed then how you hear; for to him*
> *who has will more be given, and from him*
> *who has not, even what he thinks that he*
> *has will be taken away.*

1. Pray that God would give you a good and honest heart.
The heart we need is a work of God. That's why we pray for it. "I will give you a new heart" (Ezekiel 36:26). "I will give them a heart to know Me" (Jeremiah 24:7). Let's pray, "O Lord, give me a heart for you. Give me a good and honest heart. Give me a soft and receptive heart. Give me a humble and meek heart. Give me a fruitful heart."

2. Meditate on the Word of God.
"Oh taste and see that the LORD is good" (Psalm 34:8). On Saturday night, read some delicious portion of your Bible with a view to stirring up hunger for God. This is the appetizer for Sunday morning's meal.

3. Purify your mind by turning away from worldly entertainment.

"*Putting aside all filthiness and all that remains of wickedness,* in humility receive the word implanted, which is able to save your souls" (James 1:21, emphasis added). It astonishes me how many Christians watch the same banal, empty, silly, trivial, titillating, suggestive, immodest TV shows that most unbelievers watch. This makes us small and weak and worldly and inauthentic in worship. Instead, turn off the television on Saturday night and read something true and great and beautiful and pure and honorable and excellent and worthy of praise (Philippians 4:8). Your heart will unshrivel and be able to feel greatness again.

4. Trust in the truth that you already have.

The hearing of the Word of God that fails during trial has no root (Luke 8:13). What is the root we need? It is trust. Jeremiah 17:7–8 says, "Blessed is the man who *trusts* in the LORD, and whose *trust* is the LORD. For he will be like a tree planted by the water, that extends its *roots* by a stream" (emphasis added). Trusting in the truth you already have is the best way to prepare yourself to receive more.

5. Rest long enough Saturday night to be alert and hopeful Sunday morning.

"All things are lawful for me, but I will not be enslaved by anything" (1 Corinthians 6:12, RSV). I am not laying down any law here. I am saying there are Saturday night ways that ruin Sunday morning worship. Don't be enslaved by them. Without sufficient sleep, our minds are dull, our emotions are flat, our proneness to depression is higher, and our fuses are short. My counsel: Decide when you must get up on Sunday in order to have time to eat, get dressed, pray and meditate on the Word, prepare the family, and travel to church; and then compute backward eight hours and be sure that you are in bed fifteen minutes before that. Read your Bible in bed and fall asleep with the Word of God in your mind. I especially exhort parents to teach teenagers that Saturday is *not* the night to stay out late with friends. If there is a special late night, make it Friday. It is a terrible thing to teach children that worship is so optional that it doesn't matter if you are exhausted when you come.

6. Forbear one another Sunday morning without grumbling and criticism.

"They grumbled in their tents; they did not listen to the voice of the LORD" (Psalm 106:25). Sunday morning grumbling and controversy and quarreling can ruin a worship service for a family. When there is something you are angry about or some conflict that you genuinely think needs to be talked about, forbear. Of course if *you* are clearly the problem and need to apologize, do it as quickly as you can (Matthew 5:23–24). But if you are fuming because of the children's or spouse's delinquency, forbear, that is, be slow to anger and quick to listen (James 1:19). In worship, open yourself to God's exposing the log in your own eye. It may be that all of you will be humbled and chastened so that no serious conflict is necessary.

7. Be meek and teachable when you come.

"Receive with meekness the implanted word, which is able to save your souls" (James 1:21, RSV). Meekness and teachability are not gullibility. You have your Bible and you have your brain. Use them. But if we come with a chip on our shoulders and a suspicion of the preaching, week after week, we will not hear the Word of God. Meekness is a humble openness to God's truth with a longing to be changed by it.

8. Be still as you enter the room and focus your mind's attention and heart's affection on God.

"Be still, and know that I am God" (Psalm 46:10, NKJV). As we enter the sanctuary, let us come on the lookout for God, and leave on the lookout for people. Come with a quiet passion to seek God and his power. We will not be an unfriendly church if we are aggressive in our pursuit of *God* during the prelude and aggressive in our pursuit of *visitors* during the postlude.

9. Think earnestly about what is sung and prayed and preached.

"Brethren, do not be children in your *thinking*; yet in evil be infants, but in your *thinking* be mature" (1 Corinthians 14:20, emphasis added). So Paul says to Timothy, "*Think* over what I say, for the Lord will grant you understanding in everything" (2 Timothy 2:7, RSV, emphasis added). Anything worth hearing is worth thinking about. If you would take heed how you hear, think about what you hear.

10. Desire the truth of God's Word more than you desire riches or food.
"Like newborn babies, long for [desire] the pure milk of the word, so that by it you may grow in respect to salvation" (1 Peter 2:2, author's translation). As you sit quietly and pray and meditate on the text and the songs, remind yourself of what Psalm 19:10–11 says about the words of God: "More to be *desired* are they than gold, even much fine gold; sweeter also than honey and drippings of the honeycomb."

116

"Why Do You Call Me Good? God Alone Is Good"

*What the Rich Ruler Needed to Learn
About the Goodness of God*

I

n Luke 18:18–19 we read, "And a certain ruler questioned Him, saying, 'Good Teacher, what shall I do to inherit eternal life?' And Jesus said to him, 'Why do you call Me good? No one is good except God alone.'"

Why does Jesus say this? The question is not merely why Jesus would deflect the ascription of good from himself onto God, but why he would take this tack at all? Why pick out what seems to be an incidental word from the man's sentence and focus on it, instead of immediately taking up his question about eternal life? There is more here than meets the eye. Ponder with me what Jesus means when he says to this rich ruler, "God alone is good."

1. Jesus means: "You are not good. If God alone is good, and you are not God, then you are not good. And your quest for eternal life will not find fulfillment, if you look to yourself for goodness. Being good is what God is. You are evil (Matthew 7:11). Beware, then of what you are about to say, 'All these [commandments] I have kept from my youth' (Luke 18:21)".

2. Jesus means: "The goodness of God is your only hope of eternal life. This is why I mention God's goodness at the very outset. I am not picking on an incidental word in your question to me (*'Good* Teacher, what shall I do to inherit eternal life?'). I am focusing your attention on the source of what you

want, eternal life. God's goodness, not yours—or any other man's (as you view me) will help. I know you do not view me as God, but only as a mere man. That is why I deflect the term goodness away from me to God. It is your view, not mine, that prompts me to do this. As long as you view me as a mere man, I will resist your calling me good."

3. Jesus means: "Your only hope is not to speak to good teachers, but to cry out to God and say, 'Good Savior, satisfy me in the morning with your goodness (Psalm 90:14) and show me your goodness in granting me eternal life as I look not to myself or any man, but to you for goodness.'"

4. Jesus means: "My focus on the all-satisfying goodness of God alone is the point of the first four of the Ten Commandments—which is why I do not mention them in my commandments to you ('You know the commandments: "Do not commit adultery, do not kill, do not steal, do not bear false witness, honor your father and mother,"' Luke 18:20, RSV). God *alone* is good. That's the point of the first table of the Law. Have no other gods before this all-good God, do not take his good name in vain, hallow his wonderful goodness every seven days with the enjoyment of his good gift of rest, and do not try to make an idol that you can worship because God and God alone is good."

5. Jesus means: "The commandments I quote are the ones that will show that you have come to value God alone as the all-satisfying good in your life: If you kill or lie or commit adultery or steal, you are obviously cherishing some good above God."

6. Jesus means: "When I quote the second table of the Ten Commandments, I leave out the command not to *covet* because I want to make that one more pointed and show you that you have not complied with it: Go sell what you have, give it to the poor, and come follow me. That is, stop coveting wealth and security. Instead, start resting in the goodness of God alone. Stop letting your love of status and power and ease make you callous to the poor. The issue in your life is a failure to see and enjoy how good God is."

7. Jesus means: "When I say, 'Follow me,' I mean, 'Join those who are ready to leave all and find in my presence and fellowship the goodness of God.' If you follow me, you will know sooner, rather than later, how close and how far you were from the kingdom in calling me good."

Oh, merciful Father, you are good. We come to you to learn of goodness and to taste goodness. No man is good. And if Jesus were not one with you in the mystery of the incarnation, he would be a mere man and not good. He is good because he is one with you, and you are good. Your heart is good and your promises are good and your warnings are good and your commandments are good. We have no good apart from you. We turn from all the "good" of the world and all the "goods" of the world. Our treasure is in you. Keep us on this narrow path that leads to life. And may our freedom from this world give glory to the goodness of your heart. On earth there is nothing that we desire besides you.

117

YOU ALMOST CAN'T TEACH AN OLD DOG NEW TRICKS

Thoughts on the Possibilities of Change

Someone suggested to me after I had taught on Luke 5:39 ("No one who drinks old wine desires the new, because he says the old is good" [RSV]), "Maybe what he meant is, 'You can't teach an old dog new tricks.'" That's almost right. The point was this: Jesus and his teaching were the new wine coming into the world, but the scribes and Pharisees could not bring themselves to even try the new, let alone enjoy it.

When it comes to changing long-held religious convictions, changing is almost impossible. Suppose you have held a doctrinal conviction for fifty years and have taught it in Sunday school classes and have rejoiced in it in your private meditations. And suppose you are wrong. Somebody comes along and offers the new wine of a contrary doctrinal view and has totally compelling biblical support plus a grand historical tradition. Can you, the "old dog," learn the "new trick"? The hindrances are huge.

First, in order to change my conviction at sixty-five, I must admit that I have thought and believed wrong for decades. This is very hard on my ego. How could I have overlooked the true evidence so long? How could I have been illogical all this time? Or have I willfully shut my eyes, indifferent to truth? Our human nature rebels so much against making these admissions that we can almost always find excuses not to accept the "new trick," no matter how compelling the biblical support.

Second, all these years I have channeled my relation to God through a misconception. I have delighted in a view that is not true. This is not only hard on my ego, but threatens to make my relation to God look artificial and unreal.

Third, if I am wrong on this point, then I have been misleading other people all these years. I have taught my children wrong and my Sunday school classes and my congregation. The disposition to reject such an indictment of my ministry to others is so strong that my subconscious engages in an all-out smear campaign to discredit the "new wine."

But I still say, You *almost* can't teach an old dog new tricks. There are reasons that change is possible. The most important one is that the Holy Spirit gives the fruit of humility, so the threats to our ego are nullified. He opens our hearts to give heed to what we have resisted (Acts 16:14). What flesh and blood cannot do, God can do: "Flesh and blood did not reveal this to you, but My Father who is in heaven" (Matthew 16:17). Paul had a great deal of confidence in this work of God. He expressed it in Philippians 3:15, "Let those of us who are mature be thus minded; and if in anything you are otherwise minded, *God will reveal that also to you"* (RSV, emphasis added). The old dogs at Philippi would be changed in due season.

One of the ways the Spirit helps us change is by teaching us that God is merciful with our inadequate notions of him and is willing not only to commune with us, but also bless others in spite of our flawed conceptions. Paul reminds us, "For our knowledge is imperfect…but when the perfect comes, the imperfect will pass away…. For now we see in a mirror dimly, but then face to face. Now I know in part; then I shall understand fully, even as I have been fully understood" (1 Corinthians 13:9–12, RSV). So we may be relieved that our walk with God has been authentic and people have been blessed by our ministry even if we have had flawed ideas about God and his ways.

This does not mean truth doesn't matter. Bad theology will eventually hurt people and dishonor God in proportion to its badness. J. I. Packer reminds us, "Evangelical theology is precise and sharp honed as a result of centuries of controversy reflecting the conviction that *where truth fails, life will fail, too" (Keep in Step with the Spirit* [Old Tappan, N.J.: Fleming H. Revell Co., 1984], 173). Nevertheless, God is patient and merciful as faith gropes its way toward understanding. And this, as much as anything, frees us old dogs to make the adjustments necessary, as we strive to eliminate the wood, hay and stubble that will be burned up in the last day (1 Corinthians 3:12–13). Packer gives a hope-filled and balanced view of crucial truth and compassionate tolerance in the heart of God:

> It is certain that God blesses believers precisely and invariably by blessing to them something of his truth, and that misbelief, as such, is in its own nature spiritually barren and destructive. Yet anyone who deals with souls will again and again be amazed at the gracious generosity with which God blesses to needy ones what looks to us like a very tiny needle of truth hidden amid whole haystacks of mental error. As I have said, countless sinners truly experience the saving grace of Jesus Christ and the transforming power of the Holy Spirit while their notions about both are erratic and largely incorrect. (Where, indeed, would any of us be if God's blessing had been withheld till all our notions were right? Every Christian without exception experiences far more in the way of mercy and help than the quality of his notions warrants.) (*Keep in Step with the Spirit,* 20)

118

SENECA, C. S. LEWIS, AND A SALE

How Does Death Steal Our Days?

Strange how these things fell together. I was reading Seneca's letter on saving time and came across this insight: "We are mistaken when we look forward to death; the major portion of death has already passed. Whatever years lie behind us are already in death's hands" *(Ad Lucilium Epistulae Morales,* I, 1, Loeb Classical Library [London: William Heinemann Ltd., 1967], 3). I have not been able to shake off this sober sentence. It is true. Death is the taking away of future days on earth. But are not our future days being taken from us one by one every day, irrevocably? "Whatever years lie behind us are already in death's hands." Two days cannot be lived: yesterday and the day after you die. Yesterday is dead. It is utterly calcified as historical fact. You cannot alter the past. Something will die today, namely, all the opportunities of today.

Then I picked up a new book that Noël brought home from the library. It was the diaries of C. S. Lewis's brother, called *Brothers and Friends.* I read these words, written by Warren Lewis about his brother, whom he called Jack: "Oddly enough, as time goes on the vision of Jack as he was in his later years grows fainter, that of him in earlier days more and more vivid. It is the Jack of the attic and the little end room, the Jack of Daudelspiels and walks and jaunts, the Jack of the early and middle years, whom I miss so cruelly. An absurd feeling, for even had he lived, that Jack had already died" *(Brothers and Friends,* ed. Clyde S. Kilby and Marjorie Mead [San Francisco: Harper and Row Publishers, 1982], 255). There it was again, the gaping grave of the past, swallowing up one day after the other until its teeth clamp down once and for all. "Whatever years lie behind us are already in death's hands."

But someone will say: "There is a difference. The days taken from us by the past have at least been lived. But the days taken from us by death are in the future and have not been lived." That's true. And it leads to the final thing that fell together. Last Friday, the Word I brought up from the basement for the family's awakening at 6:30 a.m. was Colossians 4:5, "Walk in wisdom toward those outside, purchasing the time." Do we purchase what is already ours? No. We purchase what is offered to us. Each day is on sale for anyone who will purchase it. If we do not purchase it, we lose it—forever. And we may as well not have lived it. It was no more ours than tomorrow is ours. When the past consumes a day unpurchased, it consumes it as fully as death consumes the future. Oh, how many hours are squandered! As Seneca says, "What man can you show me who places any value on his time, who reckons the worth of each day, who understands that he is dying daily?" *(Ad Lucilium, 3)*.

This is the wisdom of God: Purchase the day! Purchase the hour! Purchase the moment! Spend whatever it takes to buy each hour and harness it in the chariot of your highest, eternal goal—the glory of God.

⟡

119

JESUS DELIVERS US FROM THE WRATH TO COME

How Shall Happiness Not Be Thin?

Meditation on 1 Thessalonians 1:10, RSV

Jesus...delivers us from the wrath to come.

I have said once before in these pages that it was good for me as a boy to hear my preacher-father say with the most earnest expression that I could then imagine, "It is appointed unto men once to die, but after this the judgment..." (Hebrews 9:27, KJV). It brought a certain weight to my life. And I am so thankful.

In order for the gospel to make sense, we must expect and fear the wrath of God. But for the wrath of God to be expected and feared, we must despise sin as an offense against God. But for sin to be despised in this way, we must know and love God as supremely pure and holy and righteous. This is why the mission statement of our church is so relevant: "We exist to spread a passion for the *supremacy of God* in all things for the joy of all peoples through Jesus Christ." Until there is a passion for his supremacy, there will be little fear of his wrath. And without the fear of his wrath, who will sing and shout over the words, "Jesus...delivers us from the wrath to come" (1 Thessalonians 1:10)? And if *we* are not singing and shouting over the good news, why would we bother to tell others?

We need to dwell on the biblical worldview until it displaces the secular air we breathe every day. And one aspect of that worldview is the reality of the wrath of God. It is so little spoken of. But what could be a more weighty and relevant topic? Without knowing it and feeling it as we ought, our seriousness will be superficial and our happiness will be thin. So, for the sake of your authenticity as a Christian, and for the sake of your joy, and for the sake of ballast in your ship when the winds of silliness threaten your soul, think on the wrath of God. (Emphasis added in the following verses.)

Romans 1:18—For the *wrath of God* is revealed from heaven against all ungodliness and unrighteousness of men, who suppress the truth in unrighteousness.

Romans 2:5–8—Because of your stubbornness and unrepentant heart you are storing up wrath for yourself in the *day of wrath* and revelation of the righteous judgment of God, who will render to every man according to his deeds: to those who by perseverance in doing good seek for glory and honor and immortality, eternal life; but to those who are selfishly ambitious and do not obey the truth, but obey unrighteousness, *wrath and indignation.*

Romans 9:22—What if God, because he desires to demonstrate *his wrath* and to make his power known, endured with much patience vessels of wrath prepared for destruction? (author's translation)

Romans 12:19—Never take your own revenge, beloved, but leave room for the wrath of God, for it is written, *"Vengeance is mine, I will repay,"* says the Lord.

Ephesians 2:3—[We] were by nature *children of wrath,* even as the rest.

Ephesians 5:6—The *wrath of God* comes upon the sons of disobedience.

Colossians 3:5–6—Immorality, impurity, passion, evil desire, and greed, which amounts to idolatry…it is on account of these things that the *wrath of God* will come.

Revelation 6:16–17, RSV—They will say to the mountains and to the rocks, "Fall on us and hide us…from *the wrath of the Lamb;* for *the great day of…wrath* has come; and who is able to stand?"

1 Thessalonians 5:9–10—God has not destined us for *wrath,* but for obtaining salvation through our Lord Jesus Christ.

"Jesus…delivers us from the wrath to come!"

120

A Surprise Endorsement for Doctrine

Teach Us What the Bible Says

God gives good press to doctrine. But surveys of evangelicals usually do not—until recently. In God's book, knowing his Son and believing true things about him is liberty. "You will know the truth, and the truth will set you free" (John 8:32). God's self-revelation in the Bible is not a wax nose. Paul calls it "the standard of teaching to which you were committed" (Romans 6:17). It's a standard, a yardstick, a pattern. You measure truth by it. Elsewhere he calls it "the whole counsel of God" (Acts 20:27), and the "pattern of the sound words" and "the good deposit entrusted to you" (2 Timothy 1:13–14). It does not change. Our everlasting salvation is determined by whether we believe it: "Whoever abides in the teaching has both the Father and the Son" (2 John 1:9). Depart from the doctrine, and you depart from Christ. Or, better, keep watch over your doctrine and "you will save...yourself" (1 Timothy 4:16).

That's high praise for good doctrine. You would think evangelicals would agree. But we are more likely to hear things like, "Christ unites; doctrine divides," or, "Ask, 'Whom do you trust?', not 'What do you believe?'" The minimization of biblical doctrine is common. But if we are not willing to get a high estimation of doctrine from God, perhaps we can get it from George Barna.

He has been surveying American evangelicals to see if we practice what we preach. He is finding that we don't preach doctrine from the Bible, and therefore don't practice differently from the world. For example, he says that evangelicals divorce at about the same rate as the nation at large. Only 9 percent of evangelicals tithe. Of twelve thousand teenagers who took the pledge to wait for marriage, 80 percent had sex outside marriage in the next seven years. Twenty-six percent of traditional evangelicals do not think premarital sex is wrong. White evangelicals are more likely than Catholics and mainline Protestants to object to having black neighbors.

According to Barna's definition an "evangelical" is willing to say, "I have made a personal commitment to Jesus Christ that is still important in my life today." In addition, they agree with several other things like: Jesus lived a sinless life; eternal salvation is only through grace, not works; Christians have a personal responsibility to evangelize non-Christians; Satan exists. Barna says that 7 to 8 percent of the U.S. population is in this group. And they do not live substantially differently than the world.

But Barna has now developed a new set of criteria that defines a group within evangelicalism who has a "biblical worldview." This means they say that "the Bible is the moral standard" and "absolute moral truths exist and are conveyed through the Bible." In addition they believe that God is the all-knowing, all-powerful Creator who still rules the universe, and that salvation cannot be earned by their deeds, and that the Bible is totally accurate in all it teaches. This group is substantially smaller than the broad evangelical group.

For those who belittle doctrine as troublesome, it may come as a surprise that this group lives differently from the world. Ronald Sider, in his new book, *The Scandal of the Evangelical Conscience*, describes the difference:

> They are 9 times more likely than all the others to avoid 'adult-only' material on the Internet. They are 4 times more likely than other Christians to boycott objectionable companies and products and twice as likely to choose not to watch a movie specifically because of its bad content. They are 3 times more likely than other adults not to use tobacco products and twice as likely to volunteer time to help needy people. Forty-nine percent of all born-again Christians with a biblical world view have volunteered more than an hour in the previous week to an organization serving the poor, whereas only 29 percent of born-

again Christians without a biblical world view and only 22 percent of non-born-again Christians had done so.

The conclusion is that doctrine matters. Sider puts it like this:

Barna's findings on the different behavior of Christians with a biblical worldview underline the importance of theology. Biblical orthodoxy does matter. One important way to end the scandal of contemporary Christian behavior is to work and pray fervently for the growth of orthodox theological belief in our churches.

Who would have thought that the very survey system that lures so many to put their finger in the wind of opinion would tell them, Take your finger down and teach the people what the Bible says?

⊙〰〰〰〰⊙

121

A JEWISH RESPONSE TO
THE PASSION OF THE CHRIST

An Open Letter to Rabbi Marcia Zimmerman,
Temple Israel

March 3, 2004

Dear Rabbi Zimmerman,

Thank you for your e-mail of 2-27-04 addressed to some of us among the downtown clergy concerning Mel Gibson's movie, *The Passion of the Christ.* I read most of your letter to our people on Sunday morning as part of my sermon. We take heart from your expression of a "deep and abiding commitment to understand each other [with] a willingness to discuss difficult issues." With that in view I thought I would write, for you and for our people, a response to your letter and to the movie from a New Testament perspective.

We believe that the New Testament, as well as the Tanach, are the inspired Word of God and provide a progressive revelation of God's dealings with humankind—a revelation that is unified and reliable. Therefore we try, all too imperfectly, to bring our lives into conformity to what the New Testament teaches about Jesus Christ as the fulfillment of all the Scriptures.

We respect the misgivings you have about the portrayal of Jews in the film and the possibility, as you say, "of the potential rifts this film could open once again…between Jews and Christians." There are "rifts" that we do not want to open—rifts of hostility, or stereotyping prejudice, or violence. These we renounce. Indeed we apologize for them and repent of such behavior toward Jews in history from the Christian community.

But there is a tension, isn't there, between what you call "responsible, accurate and sensitive portrayals of the Passion," on the one hand, and the "mission to build bridges of understanding and peace"? What shall we do when a "responsible, accurate and sensitive" portrayal of the Passion of Jesus builds a bridge of understanding but not always peace? What if the bridge of understanding produces anger? This was sometimes the experience of such bridge-building in the New Testament, and has been the experience of some of us today.

We believe that a responsible, accurate, sensitive portrayal of Jesus' suffering includes the statement of its loving purpose. Here are several New Testament examples: "Christ Jesus came into the world to save sinners, of whom I am the foremost" (1 Timothy 1:15); "God shows his love for us in that while we were yet sinners Christ died for us" (Romans 5:8); "God so loved the world that he gave his only Son, that whoever believes in him should not perish but have eternal life" (John 3:16).

Most Jews do not mind Christians enjoying these religious sentiments. The "rift" comes when the accurate, responsible, sensitive portrayal of Jesus includes his claim to be the only way to God. He made this claim repeatedly. "I am the way, and the truth, and the life. No one comes to the Father except through me" (John 14:6); "Whoever believes in the Son has eternal life; whoever does not obey the Son shall not see life, but the wrath of God remains on him" (John 3:36); "Everyone who acknowledges me before men, I also will acknowledge before my Father who is in heaven, but whoever denies me before men, I also will deny before my Father who is in heaven" (Matthew 10:32–33).

The bridge that we desire to cross between the Jewish and Christian faith is one that was built for us in the New Testament. It includes an explanation and invitation to all of us—Jews and Gentiles—to know Jesus as the magnificent fulfillment of Isaiah 53. "Out of the anguish of his soul he shall see and be satisfied; by his knowledge shall the righteous one, my servant, make many to be accounted righteous, and he shall bear their iniquities" (verse 11). The bridge is single. There is one way to God together: the way of faith in Jesus, the Jewish Messiah.

Peace and reconciliation between humans and God, and between Jew and Gentile, are one of the great achievements of the gospel of Christ. We Gentile Christians stand amazed that we have been included in the covenant God made through Abraham. The apostle Paul celebrates this astonishing grace: "But now in Christ Jesus you [Gentiles] who once were far off have been brought near by the blood of Christ. For he himself is our peace, who has made us both [Jew and Gentile] one and has broken down in his flesh the dividing wall of hostility by abolishing the law of commandments and ordinances, that he might create in himself one new man in place of the two, so making peace, and might reconcile us both to God in one body through the cross, thereby killing the hostility" (Ephesians 2:13–16).

This is the one bridge to God and each other—the cross of Christ, which Mel Gibson's movie so powerfully portrays. May God give us grace to cross this bridge together. I enclose a copy of my book, *The Passion of Jesus Christ,* with the hope that it will help advance the aim we share "to understand each other [with] a willingness to discuss difficult issues."

John Piper, Pastor
Bethlehem Baptist Church

122

Use Means, but Don't Trust in Means; Trust in God

A Lesson from George Mueller's Life and Teaching

This sounds so simple. In principle it is. But in practice we sinners are wired to trust in means, not God. Over and over I devise plans, and then find my initial enthusiasm rise or fall as the plan seems smart or not. This is trust in plans, not trust in God. There is no doubt God wants us to use means to get his work done. But just as clearly he wants us not to trust in these means. "The horse is made ready for the day of battle, but the victory belongs to the LORD" (Proverbs 21:31). Therefore, our confidence should not be in the horse, but in the Lord. "Some trust in chariots and some in horses, but we trust in the name of the LORD our God" (Psalm 20:7).

George Mueller's life was devoted to vindicating this truth. He explained once how it relates to our vocation. We should work to earn a living and supply our needs, but we should not trust in our work but in God. Otherwise we will be ever anxious that our needs will not be met if we can't work. But if we are trusting God, not our work, then if God ordains that we lose our job, we can be confident he will meet our needs, and so we do not need to be anxious. Here is the way he put it.

> "Why do I carry on this business, or why am I engaged in this trade or profession?" In most instances, so far as my experience goes, which I have gathered in my service among the saints during the last

fifty-one years and a half, I believe the answer would be: "I am engaged in my earthly calling, that I may earn the means of obtaining the necessaries of life for myself and family." Here is the chief error from which almost all the rest of the errors, which are entertained by children of God, relative to their calling, spring. It is no right and scriptural motive, to be engaged in a trade, or business, or profession, merely in order to earn the means for the obtaining of the necessaries of life for ourselves and family; but we should work, because it is the Lord's will concerning us. This is plain from the following passages: 1 Thess. 4:11–12; 2 Thess. 3:10–12; Eph. 4:28.

It is quite true that, in general, the Lord provides the necessaries of life by means of our ordinary calling; but that that is not THE REASON why we should work, is plain enough from the consideration, that if our possessing the necessaries of life depended upon our ability of working, we could never have freedom from anxiety, for we should always have to say to ourselves, and what shall I do when I am too old to work? or when by reason of sickness I am unable to earn my bread? But if on the other hand, we are engaged in our earthly calling, because it is the will of the Lord concerning us that we should work, and that thus laboring we may provide for our families and also be able to support the weak, the sick, the aged, and the needy, then we have good and scriptural reason to say to ourselves: should it please the Lord to lay me on a bed of sickness, or keep me otherwise by reason of infirmity or old age, or want of employment, from earning my bread by means of the labor of my hands, or my business, or my profession, He will yet provide for me. (*A Narrative of Some of the Lord's Dealing with George Mueller, Written by Himself, Jehovah Magnified. Addresses by George Mueller Complete and Unabridged,* vol. 1 [Muskegon, Mich.: Dust and Ashes Publications, 2003], 393)

This truth applies not only to our vocation but to all areas of life. Moment by moment we use means to keep us alive and accomplish the purposes of God (food, houses, phones, cars, medicines, doctors, builders, advisers, etc). The lesson we need to learn is not to trust in these things when we use them, but to trust wholly in God. This applies also to planning for our church. We plan. We budget. We teach and preach and counsel. The temptation continually is to trust in these things and not in God to work in and through and without these things. So as we dream toward ministry and missions, let us use means, but let us trust God. His promises are the only sure thing. All our means are fallible.

Mueller summed up the principle like this: "This is one of the great secrets in connection with successful service for the Lord; to work as if everything depended upon our diligence, and yet not to rest in the least upon our exertions, but upon the blessing of the Lord." (*Narrative*, vol. 2, 290). Or, as the Bible more carefully says it: "Work out your own salvation with fear and trembling, for it is God who works in you, both to will and to work for his good pleasure" (Philippians 2:12–13). Even more to the point, Paul says: "By the grace of God I am what I am, and his grace toward me was not in vain. On the contrary, I worked harder than any of them, though it was not I, but the grace of God that is with me" (1 Corinthians 15:10).

How to Speak About God When He Hurts Us

Eleven Truths from the Book of Lamentations

The book of Lamentations is the heart-cry of Jeremiah when he and his people were being hurt by God, and by their enemies, and by their own sin. How he speaks of this divine hurting shows us some of the various ways we may speak about God in our own pain. If we affirm them all, then not one of them will be taken amiss.

The Lord directly does the hurting (2:1–4).

> "The Lord in his anger has set the daughter of Zion under a cloud!... The Lord has swallowed up without mercy all the habitations of Jacob;... He has cut down in fierce anger all the might of Israel;... He has burned like a flaming fire in Jacob, consuming all around.... He has killed all who were delightful in our eyes in the tent of the daughter of Zion."

The enemies have done the hurting and God has exalted their might (2:16–17).

> "All your enemies rail against you; they hiss, they gnash their teeth, they cry.... The Lord has done what he purposed;... He has made the enemy rejoice over you and exalted the might of your foes."

The enemy has done the hurting, as if the Lord were not watching! (1:9–11; 3:49–50).

> "Her fall is terrible; she has no comforter. 'O Lord, behold my affliction, for the enemy has triumphed!... Look, O Lord, and see, for I am despised.'... My eyes will flow without ceasing, without respite, until the Lord from heaven looks down and sees."

The hurting happens as if by God's "forgetting" and "forsaking" them (5:20).

> "Why do you forget us forever, why do you forsake us for so many days?"

The Lord will repay the enemies who did the hurting on earth (3:64).

> "You will repay them, O Lord, according to the work of their hands."

The Lord will follow his hurting with compassion (3:32).

> "Though he cause grief, he will have compassion according to the abundance of his steadfast love."

God's hurting us is not "from his heart"—not his deepest delight (3:33).

> "He does not willingly [literally "from his heart" *millibbo*] afflict or grieve the children of men."

In his hurting the Lord shows mercy every morning (3:22–23).

> "The steadfast love of the Lord never ceases; his mercies never come to an end; they are new every morning; great is your faithfulness."

God's decisive mercy is his causing the erring people to repent; he removes the cause of his own wrath (5:21).

> "Cause us to return (*hasibenu*) to yourself, O Lord, and we will return (*wunasub*)! Renew our days as of old."

When God is hurting us, wait patiently for the salvation of the Lord (3:26).

> "The Lord is good to those who wait for him, to the soul who seeks him. It is good that one should wait quietly for the salvation of the Lord. It is good for a man that he bear the yoke in his youth. Let him sit alone in silence when it is laid on him."

In and after God's hurting us, he is our only hope and portion (3:24).

> "'The Lord is my portion,' says my soul, 'therefore I will hope in him.'"

124

WHAT DID CHRIST PURCHASE FOR YOUR CHILDREN WITH HIS BLOOD?

The Blessings and Limits of Christian Ancestry

Thankfully, the blood of Christ divides and unites families. "Do you think that I have come to give peace on earth? No, I tell you, but rather division…. They will be divided, father against son and son against father, mother against daughter and daughter against mother" (Luke 12:51–53). "Whoever loves father or mother more than me is not worthy of me" (Matthew 10:37). This is good news. It means that coming from an unbelieving family is no sure curse. A family may be graciously broken by the belief of a child.

When Paul said to Gentile converts, "You were bought with a price" (1 Corinthians 6:20; 7:23), he knew that the blood of Christ had broken a family line of unbelief. If you are the offspring of unbelievers it is good news to hear Paul say, "It is not the children of the flesh who are the children of God, but the children of the promise are counted as offspring" (Romans 9:8).

Biology seals no curse and guarantees no blessing. That is a warning against despair for the offspring of pagans and against presumption for Christian parents.

But did the blood of Christ purchase no privileges for the children of believers? Did the blood of Christ not unite families across generations? What about Acts 2:39? "For the promise is for you and for your children and for all who are far off, everyone whom the Lord our God calls to himself." What about Psalm

103:17–18? "The steadfast love of the LORD is from everlasting to everlasting on those who fear him, and his righteousness to children's children, to those who keep his covenant and remember to do his commandments." Or Exodus 20:5–6? "I the LORD your God am a jealous God, visiting the iniquity of the fathers on the children to the third and the fourth generation of those who hate me, but showing steadfast love to thousands of those who love me and keep my commandments."

Yes. Christ did purchase privileges for the children of believers. But he did not guarantee their salvation. Each of those three texts makes clear that the blessing which comes to the future generations of believers comes only to those who are "called by God" (Acts 2:39), "keep his covenant" (Psalm 103:18), and "love him" (Exodus 20:6). Do all the children of believers love God and keep covenant with him by faith in Christ? No. There are enough examples of believers in the Bible whose children did not believe to show us that a parent's faith does not secure a child's.

The point of Romans 9:7–13 is to show that Isaac not Ishmael, and Jacob not Esau, received the full blessing of being born to believing parents. The blood of Jesus divides not just when parents are unbelieving, but also when children are unbelieving. This is what Jesus had in mind when he said, "A person's enemies will be those of his own household.... Whoever loves son or daughter more than me is not worthy of me." A Christian parent may face this choice: allegiance to Christ or allegiance to child?

But I say again, yes, Christ did purchase privileges for the children of believers. It would seem to be pointless to say, "The promise is for you and for your children" (Acts 2:39), and to say, "His righteousness is to children's children" (Psalm 103:18), if there was no more significance to a Christian ancestry than a pagan one. There is a good that comes to the children of believers.

God says in Jeremiah 32:39, "I will give them one heart and one way, that they may fear me forever, *for their own good and the good of their children after them.*" This "good" is not the guarantee of faith, but the gift of God's word (Deuteronomy 6:6–7), the restraint of God's discipline (Ephesians 6:4), the demonstration of God's love (Colossians 3:21), and the power of prayer (Job

1:5). God has ordained, regularly and normally, to work through these means for the salvation of the children of believers.

For this Christ died. Christian parents honor the blood of Jesus when they follow his ways for the sake of their children.

⟳

125

How the Archbishop Got
It Wrong

Humane Confidence Versus Destructive Doubt

When calamity brings horrific death and suffering, as in Beslan, Russia, we do not honor the dead or the dignity of human beings by making doubt the measure of their worth. But the archbishop of Canterbury, Rowan Williams, seems to think otherwise. His interview on the BBC was sensitive and caring, but its ending was disheartening. He said that the Beslan catastrophe caused his faith to tremble. That is good. We should tremble indeed in a world so ripe for judgment, where we know our own sins keenly. But he went further and said something that should dismay us when we consider his rank and influence as a leader of Christ's people. "When you see the depth of energy that people can put into such evil, then…there is a flicker, there is a doubt. It would be inhuman, I think, not to react in that way."

I find that statement, coming from the shepherd of millions of Anglicans, to be incredible. Perhaps it was a slip. If so, I am happy that this article does not apply to the archbishop. But it is likely that for many, it would be no slip. Many would indeed say what the archbishop implied: To be humane in the face of great suffering, one must at least have a flicker of doubt toward God! This statement is symptomatic not of deep compassion, but of deep confusion—or worse, unbelief. Against this fragile vision of God's goodness and power, may there rise from millions of Christ's people a sad and sorrowing, "Not so, Reverend Williams! Not so."

It does not belittle people or make light of their pain when we hold fast to God's power and goodness while we hold out our hand to the suffering in help and prayer. I would venture to say that the most compassionate and merciful saints in history have sacrificed themselves for the suffering, precisely because their faith in God's sovereign goodness was unshakable. They would have found the archbishop's final comment unintelligible.

Nor do we learn such counsel from Jesus. Never, never did he doubt the goodness or power of his Father while confronting the worst evils in the universe. And this did not make him "inhuman." It made him perfectly human. His combination of compassion for people and confidence in God is the call on our lives for how to respond to suffering. It is unthinkable that Jesus would make doubt in his Father the test of compassion for suffering Russians.

Never did he teach us, or even hint, that we should doubt the reality of God's goodness and power when facing unspeakable evil. When people confronted him with the slaughter of the Galileans whose blood Pilate mingled with their sacrifices, he spoke very differently from the archbishop: "He answered them, 'Do you think that these Galileans were worse sinners than all the other Galileans, because they suffered in this way? No, I tell you; but unless you repent, you will all likewise perish'" (Luke 13:2–3).

For those who are saturated and shaped by all the words and ways of Jesus, not only does horrific evil today not bring doubt of God, it does not even bring surprise. Jesus labored to help us be ready for the worst of evils, even Islamic terrorists. He taught us that there would be "terrors" (an amazingly relevant word for what "terrorists" cause—Luke 21:11). He said that there would be terrible famines and plagues. Betrayal would become common and even parents would hand over children, "and some of you they will put to death" (Luke 21:16). People will be "fainting with fear and with foreboding of what is coming on the world" (Luke 21:28). And, perhaps most relevant of all in this day of religious terrorism, Jesus said, "The hour is coming when whoever kills you will think he is offering service to God" (John 16:2).

But in spite of all this evil and suffering, Jesus did not even remotely suggest that we should have a flicker of doubt toward the goodness and sovereignty of God, or that somehow it would be less humane to hold fast to God with unshakable hope and undoubting faith. Rather Jesus did the opposite. He strove to help us maintain faith in the face of horrifying evil: "When you see these things taking place, you know that the kingdom of God is near" (Luke 21:31). This is not the suggestion of doubt, but the certainty of hope. Again he says that when you see these unspeakable evils happening around you, you should "raise your heads, because your redemption is drawing near" (Luke 21:38). This is not a time for weakening faith, but unwavering hope.

The gift that followers of Christ bring to the suffering world is not the empathy of doubt, but the power of hope. We do not join the world in their anger at God or their questioning of his existence or justice or mercy. The very thing that survivors of suffering need most is hope in God through Jesus Christ. This will not be given by those who make its uncertainty the measure of our compassion. It is unbiblical and unmerciful to say that what suffering people need most must be doubted in order to prove our love for them.

126

SIN, CIVIL RIGHTS, AND MISSIONS

The Amazing Role of Sober Truth

The biblical doctrine [of?] human depravity is a great antidote to racism. I have seen this recently in two very different articles. One is by Andrew Walls called "The Evangelical Revival, the Missionary Movement, and Africa" (*The Missionary Movement in Christian History* [Maryknoll, NY: Orbis Books], 79–101). He points out that the Great Awakening in America and England (1730s and '40s) gave rise to the modern foreign missionary movement. One of the ways it did so was by clarifying the unity between the sinful homeland and the sinful heathen.

> There was no difference between the spiritual state of a pleasure-seeking duchess (though baptized and adhering to the prevailing religious system of the higher and middle classes) and that of a South Sea Islander. That spiritual parity of the unregenerate of Christendom and the heathen abroad had important missionary consequences.... A consistent view of human solidarity in depravity shielded the first missionary generation from some of the worst excesses of racism. (79)

In other words, a dark view of our own depraved hearts, and a sense of brokenness before God, and a dependence on mercy in Christ make it harder for us to view other humans—whatever race—as less advantaged before God. The doctrine of total depravity unites us in desperate dependence on mercy. The early missionaries—with all their flaws and biases—knew this. And it helped them count others better than themselves for the sake of Christ (Philippians 2:3).

The other illustration of how the doctrine of depravity works against racism comes from a review of the book *A Stone of Hope: Prophetic Religion and the Death of Jim Crow* by David L. Chappell. Elisabeth Fox-Genovese shows how the theological convictions of the black leaders of the civil rights movement were very different from those of the white liberals who supported the movement. Liberalism as a movement has a high degree of confidence in human reason and in the inevitability of human progress away from barbarism. So they saw the civil rights movement in those terms and supported it.

But Martin Luther King and most of the other black leaders were cut from another cloth. They "believed that the natural tendency of this world and of human institutions (including churches) is toward corruption." This did not produce despair, but a "hopeful pessimism." Humans are bad, but God is good and powerful. He can and will establish justice. The bond of human depravity among all humans and all races, linked with the hope of redemption in Jesus Christ, provided a deep and powerful impulse for the civil rights movement that many of its white liberal participants did not understand.

> Seen through the lens of the leading black activists' view of the fallen and depraved character of human nature, liberal optimism seemed more than slightly facile, especially liberal views about the natural— indeed, inevitable—improvement of the position of minorities in general and black Americans in particular…. It is common to assume that southern blacks readily saw whites as sinful—and often with good reason. It is much less common to recognize that leaders like [Martin Luther] King also acknowledged the inherent sinfulness of black southerners. For all but racists on either side, the conclusion is inescapable: if, "of one blood He made them," then it inexorably follows that sinfulness adheres to the human condition shared by people of all races. The whole point of the civil rights movement was to affirm that fundamental equality of condition, yet many find irresistible the temptation to paint one side as entirely good and the other as entirely evil…. A heroism grounded in optimism is admirable and uplifting, but a heroism

grounded in the pessimism of prophetic faith is decisively more impressive and moving. (Elisabeth Fox-Genovese, "Hopeful Pessimism," in *Books and Culture*, July/August 2004, 9)

Stop and ponder these amazing illustrations of the role of sober truth—even truth about total depravity—in the global missionary movement and the civil rights movement. Oh, let us hold fast to the truth of Scripture! It will break out and do its good work in ways we never dreamed.

127

"ABHOR WHAT IS EVIL"

The Part About Mercy I Left out of the Sermon

In a recent sermon I exhorted our people to build their lives on the mercies of God in Jesus Christ. "I appeal to you therefore brothers, by the mercies of God…" (Romans 12:1). The part I left out is that mercy toward one person may require opposition, even pain, toward another.

We will see this when we get to verse 9. Back to back: love and hate. "Let love be genuine. Abhor what is evil." The word "abhor" is really strong. When you love deeply, you must hate passionately. Why? Because there are evils in the world that would destroy the beloved. If you are indifferent to what would destroy the one you love, you do not love.

The painful reality is that this evil almost always lodges in the heart of another human being. This means that hating the evil that humans can do to humans involves opposing the desires and actions of some people. That opposition (like Jesus' opposing the Pharisees with fierce words, or driving the money changers out of the temple) is not tender and may not look merciful. It may look at first like worldly anger and revenge. The difference is that mercy weeps with longing while it hates the evil.

Jesus embodied this in one vivid scene from Mark 3:5 where merciless leaders opposed his healing on the Sabbath: "He looked around at them with anger, grieved at their hardness of heart." Anger and grief. Hatred of evil and tears. Mercy grieves over the evil that it must oppose.

Mercy is not absolute. We cannot even know what mercy is until we know an absolute good besides mercy. Mercy aches to do people good. But until we know what is ultimately good for people, mercy doesn't know what to do. Therefore, mercy is not absolute. Christ is absolute. What is ultimately good for people is knowing and trusting and being satisfied with Christ. Mercy pities people who do not have this good. Mercy gets angry at forces in the world that discount Christ and keep people from seeing and trusting and loving Christ. But, like Jesus, Christian mercy looks on the world "with anger, grieved." It weeps as it opposes. Until we are able to weep over evil, we are probably not ready to fight evil.

One clear illustration of the way mercy demands abhorrence is Judge Phyllis Hamilton's nullification on June 1, 2004, of the ban on partial birth abortion. The congress had passed this ban into law in March of this year. The procedure of delivering a viable child partway out of the mother, then sucking the brains out of his or her head, is barbaric. The defense of it by the *Minneapolis Star Tribune* in Sunday's paper is appalling. Words fail to describe the outrage appropriately.

Here is the key sentence from the article in Sunday's paper: "Considerable evidence shows the procedure is often the safest option for a woman undergoing a lamentable late-term abortion." Think about that. Translation: "When a woman decides to kill her baby in the third trimester, the way to do it with least difficulty to the mom is to deliver the baby partway and then suck his brains out."

This is the world we live in. Without the biblical description about the depth of sin, it would be incomprehensible. What should mercy do? Defend the voiceless, helpless children. Offer every assistance to the mom before and after birth. Oppose the defenders of child-killing. And weep while you work. I thank God that thousands of crisis pregnancy centers around the country do that. Support them. And ask the Lord what more you should do.

128

GOD WORKS WONDERS

In Steady-State Obedience and in

Total Disobedience

1. Don't dream too small or pray too small about what God may do to save sinners and glorify his name in the midst of steady-state obedience.

God ordinarily works his wonders of mercy and salvation in the midst of our steady-state obedience. For example, in 2 Timothy 2:24–26 Paul says:

> The Lord's servant must not be quarrelsome but kind to everyone, able to teach, patiently enduring evil, 25 correcting his opponents with gentleness. God may perhaps grant them repentance leading to a knowledge of the truth, 26 and they may escape from the snare of the devil, after being captured by him to do his will.

Our duty is steady-state obedience: don't be quarrelsome, be kind, teach well, be patient, don't return evil for evil, correct with gentleness. In the midst of this steady-state obedience, "God may perhaps grant them repentance." We should not assume that nothing extraordinary will happen while we persevere in daily faithfulness. That is where God loves to act in supernatural ways.

Therefore, we should pray: "O Lord, make the fruit of our lives utterly disproportionate to the measure of our faithfulness."

2. Don't dream too small or pray too small about what God may do to save sinners and glorify his name in the midst of total disobedience.

God is not limited to work only where we are obeying and praying and dreaming of his intervention.

For example, in Acts 22:5–8 Paul tells us about how Christ broke into his totally disobedient life when no human being had planned or dreamed it.

> I journeyed toward Damascus to take those also who were there and bring them in bonds to Jerusalem to be punished. 6 "As I was on my way and drew near to Damascus, about noon a great light from heaven suddenly shone around me. 7 And I fell to the ground and heard a voice saying to me, 'Saul, Saul, why are you persecuting me?' 8 And I answered, 'Who are you, Lord?' And he said to me, 'I am Jesus of Nazareth, whom you are persecuting.'"

In the midst of Paul's total disobedience God broke in and made Paul into a great missionary. Here's a contemporary version of God's inbreaking power: D. James Kennedy, pastor of Coral Ridge Presbyterian Church, tells the story of his conversion in *Indelible Ink,* edited by Scott Larsen (WaterBrook Press, 2003):

> At the age of twenty-three, I was a spiritual derelict. Worse than that, I was thoroughly satisfied with my secular lifestyle as a ballroom dance instructor in Tampa's Arthur Murray Studio. I was a college dropout, but making good money in a job that I immensely enjoyed. I was single, popular, and pretty well unhampered by moral restraints. Nor could I recall ever having heard the gospel....
>
> That was before my clock radio, in my rented apartment on South Boulevard in Tampa, threw me a curve. I had come in from an all-night dance party and thought I had set the appliance to wake me at the proper time with appropriate music for a soothing return to consciousness. But what I heard that Sunday afternoon was...the thundering voice of Dr. Donald Gray Barnhouse, pastor of Philadelphia's Tenth Presbyterian Church. I jumped out of bed to switch the dial but was

stopped almost in mid-flight by a question I couldn't brush aside.

In the penetrating, stentorian tones for which he was famous, this great preacher and broadcast evangelist asked, "Suppose that you were to die today and stand before God, and He were to ask you, 'What right do you have to enter into my heaven?'—what would you say?" I was completely dumbfounded. I had never thought of such a thing as that, and my nonchalance suddenly evaporated into thin air.

I sat on the edge of my bed, as though transfixed, groping for an answer to this simple question. I had enough common sense to realize that, even though I had no background in the Bible, this was the most important question that had ever entered my mind. (69–70)

In mercy, God led Kennedy to a nearby corner newsstand where he asked simply, "Do you have any religious books?" He was given Fulton Oursler's *The Greatest Story Ever Told*. In this way, with no human design or dream, God saved D. James Kennedy.

Therefore, let us pursue steady-state obedience, but let us also pray, "O Lord, grant new life, and glorify your name, where no human has dreamed it or designed it."

129

SURRENDERING AND DEMANDING RIGHTS: TWO KINDS OF LOVE

Thoughts on Mercy and Justice in
2 Thessalonians 3:6–15

*Now we command you, brothers, in the name
of our Lord Jesus Christ, that you keep away
from any brother who is walking in idleness
and not in accord with the tradition that you
received from us. ⁷ For you yourselves know
how you ought to imitate us, because we were
not idle when we were with you, ⁸ nor did we
eat anyone's bread without paying for it, but
with toil and labor we worked night and day,
that we might not be a burden to any of you.
⁹ It was not because we do not have that right,
but to give you in ourselves an example to
imitate. ¹⁰ For even when we were with you, we
would give you this command: If anyone is not
willing to work, let him not eat. ¹¹ For we hear
that some among you walk in idleness, not
busy at work, but busybodies. ¹² Now such
persons we command and encourage in the
Lord Jesus Christ to do their work quietly and*

to earn their own living. 13 As for you,

brothers, do not grow weary in doing good.

14 If anyone does not obey what we say in this

letter, take note of that person, and have

nothing to do with him, that he may be

ashamed. 15 Do not regard him as an enemy,

but warn him as a brother.

By surrendering and demanding a right at the same time, Paul modeled two forms of love.

In verses 8–9 he surrendered the right to be paid by the church for his ministry: "With toil and labor we worked night and day, that we might not be a burden to any of you. It was not because we do not have that right, but to give you in ourselves an example to imitate." So Paul has the right to be paid simply for preaching. But he surrenders that right in this case to accomplish something else: giving an example to the church of secular work for self-support.

But Paul also demanded a right in verse 10—the right to receive work for pay: "If anyone is not willing to work, let him not eat."

Both of these—the surrender of a right, and the demand of a right—are forms of love. Surrendering a right is love because Paul sacrifices his own right in order to model a productive way to live. Demanding a right is love because it aims not at self-aggrandizement, but at the good of the brother. This is what verses 14–15 make plain:

> If anyone does not obey what we say in this letter, take note of that person, and have nothing to do with him, that he may be ashamed. 15 Do not regard him as an enemy, but warn him as a brother.

The aim is not alienation, but restoration from destructive behavior through tough love that insists on change.

Another way to say it is that Paul was modeling mercy and justice. Mercy: because, in working a secular job for his bread, he gave more time and effort than was required, and demanded less than he had a right to receive. Justice: because, in demanding that others work, he was forbidding them to demand mercy from the church and insisting that they earn their food.

Now when should we do which? How do you know when to love with mercy and when to love with justice? Three guidelines:

Know your personality well and be vigilant not to indulge your bent carelessly. If you are naturally merciful, consider justice seriously. If you are naturally judicial, consider mercy seriously. We are very likely to indulge our natural bent at the expense of love.

The more personal and private a matter is, the more likely surrendering rights will be the loving way. But the more communal and public a matter is, the more likely demanding rights will be the loving way. The reason for this is that, in public, demanding rights can be seen as a way of caring for others, not just yourself; but in private a demanded right will almost surely communicate self-aggrandizement, and a failure to treasure Christ above all.

Be sure in either case—loving with mercy, or loving with justice—that your burden is the greatest good for the greatest number. That is, seek to help the greatest number enjoy making much of Christ forever.

⟨⟩⟩

130

SHOULD ONLY UNANIMOUS DECISIONS GUIDE THE CHURCH?

Letter to a Friend on How Leadership Works

Someone challenged me recently to show why all decisions in church leadership should not be unanimous. In other words, why would you ever move forward without a unanimous leadership? The form of the question was, "Where is there an instance in the Bible in which disagreement didn't include sin by one of the parties or where it didn't lead to a parting of ways? Where is an example of disagreeing on a particular issue but maintaining fellowship and working together?"

We love unity and even unanimity at our church, and we want as much agreement as possible when the whole church votes on something. But we do not demand unanimity in order to move ahead. Here is what I wrote to explain why.

First of all, I sense a perfectionistic mindset behind the question. This mindset has a hard time living with ambiguities and imperfections and uncertainties. It tends to demand biblical warrant for things that may not be there. I think it is fundamentally flawed to approach Scripture with the notion that the absence of teaching on the necessity of unanimity can be replaced by the uniform presence of unanimity (even if it were there, which I doubt). This would be the same mindset that asks, "Is there a single place in the New

Testament where there was a church building?" Conclusion: Don't build church buildings; worship in homes. This mindset tends toward sectarian isolation with a growing perfectionism that makes visionary outreach and missions almost impossible because methods are always being second-guessed as insufficiently "biblical."

But now to your question. I would go first to Romans 14. Here we have manifest disagreements. Paul's goal here was not to create unanimous thinking (as wonderful as that would be, and as much as we should pray toward it), but to help them see their way through to unity without unanimity on the issue at hand. For example, verse 5: "One person esteems one day as better than another, while another esteems all days alike. Each one should be fully convinced in his own mind."

Then I would go to Philippians 3. Here Paul would like for them to come to one mind (as he often pleads), but he does not envision an inability to continue working together until that unanimity happens. He says, "I press on toward the goal for the prize of the upward call of God in Christ Jesus. Let those of us who are mature think this way, and if in anything you think otherwise, God will reveal that also to you. Only let us hold true to what we have attained" (3:14–16). This strikes me as amazingly realistic. There are some people who are not yet persuaded. If they took a vote now, there would be differences. But Paul does not talk in either-or terms for the fellowship. He sees process and movement. There is no reason to think the whole church is paralyzed till the minority arrives at agreement. That can even happen after a vote that they disagreed on.

Third, I would go to those texts that portray leaders admonishing the immature. For example, 1 Thessalonians 5:14: "Be at peace among yourselves. And we urge you, brothers, admonish the idle, encourage the fainthearted, help the weak, be patient with them all." This seems to me to imply that there will always be a range of maturity and wisdom in the church, and that there will always be people less able to see the wise path which others see. It would be very unwise to assume that there must be a time in the life of a church when these sins and flaws disappear long enough to take a vote on some issue with no flawed thinking or feeling or acting coming into play. There is a theology of grace and sovereignty that holds sway here. God rules over endless imperfect decisions. That is the only kind there are.

Bottom line: It is a tragedy when a body of spiritual leaders, or a body of believers in general, give the least mature people the veto power over wise counsel. There is simply nothing in the Bible that says a weak and unspiritual person in the church should be able to paralyze the advance of God's people. There will always be such people. The mindset that says God only leads his people by creating a community where there is no such weakness and carnality and finiteness is, in my judgment, an unbiblical and harmful mindset.

꧁꧂

131

TSUNAMI AND REPENTANCE

The Point of All Pleasure and Pain

From pulpits to news programs, from the *New York Times* to the *Wall Street Journal*, the message of the tsunami was missed. It is a double grief when lives are lost and lessons are not learned. Every deadly calamity is a merciful call from God for the living to repent. "Weep with those who weep," the Bible says. Yes, but let us also weep for our own rebellion against the living God. Lesson one: Weep for the dead. Lesson two: Weep for yourselves.

Every deadly calamity is a merciful call from God for the living to repent. That was Jesus' stunning statement to those who brought him news of calamity. The tower of Siloam had fallen, and eighteen people were crushed. What about this, Jesus? they asked. He answered, "Do you think that they were worse offenders than all the others who lived in Jerusalem? No, I tell you; but unless you repent, you will all likewise perish" (Luke 13:4–5).

The point of every deadly calamity is this: Repent. Let our hearts be broken that God means so little to us. Grieve that he is a whipping boy to be blamed for pain, but not praised for pleasure. Lament that he makes headlines only when man mocks his power, but no headlines for ten thousand days of wrath withheld. Let us rend our hearts that we love life more than we love Jesus Christ. Let us cast ourselves on the mercy of our Maker. He offers it through the death and resurrection of his Son.

This is the point of all pleasure and all pain. Pleasure says: "God is like this, only better; don't make an idol out of me. I only point." Pain says: "What sin deserves is like this, only worse; don't take offense at me. I am a merciful warning."

But the topless sunbathers amid the tsunami aftermath in Phuket, Thailand, did not get the message. Neither did the man who barely escaped the mighty wave with the help of a jungle gym and palm-leaf roof. He concluded, "I am left with an immense respect for the power of nature." He missed it. The point is: reverence for the Creator, not respect for creation.

Writing in the *New York Times*, David Brooks rightly scorns the celebration of nature's might: "When Thoreau [celebrates] savage wildness of nature, he sounds, this week, like a boy who has seen a war movie and thinks he has experienced the glory of combat." But Brooks sees no message in the calamity: "This is a moment to feel deeply bad, for the dead and for those of us who have no explanation."

David Hart, writing in the *Wall Street Journal*, goes beyond Brooks and pronounces: "No Christian is licensed to utter odious banalities about God's inscrutable counsels or blasphemous suggestions that all this mysteriously serves God's good ends."

These responses are foreseen in Scripture: "I killed your young men with the sword…yet you did not return to me, declares the Lord" (Amos 4:10). "They cursed the name of God who had power over these plagues. They did not repent and give him glory" (Revelation 16:9).

Contrary to Hart's pronouncement, the Christian Scriptures do indeed license us to speak of God's "inscrutable counsels" and how he works in all things for mysterious good ends. To call this banal and blasphemous is like a bird calling the wind under its wing wicked.

Jesus said that the minutest event in nature is under the control of God. "Are not two sparrows sold for a penny? And not one of them will fall to the ground apart from your Father" (Matthew 10:29). He said this to give hope to those who would be killed for his name.

He himself stood on the sea and stopped the waves with a single word (Mark 4:39). Even if Nature or Satan unleashed the deadly tidal wave, one word from Jesus would have stopped it. He did not speak it. This means there is design in this suffering. And all his designs are wise and just and good.

One of his designs is my repentance. Therefore I will not put God on trial. I am on trial. Only because of Christ will the waves that one day carry me away bring me safely to his side. Come. Repentance is a good place to be.

132

"FACT! FAITH! FEELING!"

Testing a Common Slogan

The virtue of slogans is brevity. Their vice is ambiguity. So they are risky ways of communicating. They are powerful and perilous. So we should exploit the power and explain the peril. I would like to venture a corrective explanation to the slogan "Fact! Faith! Feeling!"

It's an old and common evangelical slogan. F. B. Meyer, A. T. Pearson, and L. E. Maxwell all preached sermons by this title. Today a Campus Crusade booklet uses it powerfully. The point of the slogan is the order. First, the facts about Christ. Second, the response of faith. Third, the feelings that may or may not follow.

So what's the ambiguity? There are two: changed "feelings" may be essential to true Christian conversion, not incidental; and "faith" may not be completely distinct from feeling.

In the Campus Crusade booklet the slogan appears as a train: The locomotive is "fact." The coal car is "faith." The caboose is "feeling." The explanation reads: "The train will run with or without the caboose. However, it would be futile to attempt to pull the train by the caboose." But what are the "feelings" the train of Christian living can run without? Do "feelings" refer merely to physical experiences like sweaty palms, knocking knees, racing heart, trembling lips, tearful eyes? If so, the slogan is clear and accurate.

But most people don't think of feelings that way. Feelings include things like gratitude, hope, joy, contentment, peacefulness, desire, compassion, fear, hate, anger, grief. None of these is merely physical. Angels, demons, and departed saints without bodies can have these "feelings."

Apart from the Bible I think Jonathan Edwards has written the most important book on feelings in the Christian life. It's called *The Religious Affections*. The definition of these "affections" (or what most people today mean by feelings) is: "the more vigorous and sensible exercises of the inclination and will of the soul." In other words, the feelings that really matter are not mere physical sensations. They are the stirring up of the soul with some perceived treasure or threat.

There is a connection between the feelings of the soul and the sensations of the body. This is owing, Edwards says, to "the laws of union which the Creator has fixed between the soul and the body." In other words, heartfelt gratitude can make you cry. Fear of God can make you tremble. The crying and the trembling are in themselves spiritually insignificant. The train can run without them. That's the truth in the slogan. But the gratitude and the fear are not optional in the Christian life. But these are what most people call feelings. That is the peril of the slogan. It seems to make optional what the Bible makes essential.

Minimizing the importance of transformed feelings makes Christian conversion less supernatural and less radical. It is humanly manageable to make decisions of the will for Christ. No supernatural power is required to pray prayers, sign cards, walk aisles, or even stop sleeping around. Those are good. They just don't prove that anything spiritual has happened. Christian conversion, on the other hand, is a supernatural, radical thing. The heart is changed. And the evidence of it is not just new decisions, but new affections, new feelings.

Negatively, the apostle Paul says that those who go on in the same old way of "hostility," "jealousy," "rage," and "envy" "will not enter the kingdom of God" (Galatians 5:20–21). These are all feelings. They must change. The train won't get to heaven without them. Positively, Christians are commanded to have God-honoring feelings. We are commanded to feel joy (Philippians 4:4), hope (Psalm 42:5), fear (Luke 12:5), peace (Colossians 3:15), zeal (Romans 12:11), grief (Romans 12:15), desire (1 Peter 2:2), tenderheartedness (Ephesians 4:32), brokenness and contrition (James 4:9).

Moreover, faith itself has in it something that most people would call feeling. Saving faith means "receiving Christ." "To all who did receive him, who believed in his name, he gave the right to become children of God" (John 1:12). But receive as what? We usually say, as "Lord and Savior." That's right. But something more needs to be said. Saving faith also receives Christ as our Treasure. A non-treasured Christ is a non-saving Christ. Faith has in it this element of valuing, embracing, prizing, relishing of Christ. It is like a man who found a treasure hidden in a field and "from joy" sells all his treasures to have that field (Matthew 13:44).

Therefore, let us affirm the slogan when it means that physical sensations are not essential. But let us also make clear that the locomotive of fact is not headed for heaven if it is not followed by a faith that treasures Christ, and if it is not pulling a caboose-load of imperfect, but new, affections.

133

IF CHRIST PREDICTED WAR, MAY CHRISTIANS PRAY FOR PEACE?

Distinguishing God's Work and Ours

I ask this question because some Bible-believing Christians feel that prayer for peace in these "last days" would be contrary to God's will, since Jesus said, "When you hear of wars and rumors of wars, do not be alarmed. This must take place, but the end is not yet" (Mark 13:7). If war "must take place," how can you pray for peace without opposing God?

Our prayers should be guided by what is morally right for men to do, not by what God, in his sovereign providence, may will to take place. Rarely, if ever, should we pray for moral evil to take place, but God may will that moral evil prevail for a season. For example: 1) God willed that Christ be crucified. Many of the necessary acts involved in crucifying Christ were morally evil. Therefore, God willed that this moral evil prevail for a season (Acts 2:23; 4:27–28). 2) God willed that Joseph's brothers sell him into slavery in Egypt, even though this was evil for them to do (Genesis 50:20). 3) And God ordains the sinful ravages of the end times (Revelation 17:17).

In other words, God ordains and predicts that moral evil prevail for certain seasons, but this does not mean we should pray for moral evil to happen. We should pray according to the way God has commanded us to live—in righteousness and love. We should pray that God's will be done on earth the way it's done in heaven by the perfectly holy angels (Matthew 6:10), not the way it's done on earth through the agency of sinful men.

In fact, Paul teaches us to pray for peace among nations for the sake of the gospel. The crucial text relating to prayer and peace is 1 Timothy 2:1–4. "First of all, then, I urge that supplications, prayers, intercessions, and thanksgivings be made for all people, for kings and all who are in high positions, that we may lead a peaceful and quiet life, godly and dignified in every way. This is good, and it is pleasing in the sight of God our Savior, who desires all people to be saved and to come to the knowledge of the truth."

Notice the link between praying for 1) national leaders, 2) the preservation of peace and order, and 3) the "desire for all to be saved." There is a connection between 1) national leadership, 2) peace, and 3) evangelism and missions. It is true that the church may grow in times of hostilities and war. But it is also true that wars have devastated the church in many areas. It is not our business to decide the sovereign purpose of God in ordaining that some wars happen. Our business is to pray that justice, peace, and the proclamation of the gospel prevail. Our business is to pray that the Christian church not be complicit in national affairs as if nation and church were one. Ours is to pray that the church be seen as aliens in the cause of Christ-exalting love and justice with no supreme allegiances to any nation.

This leaves open the possibility that Christians might support a just war. God has given to the governing authorities the right to bear the sword (Romans 13:1–6). There are occasions when justice and love painfully call for military force for the sake of opposing aggression or liberating the oppressed. In such cases our prayers would be for the minimizing of misery and the speedy triumph of justice and the restraint of animosities and cruelties.

So let us pray for the love and wisdom and courage and power and fruitfulness of the church of Jesus Christ around the world. Let us plead that she would be distinct from all the nations and all the national and ethnic manifestations of pride. Let us plead that she would be a peace-making presence of salt and light everywhere. And that she would be unafraid to call every nation into question for the sake of justice and humility. And that Jesus Christ would be magnified as no national deity, but as Lord of lords and King of kings. And let us pray that all lords and all kings see this and humble themselves and make way for the Lord of glory.

134

THE TRANSFORMING POWER OF FEELING MERCY

Using Imagination and Revelation to Know Our Condition

What a difference it makes in everything, if we feel like we have just been rescued from torment and death! Picture your attitude on a Navy ship after being plucked from the ocean where you spent weeks adrift on a life raft. Or picture yourself rescued from a deep, collapsing mine in Pennsylvania. Or think of a nine-month battle with malignant cancer, only to hear the doctor say, "I can't explain it, but it's gone." Think about your powers of patience and kindness and forgiveness in those early hours of relief and rejoicing.

Now add this to your imagination (though it shouldn't take imagination, only biblical revelation), that you don't deserve to be rescued. Let it sink in—pray right now that God would make it sink in—that you and I deserve nothing but trouble and persecution and sickness and death and hell. We are, the Bible says, "by nature children of wrath like the rest of mankind" (Ephesians 2:3). "All...are under sin...and every mouth [is] stopped, and the whole world...accountable to God" (Romans 3:9, 19). The "wages" of our sin is eternal death (Romans 6:23). We are under the curse of God's law, because "cursed be anyone who does not confirm the words of this law by doing them" (Deuteronomy 27:26). Our natural mind is "hostile to God" (Romans 8:7). We are "strangers to the covenants of promise, having no hope and without God in the world" (Ephesians 2:12). We are destined to be cast into "outer darkness" where there is "weeping and gnashing of teeth" (Matthew 8:12; 25:30). If something doesn't intervene, our lot will be in the lake of fire where "the smoke of their torment goes up forever and ever, and they have no rest" (Revelation 14:11).

Therefore, all you Christians—all you believers rescued by the blood of Christ, who has become a curse for us—add to the relief and happiness of your rescue the bewildering wonder and the brokenhearted joy that you deserve none of this, but are lavished with unceasing mercy.

Then look upon your afflictions in this light. Think with Jonathan Edwards on your condition:

> How far less [are] the greatest afflictions that we meet with in this world...than we have deserved.... The greatest outward troubles and calamities that we meet with...must needs appear very little things to the misery which we have deserved.... A man may meet with very great losses...his cattle may die, his corn may be blasted, his barn may be burnt down and all the goods consumed, and he may be brought from a comfortable living to a poor, low, stricken state. This is very hard to bear, but alas, how little reason have such to complain if they do but consider how little this is, compared with that eternal destruction that we have been informed of." (Jonathan Edwards, *The Works of Jonathan Edwards* [New Haven: Yale University Press, 1997], 321)

Is it any wonder that Paul said to such people, "Do all things without grumbling" (Philippians 2:14)? Ponder how you would react to things if you lived hour by hour in the heartfelt awareness that you are rescued from horrible death and eternal suffering, and that, in spite of deserving no help, you are lavished with mercy every day (even in the hard things) and will be made perfectly and eternally happy in the age to come.

Then add one more thing to your thinking. The one who rescued you had to die to do it, and he is the one Person in the universe who did NOT deserve to die. "Christ suffered once for sins, the righteous for the unrighteous, that he might bring us to God" (1 Peter 3:18).

Oh, Christian, know your condition—the misery and the mercy. And let the horror from which you have been rescued, and the mercy in which you live, and the price that Christ paid, make you humble and thankful and patient and kind and forgiving. You have never been treated by God worse than you deserve. And in Christ you are treated ten million times better. Feel this. Live this.

∽⟶

135

THE GREATEST EVENT IN HISTORY

Two Paradoxes in the Death of Christ

Not surprisingly, the greatest event in the history of the world is complex. For example, since Jesus Christ is man and God in one person, was his death the death of God? To answer this we must speak of the two natures of Christ, one divine and one human. Ever since AD 451 the Chalcedonian definition of Christ's two natures in one person has been accepted as the orthodox teaching of Scripture. The Council of Chalcedon said,

> We, then,...teach men to confess...one and the same Christ, Son, Lord, Only-begotten, to be acknowledged in two natures, inconfusedly, unchangeably, indivisibly, inseparably; the distinction of the natures being by no means taken away by the union, but rather the property of each nature being preserved, and concurring in one Person and One Subsistence, nor parted or divided into two persons, but one and the same Son, and only begotten, God, the Word, the Lord Jesus Christ.

The divine nature is immortal (Romans 1:23; 1 Timothy 1:17). It cannot die. That is part of what it means to be God. Therefore, when Christ died, it was his human nature that suffered death. The mystery of the union between the divine and the human natures, in that experience of death, is not revealed to us. What we know is that Christ died, and that in the same day he went to Paradise

("Today you will be with me in Paradise," Luke 23:43). Therefore there seems to have been consciousness in death, so that the ongoing union between the human and divine natures need not have been interrupted, though Christ, only in his human nature, died.

Another example of the complexity of the event of Christ's death is how God the Father experienced it. The most common evangelical teaching is that the death of Christ is Christ's experience of the Father's curse. "Christ redeemed us from the curse of the law by becoming a curse for us, for it is written, 'Cursed is everyone who is hanged on a tree'" (Galatians 3:13). Whose curse? One could soften it by saying, "the curse of the law." But the law is not a person to curse anyone. A curse is a curse if there is one who curses. The one who curses through the law is God, who wrote the law. Therefore the death of Christ for our sin and for our law breaking was the experience of the Father's curse.

This is why Jesus said, "My God, my God, why have you forsaken me?" (Matthew 27:46). In the death of Christ God laid on him the sins of his people (Isaiah 53:6) which he hated. And in hatred for that sin, God turned away from his sin-laden Son and gave him up to suffer the full force of death and cursing. The Father's wrath was poured out on him instead of us so that his wrath toward us was "propitiated" (Romans 3:25) and removed.

But here is the paradox. God deeply and joyfully approved of what the Son was doing in that hour of sacrifice. In fact, he had planned it all together with the Son. And his love for the God-Man, Jesus Christ, on earth was owing to the very obedience that took Jesus to the cross. The cross was Jesus' crowning act of obedience and love. And this obedience and love the Father profoundly approved and enjoyed. Therefore Paul says this amazing thing: "Christ loved us and gave himself up for us, a fragrant offering and sacrifice to God" (Ephesians 5:2). The death of Jesus was a fragrance to God.

So here we have one more glorious complexity. The death of Christ was the curse of God and the wrath of God; and yet, at the same time, it was pleasing to God and a sweet fragrance. While turning from his Son and giving him up to die laden with our sin, he delighted in the obedience and love and perfection of the Son.

Therefore, let us stand in awe and look with trembling joy on the death of Jesus Christ, the Son of God. There is no greater event in history. There is no greater thing for our minds to ponder or our hearts to admire. Stay close to this. Everything important and good gathers here. It is a wise and weighty and happy place to be.

136

A CALL FOR CHRISTIAN RISK

How the Removal of Eternal Risk Creates the Call for Temporal Risk

By removing eternal risk, Christ calls his people to continual temporal risk. For the followers of Jesus the final risk is gone. "There is now no condemnation for those who are in Christ Jesus" (Romans 8:1). "Neither death nor life...will be able to separate us from the love of God in Christ Jesus our Lord" (Romans 3:38–39). "Some of you they will put to death.... But not a hair of your head will perish" (Luke 21:16, 18). "Whoever believes in me, though he die, yet shall he live" (John 11:25).

When the threat of death becomes a door to paradise the final barrier to temporal risk is broken. When a Christian says from the heart, "To live is Christ and to die is gain," he is free to love no matter what. Some forms of radical Islam may entice martyr-murderers with similar dreams, but Christian hope is the power to love, not kill. Christian hope produces life-givers, not life-takers. The crucified Christ calls his people to live and die for their enemies, as he did. The only risks permitted by Christ are the perils of love. "Love your enemies, do good to those who hate you, bless those who curse you, pray for those who abuse you" (Luke 6:27–28).

With staggering promises of everlasting joy, Jesus unleashed a movement of radical, loving risk-takers. "You will be delivered up even by parents...and some of you they will put to death" (Luke 21:16). Only some. Which means it might be you and it might not. That's what risk means. It is not risky to shoot yourself in the head. The outcome is certain. It is risky to serve Christ in a war zone. You might get shot. You might not.

Christ calls us to take risks for kingdom purposes. Almost every message of American consumerism says the opposite: Maximize comfort and security— now, not in heaven. Christ does not join that chorus. To every timid saint, wavering on the edge of some dangerous gospel venture, he says, "Fear not, you can only be killed" (Luke 12:4). Yes, by all means maximize your joy! How? For the sake of love, risk being reviled and persecuted and lied about, "for your reward is great in heaven" (Matthew 5:11–12).

There is a great biblical legacy of loving risk-takers. Joab, facing the Syrians on one side and the Ammonites on the other, said to his brother Abishai, "Let us be courageous for our people…and may the LORD do what seems good to him" (2 Samuel 10:12). Esther broke the royal law to save her people and said, "If I perish, I perish" (Esther 4:16). Shadrach and his comrades refused to bow down to the king's idol and said, "Our God whom we serve is able to deliver us…. But if not, be it known to you, O king, that we will not serve your gods" (Daniel 3:16–18). And when the Holy Spirit told Paul that in every city imprisonment and afflictions await him, he said, "I do not account my life of any value nor as precious to myself, if only I may finish my course" (Acts 20:24).

"Every Christian," said Stephen Neil about the early church, "knew that sooner or later he might have to testify to his faith at the cost of his life" (*A History of Christian Missions*, Penguin, 1964, 43). This was normal. To become a Christian was to risk your life. Tens of thousands did it. Why? Because to do it was to gain Christ, and not to was to lose your soul. "Whoever would save his life will lose it, but whoever loses his life for my sake will find it" (Matthew 16:25).

In America and around the world the price of being a real Christian is rising. Things are getting back to normal in "this present evil age." Increasingly, 2 Timothy 3:12 will make sense: "All who desire to live a godly life in Christ Jesus will be persecuted." Those who've made gospel-risk a voluntary lifestyle will be most ready when we have no choice. Therefore I urge you, in the words of the early church, "Let us go to him outside the camp and bear the reproach he endured. For here we have no lasting city, but we seek the city that is to come" (Hebrews 13:13–14). *When God removed all risk above / He loosed a thousand risks of love.*

137

Do Jews Have a Divine Right in the Promised Land?

How Christians Should Think About the Jewish-Palestinian Conflict

How should Bible-believing Christians align themselves in the Jewish-Palestinian conflict? There are biblical reasons for treating both sides with compassionate public justice in the same way that disputes should be settled between nations generally. In other words, the Bible does not teach us to be partial to Israel or to the Palestinians because either has a special divine status.

I do not deny that Israel was chosen by God from all the peoples of the world to be the focus of special blessing in the history of redemption which climaxed in Jesus Christ, the Messiah. "The LORD your God has chosen you to be a people for his treasured possession, out of all the peoples who are on the face of the earth" (Deuteronomy 7:6).

Nor do I deny that God promised to Israel the presently disputed land from the time of Abraham onward. God said to Moses, "This is the land of which I swore to Abraham, to Isaac, and to Jacob, 'I will give it to your offspring'" (Deuteronomy 34:4).

But neither of these biblical facts leads necessarily to the endorsement of present-day Israel as the rightful possessor of all the disputed land. Israel may have such a right. And she may not. But that decision is not based on divine privilege. Why?

First, a non-covenant-keeping people does not have a divine right to hold the land of promise. Both the blessed status of the people and the privileged right to the land are conditional on Israel's keeping the covenant God made with her. Thus God said to Israel, "If you will indeed obey my voice and keep my covenant, you shall be my treasured possession among all peoples" (Exodus 19:5). Israel has no warrant to a present experience of divine privilege when she is not keeping covenant with God.

More than once Israel was denied the experience of her divine right to the land when she broke covenant with God. For example, when Israel languished in captivity in Babylon, Daniel prayed, "O Lord...we have sinned and done wrong.... To you, O Lord, belongs righteousness, but to us open shame...to all Israel...in all the lands to which you have driven them, because of the treachery that they have committed against you" (Daniel 9:4–7; see Psalm 78:54–61). Israel has no divine right to be in the land of promise when she is breaking the covenant of promise.

This does not mean that other nations have the right to molest her. She still has human rights among nations when she has no divine right. Nations that gloated over her divine discipline were punished by God (Isaiah 10:5–13).

Second, Israel as a whole today rejects her Messiah, Jesus Christ, God's Son. This is the ultimate act of covenant-breaking with God. God promised that to Israel "a son is given; and the government shall be upon his shoulder, and his name shall be called Wonderful Counselor, Mighty God, Everlasting Father, Prince of Peace" (Isaiah 9:6–7). But with tears this Prince of Peace looked out over Jerusalem and said, "Would that you...had known on this day the things that make for peace! But now they are hidden from your eyes.... You did not know the time of your visitation" (Luke 19:42–44).

When the builders rejected the beautiful Cornerstone, Jesus said, "The kingdom of God will be taken away from you and given to a people producing its fruits" (Matthew 21:43). He explained, "Many will come from east and west and recline at table with Abraham, Isaac, and Jacob in the kingdom of heaven, while the sons of the kingdom will be thrown into the outer darkness" (Matthew 8:11–12).

God has saving purposes for ethnic Israel (Romans 11:25–26). But for now the people are at enmity with God in rejecting the gospel of Jesus Christ, their Messiah (Romans 11:28). God has expanded his saving work to embrace all peoples (including Palestinians) who will trust his Son and depend on his death and resurrection for salvation. "Is God the God of Jews only? Is he not the God of Gentiles also? Yes, of Gentiles also, since God is one. He will justify the circumcised by faith and the uncircumcised through faith" (Romans 3:29–30).

The Christian plea in the Middle East to Palestinians and Jews is: "Believe on the Lord Jesus, and you will be saved" (Acts 16:31). And until that great day when both Jewish and Gentile followers of King Jesus inherit the earth (not just the land), without lifting sword or gun, the rights of nations should be decided by the principles of compassionate and public justice, not claims to national divine right or status.

138

What Is the Christian Gospel?

Exploring What Makes the "Good News" Good News

The gospel is not just a sequence of steps (say, the "Four Laws" of Campus Crusade or the "Six Biblical Truths" of *Quest for Joy*). Those are essential. But what makes the gospel "good news" is that it connects a person with the "unsearchable riches of Christ."

There is nothing in itself that makes "forgiveness of sins" good news. Whether being forgiven is good news depends on what it leads to. You could walk out of a courtroom innocent of a crime and get killed on the street. Forgiveness may or may not lead to joy. Even escaping hell is not in itself the good news we long for—not if we find heaven to be massively boring.

Nor is justification in itself good news. Where does it lead? That is the question. Whether justification will be good news depends on the award we receive because of our imputed righteousness. What do we receive because we are counted righteous in Christ? The answer is fellowship with Jesus.

Forgiveness of sins and justification are good news because they remove obstacles to the only lasting, all-satisfying source of joy: Jesus Christ. Jesus Christ is not merely the means of our rescue from damnation; he is the goal of our salvation. If he is not satisfying to be with, there is no salvation. He is not merely the rope that pulls us from the threatening waves; he is the solid beach under our feet, and the air in our lungs, and the beat of our heart, and the warm sun on our skin, and the song in our ears, and the arms of our beloved.

This is why the New Testament often defines the gospel as, simply, Christ. The gospel is the "gospel of Christ" (Romans 15:19; 1 Corinthians 9:12;

2 Corinthians 2:12; 9:13; 10:14; Galatians 1:7; Philippians 1:27; etc.). Or, more specifically, the gospel is "the gospel of the glory of Christ" (2 Corinthians 4:4). And even more wonderfully, perhaps, Paul says that the preaching of the gospel is the preaching of "the unsearchable riches of Christ" (Ephesians 3:8).

Therefore to believe the gospel is not only to accept the awesome truths that 1) God is holy, 2) we are hopeless sinners, 3) Christ died and rose again for sinners, and 4) this great salvation is enjoyed by faith in Christ—but believing the gospel is also to treasure Jesus Christ as your unsearchable riches. What makes the gospel Gospel is that it brings a person into the everlasting and ever-increasing joy of Jesus Christ.

The words Jesus will speak when we come to heaven are: "Enter into the joy of your Master" (Matthew 25:21). The prayer he prayed for us ended on this note: "Father, I desire that they also, whom you have given me, may be with me where I am, to see my glory" (John 17:24). The glory he wants us to see is the "unsearchable riches of Christ." It is "the immeasurable riches of [God's] grace in kindness toward us in Christ Jesus" (Ephesians 2:7).

The superlatives "unsearchable" and "immeasurable" mean that there will be no end to our discovery and enjoyment. There will be no boredom. Every day will bring forth new and stunning things about Christ which will cause yesterday's wonder to be seen in new light, so that not only will there be new sights of glory every day, but the accumulated glory will become more glorious with every new revelation.

The gospel is the good news that the everlasting and ever-increasing joy of the never-boring, ever-satisfying Christ is ours freely and eternally by faith in the sin-forgiving death and hope-giving resurrection of Jesus Christ.

May God give you "strength to comprehend with all the saints what is the breadth and length and height and depth, and to know the love of Christ that surpasses knowledge" (Ephesians 3:18–19).

139

A PRAYER FOR OUR CHURCH

Asking God to Build a Certain Kind of
Men and Women

Oh, Lord, by the truth of your Word, and the power of your Spirit and the
ministry of your body, build men and women at _____ ...
Who don't love the world more than God,
who don't care if they make much money,
who don't care if they own a house,
who don't care if they have a new car or two cars,
who don't need recent styles,
who don't care if they get famous,
who don't miss steak or fancy fare,
who don't expect that life should be comfortable and easy,
who don't feed their minds on TV each night,
who don't measure truth with their finger in the wind,
who don't get paralyzed by others' disapproval,
who don't return evil for evil,
who don't hold grudges,
who don't gossip,
who don't twist the truth,
who don't brag or boast,
who don't whine or use body language to get pity,
who don't criticize more than praise,

who don't hang out in cliques,
who don't eat too much or exercise too little;
But
who are ablaze for God,
who are utterly God-besotted,
who are filled with the Holy Spirit,
who strive to know the height and depth of Christ's love,
who are crucified to the world and dead to sin,
who are purified by the Word and addicted to righteousness,
who are mighty in memorizing and using the Scriptures,
who keep the Lord's Day holy and refreshing,
who are broken by the consciousness of sin,
who are thrilled by the wonder of free grace,
who are stunned into humble silence by the riches of God's glory,
who are persevering constantly in prayer,
who are ruthless in self-denial,
who are fearless in public witness to Christ's lordship,
who are able to unmask error and blow away doctrinal haze,
who are tough in standing for the truth,
who are tender in touching hurting people,
who are passionate about reaching the peoples who have no church,
who are pro-life for the sake of babies and moms and dads and the glory of God,
who are keepers of all their promises, including marriage vows,
who are content with what they have and trusting the promises of God,
who are patient and kind and meek when life is hard.

140

THE LORD ALONE WILL BE EXALTED

Making War on Pride

During our staff days of prayer and planning, one of our focuses in prayer was to wage war on pride. For help, we looked at God's attitude toward pride, the nature of pride and the remedy for pride. We are aware that our hearts are deceitful and that we must be relentlessly vigilant in the fight against pride.

GOD'S ATTITUDE TOWARD PRIDE

God is opposed to human pride and will eventually bring it all down.

For the LORD of hosts will have a day of reckoning against everyone who is proud and lofty, and against everyone who is lifted up, that he may be abased. And it will be against all the cedars of Lebanon that are lofty and lifted up, against all the oaks of Bashan, against all the lofty mountains, against all the hills that are lifted up, against every high tower, against every fortified wall, against all the ships of Tarshish, and against all the beautiful craft. And the pride of man will be humbled, and the loftiness of men will be abased, and the LORD alone will be exalted in that day. (Isaiah 2:12–17)

THE NATURE OF PRIDE

One part of pride is taking credit yourself for what God does.

I will punish the fruit of the arrogant heart of the king of Assyria and the pomp of his haughtiness. For he has said, "By the power of my hand and by my wisdom I did this, for I have understanding." Is the axe to boast itself over the one who chops with it? Is the saw to exalt itself over the one who wields it? That would be like a club wielding those who lift it, or like a rod lifting him who is not wood. (Isaiah 10:12–15)

The Remedy for Pride

Take to heart that all you have is a gift of free grace.

For who regards you as superior? And what do you have that you did not receive? But if you did receive it, why do you boast as if you had not received it? (1 Corinthians 4:7)

Trust God to exalt you in due time.

Humble yourselves, therefore, under the mighty hand of God, that He may exalt you at the proper time. (1 Peter 5:6)

Remember that the true and full revelation of God comes only to the humble.

At that time Jesus answered and said, "I praise You, O Father, Lord of heaven and earth, that You hid these things from the wise and intelligent and revealed them to babes." (Matthew 11:25)

Realize that entering the kingdom depends on humility.

Truly I say to you, unless you are converted and become like children, you shall not enter the kingdom of heaven. Whoever then humbles himself as this child, he is the greatest in the kingdom of heaven. (Matthew 18:3–4)

Rest in the truth that all things are already yours in Christ.

So then let no one boast in men. For all things belong to you, whether Paul or Apollos or Cephas or the world or life or death or things present or things to come; all things belong to you, and you belong to Christ; and Christ belongs to God. (1 Corinthians 3:21–23)

Pray with us that this will be a year of humble self-forgetfulness as we see and savor the greatness of God.

⌘

desiringGod

Desiring God is a ministry that exists to spread a passion for the supremacy of God in all things for the joy of all peoples through Jesus Christ. We love to spread the truth that God is most glorified in us when we are most satisfied in him. John Piper receives no royalties from the books he writes—they are all reinvested into the ministry of Desiring God. It's all designed as part of our vision to spread this passion to others.

With that in mind, we invite you to visit the Desiring God website at desiringGod.org. You'll find twenty years' worth of free sermons by John Piper in manuscript, and hundreds in downloadable audio formats. In addition there are free articles and information about our upcoming conferences. An online store allows you to purchase audio albums, God-centered children's curriculum, books and resources by Noël Piper, and over 25 books by John Piper. You can also find information about our radio ministry at desiringGodradio.org.

DG also has a whatever-you-can-afford policy, designed for individuals without discretionary funds. If you'd like more information about this policy, please contact us at the address or phone number below.

We exist to help you treasure Jesus Christ above all things. If we can serve you in any way, please let us know!

Desiring God
2601 East Franklin Avenue
Minneapolis, MN 55406-1103

Telephone: 1.888.346.4700
Fax: 612.338.4372
Email: mail@desiringGod.org
Web: www.desiringGod.org

Subject Index

PERSON INDEX

Scripture Index

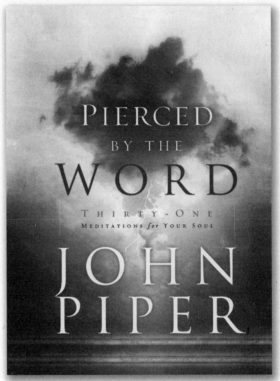

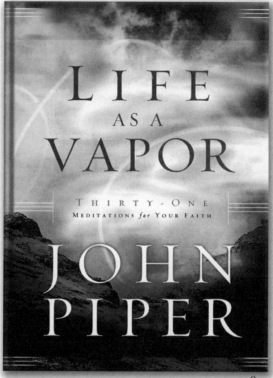

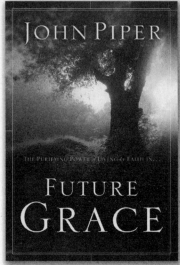

1-59052-191-9

FUTURE GRACE
BY JOHN PIPER

In *Future Grace*, pastor John Piper helps readers discover the key to overcoming sin and living a life that honors God. Many men and women attempt to walk upright merely out of gratitude for what Christ did in the past, but Piper encourages believers to look ahead to the grace God provides on a moment-by-moment basis—and put your faith into action by laying hold of God's promises.

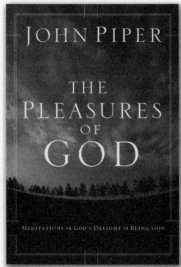

1-57673-665-2

THE PLEASURES OF GOD
BY JOHN PIPER

Fully understanding the joy of God will draw you into an encounter with His overflowing, self-replenishing, all-encompassing grace—the source of living water that all Christians desire to drink. *The Pleasures of God* will again put God at the center of Creation and leave you satisfied in Him.

www.multnomah.net/johnpiper